Frances

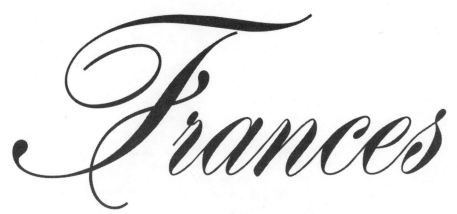

Frances

THE REMARKABLE STORY OF PRINCESS DIANA'S MOTHER

Max Riddington

and

Gavan Naden

MICHAEL O'MARA BOOKS LIMITED

First published in Great Britain in 2003 by
Michael O'Mara Books Limited
9 Lion Yard, Tremadoc Road
London sw4 7nq

A CIP catalogue record for this book is available from the British Library

ISBN 1-84317-043-4

1 3 5 7 9 10 8 6 4 2

Photograph credits:

Page 1 upper © TopFoto; page 1 lower © Edith Hodgins; page 2 © TopFoto; page 3 © authors; page 4 © Getty Images/Hulton Archive; page 5 © TopFoto; page 6 upper © Hulton Archive; page 6 lower © authors; page 7 upper © PA Photos; page 7 lower © Hulton Archive; page 8 upper © TopFoto; page 8 lower © Getty Images/Hulton Archive; page 9 upper © Getty Images/Hulton Archive; page 9 lower © Hulton-Deutsch Collection/CORBIS; page 10 upper © PA Photos; page 10 lower © Getty Images/Hulton Archive; page 11 upper © Getty Images/Hulton Archive; page 11 lower © PA Photos; page 12; © TopFoto; page 13 © PA Photos; page 14 upper © TopFoto; page 14 lower left © Rex Features; page 14 lower right © PA Photos; page 15 © PA Photos; page 16 upper © authors; page 16 lower © Murdo MacLeod/CORBIS SYGMA

Designed and typeset by Martin Bristow

Printed and bound in England by Clays Ltd, St Ives plc

Contents

THIS BOOK IS DEDICATED TO KEN FREAKLEY – WHO DIED
DURING THE WRITING OF IT. A WONDERFUL FATHER,
WHOSE LOVE, FAITH AND BELIEF NEVER FALTERED.

Acknowledgements

We are deeply indebted to: the Hon. Mrs Frances Shand Kydd; Ken Wharfe; Andrew Morton; Sharon Makepeace; Ross Langford; Steve Adcock; Lady C.; Maggie Turnbull; Sue Lewis; Gordon Honeycombe; Graeme Clark; Maureen Condon; John Prime; Nicky Johnston; Erin Pizzey; Edith Hodgins; VisitScotland; everyone at Michael O'Mara Books, especially Michael O'Mara, Gabrielle Mander, Rhian McKay, Judith Palmer and Bryony Evens, and Toby Buchan for his calm editing; Glen Saville and Martin Bristow for their designs; and those people who talked to us only on condition that they remain for ever anonymous.

I could not have completed this book without the love of my family – Kim, Tom and my lovely mum. Many thanks to Val and Ridd, and Mick and Sheila, who helped more than they will ever know – Max

To Isobel for her endless patience, love and support. To my children Holly and Oscar, whose smiley faces make everything worth while. And to Pam, Gayle and Cary. Love you all – Gavan

Foreword

WHEN I FIRST SPOKE to the Honourable Mrs Frances Shand Kydd, she put the fear of God into me. I knew that she was a former viscountess, and the mother of a princess. And not just any princess – this was the mother of Diana, Princess of Wales. This knowledge alone served to make me extremely nervous of approaching her.

Back then, my enduring image of this woman was of her looking remarkably dignified yet somehow terribly vulnerable as she arrived for Diana's funeral at Westminster Abbey, her weary, soulful eyes staring out from beneath an enormously wide-brimmed black hat. As a mother myself, I could only imagine the physical and emotional strength it must have taken to walk inside to say farewell to her youngest daughter.

I had contacted her early in 2000, while writing a series of articles based on interviews with notable personalities who are dedicated to their charity work. I was looking for high-profile people who are more than figureheads or names on the writing paper, and who have a real passion for the causes they support. Frances Shand Kydd was an obvious choice because, among many other good works, she had made repeated trips to Lourdes, acting as a personal carer for handicapped Catholic children.

I had made my request to interview her through the director of the charity in question, who replied quickly, courteously and positively, but with just one cautionary condition: 'Don't mention Diana.' I was also asked to type my questions and send them to Mrs Shand Kydd, as she was not keen to talk (I was later to learn the full extent of her wariness of journalists, and the reasons for it). I did as instructed, before faxing the list through to her home on the Isle of Seil in Scotland.

I had no idea how long it would be before she replied, and turned my mind to other matters. An hour later there was a fax waiting for me. All my questions had been answered and there, at the bottom of the page, was a message in distinctive, thick, swirling handwriting. 'Call me,' it said. She had written her telephone number after that brief request.

I made the call. A gravelly voice answered, 'Hello.' I stumbled: 'Mrs Shand Kydd? It's Max Riddington . . . You asked me to call.'

'I thought you were a man,' she laughed.

'I hope you're not disappointed,' I said, and that was enough to break the ice.

I ran through the interview with her, keeping the questions strictly professional. She was generous with her answers, and I never mentioned the 'D' word. At the end she asked me for my telephone number, although I honestly did not expect to hear from her again.

Except that Frances started to call me. At first it was to mention some snippet of interest in the news, or some aspect of her charitable work – she had, she said, loved my piece about her when it was published. Then, however, we would talk. She spoke to me when I was cooking supper, cleaning the bath, out with friends, driving my car. Once, when I was not at home, she called and talked with my son about school and his love of a particular breakfast cereal (she later labelled him 'The Coco Pops King'). On another occasion, I walked in through the back door to find my husband looking somewhat pale. 'I've just spoken to Frances for ages,' he said, reaching for a glass of red wine. When she called and my mother answered the telephone, Mum was too terrified to say who she was and pretended to be the cleaner. Frances later sent her and my father a card saying, 'Thank you for Max.' I was very touched.

And that was how the friendship went on. Notes and cards came in the post, flowers were sent, faxes went backwards and forwards. We would talk, laugh a great deal and, sometimes, she would cry. She left an excited message after a friend of hers had given birth to a baby boy, the rich delight in her voice filling the room. Frances loves babies.

On Diana's birthday, 1 July 2000, Frances called late at night. She was sobbing uncontrollably. 'I always believed the night Diana died there was life after her, but I didn't know it was going to be so tough,' she sobbed. She talked about how hard it was to be Diana's mother, but, typically, apologized for 'doing a version of a human monsoon'. It seemed that amid the widespread emotional devastation caused by Diana's death, people had forgotten that this woman lost her daughter on that night in Paris, rather than an icon.

Then, one stifling summer evening, as we talked – Frances was bemoaning her hay fever – she suddenly asked me if I would like to come to Seil. I paused, momentarily lost for words. She said we should both sleep on it. I did not get much sleep.

I took my time driving the 450 miles from my home to the west coast of Scotland. As I crawled across the tiny bridge that links Seil to the mainland, I hoped that, face to face, we would hit it off as well as we had over the telephone.

I parked the car and walked up the concrete path towards 'Callanish,' Frances's neat bungalow set on a hillside overlooking the Atlantic Ocean. Taking a steadying breath, I knocked on the heavy wooden door. Music by the boy band Boyzone was blasting out from somewhere inside the house. No one answered. I paused, then knocked again. Nothing. I looked for a bell. No luck. There was a brass letterbox that I could yell through, but I didn't dare. Eventually I attracted attention by waving through the kitchen window – hardly very sophisticated.

Frances, wearing a blue silk polo-necked sweater, slacks and Todd loafers, opened the door, tall, elegant, poised and very attractive. She kissed me on both cheeks, and seemed remarkably relaxed. I handed her a pot of marmalade flavoured with Earl Grey tea as a small present and she looked at me in surprise. 'What on earth . . . ?' she said before glancing down at the gift and laughing out loud, 'Goodness knows what this will taste like!' She ushered me into the sitting room, and then made me a cup of tea. Ronan Keating was singing his way through another number.

The bungalow was far less grand than I had imagined, although it is obviously a much loved home. We sat and talked about my journey, how my family would fare without me, and where I was staying in Oban, fifteen miles away on the mainland. Then Frances disappeared into the kitchen and I asked if I could help her. I stirred the orange sauce while she prepared the chicken for our lunch. A huge silver mobile of the number '2000', left over from the millennium celebrations, dangled near the cooker. We ate in her dining room, sitting on bamboo chairs surrounded by books, her computer and what she calls 'Catholic kitsch'. She lit two candles – one lemon-scented, and the other in the shape of Christ's head which, when lit, made it look as though His hair was on fire. 'Hideous, isn't it?' she laughed. The table was laid with a crisp, snowy white linen cloth, the china was Wedgwood, the glasses crystal. We ate orange chicken with mashed potatoes, broad beans and peas, followed by cheese in place of pudding, all washed down with pineapple juice and fizzy mineral water (Scottish, of course). There were home-made bread, water biscuits and oatcakes. When we had eaten I offered to help clear away, but Frances would not hear of it. I tell these things, not from any sense of voyeurism, but to illustrate her concern with taking trouble, and with making people both comfortable and welcome.

We retired to the sitting room, where she plied me with chocolates and very good coffee. Sitting bolt upright on her favourite chesterfield sofa, she talked about her life, serenely smoking one cigarette after another, stopping every now and again to ask me if I was warm enough. When she spoke about her father her whole face was filled with affection. I had been there for several hours, but Frances seemed comfortable, relaxed. Then she spoke about Diana.

She took a deep breath, staring through the window out over Seil bay. Her elbows slipped to her knees, and she hunched over to clasp both hands together. Speaking slowly and deliberately, pausing every so often as if she were pacing herself, she began with the words, 'The night Diana died . . .' and the hairs stood up on the back of my neck. I was painfully aware of the many pictures of Diana in the room, but also struck by the strong physical similarities between the two women. The atmosphere in the room was so intense that I hardly dared breathe.

I stayed with her until the early evening. Then I drove back to my bed-and-breakfast in Oban, and returned to Seil every day over the next four days. After driving home, this time in eight hours straight, there was a fax from Frances waiting for me, thanking me for my visit and hoping that I had got back safely.

We have met since at her favourite London restaurant, Caraffini's in Lower Sloane Street, and had drinks at her club, which is just like a quiet country house in the middle of a most exclusive part of the capital. I have been back to Seil several times and met her closest friend, Janey Milne, and we have giggled at photographs in her private albums of girlie weekends she has spent away with friends. She returned my initial gesture and handed me a pot of her own home-made marmalade – sadly, from the last batch she may ever make. She listened, unperturbed by my shaky voice, when I told her that my father had been taken ill and suddenly died soon after my last visit to Seil.

In the years I have known Frances there have been some dramatic changes. She is now more frail due to a progressive illness that makes walking and talking difficult for her, but she remains as spirited and full of life as ever. She is clearly delighted by the extension to her bungalow, which she had built to accommodate guests, or extra help for her when the time comes. 'Come and have a tour,' she said, waving me around the pretty new space.

Has life treated Frances well? To an outsider, probably not. Sometimes it seems as if there is a curse on her family. The deaths, divorces, and other tragedies beg the question, Are the Spencers set to become a kind of British version of the Kennedys? Yet Frances is indomitable. Somehow she endures. Her love of life, her faith, and an unbridled belief in the human spirit, which set her apart from most other people, also give her enormous strength of character.

On the other hand, she is not a saint, and would not care to be called one. She is human, and it is her humanity that makes her fascinating, in particular in the fact that a woman born into the aristocracy, who has moved in the highest circles guiding the Princess of Wales, can remain this unaffected, in touch, ordinary. I do not agree with everything she says and does; but I do respect her. She is not perfect – but then, neither does she pretend to be.

This book is intended to play some part in ending the damning mythology that surrounds Frances Shand Kydd. Too often she is portrayed as a bad mother who deserted her children, and who now lives as a sad recluse, seeking solace in Catholicism and alcohol after her nineteen-year-long second marriage ended. Many commentators seem desperate to pigeonhole her as a grand but sad old dame.

I have discovered a different woman, and a different story. What I have found in the time I have spent with Frances, and the many hours over which we have talked, is a funny, warm, intelligent, energetic and certainly complicated woman. She is much more than a survivor; she is someone who continues to live life to the full, despite all that it throws at her.

As always with biographies, there will be parts with which Frances does not agree. When we discussed this book and its eventual publication (and this is a measure of the woman), she feared for me as much as for herself. Yet I was encouraged by something that her son, Lord Spencer, had written to me: 'I am glad that you will write a fair biography of my mother, and I do remember her saying how rare you are – a journalist that she trusts!'

As she approaches her seventies, Frances's dearest wish is to be seen as 'just Frances' – an ordinary woman. If she is, then she is an ordinary woman who has lived, and continues to live, an extraordinary life.

MAX RIDDINGTON
August 2003

Prologue

EARLY SEPTEMBER 1997: Kensington Palace Gardens has become a shrine. People, hundreds of them, many with tear-stained faces, squeeze along the open pathways, seemingly distracted by an obscure but nonetheless overwhelming sense of loss. The scent of fresh flowers hangs heavy in the warm evening air. A sea of bouquets, dotted here and there with flickering candles, shimmers in the twilight. The world itself is all at sea: the Queen of Hearts has been killed in the most tragically ordinary of ways – in a car driven by a drunk driver. Yet that she should die in something as banal as a traffic accident does nothing to lessen the tragedy. Hers is as unbelievable a death as a life.

A tall, elegant, grey-haired woman walks quietly, straight-backed among the mournful crowds. Shattered by personal grief, Frances Shand Kydd, the Princess of Wales's mother, bends down to read the poignant messages written on cards attached to bunches of flowers, or photographs, or children's toys, or stops to murmur her thanks to people for their kindness. Hands reach out to take hers; they hold on to her and talk about her daughter as though she had been an old friend, expressing unbearable sorrow. Some call to her or reach out to touch her, while others stand silently pointing as she walks by. Almost everyone weeps for the beautiful dead woman whom they never knew.

For Frances, however, the one voice that matters, perhaps more than any other, stays silent. There is no personal commiseration, no kindly thought, no shared sense of grief, no kinship in mourning – not one word.

So when the Queen, under pressure from her advisers and from the media, but effectively forced by the will of the people, belatedly stared into a television camera's lens and broadcast to the world her tribute to Diana – 'What I say to you now, as your queen and as a grandmother, I say from my heart' – it had the hollow ring of hypocrisy.

For at no time in the long aftermath of Diana's shocking death did the Queen telephone Frances Shand Kydd to offer her condolences. There was no mother-to-mother call, no discussion between two grandmothers anxious for the welfare of their grandsons. No personal, considered attempt at reconciliation in death after the long war between the Palace and the Princess. Just the stilted broadcast of 417 words of conscience-salving platitudes, apparently designed to pacify an impatient nation and press, perhaps even to deflect a potential constitutional crisis.

To this day, Her Majesty has still not made that call.

CHAPTER ONE

Behind Closed Doors

A s a child, Frances Roche was an extraordinary creature, brave to the point of foolhardiness, and blessed with superb balance and a lively mind – some would have said too lively for her own good.

Often she would creep up on to the sloping roof of Park House, on the royal family's Sandringham Estate in Norfolk, easing her way across the brittle grey slates without looking down. Crouching on her haunches, she would untie her polished shoes, kicking them off to the side, and slip out of her white socks, placing each into the toes of her shoes. All at once she would unfurl her long-limbed body to its full height while flicking back her shock of blond hair. Looking up, passers-by would see a small, lithe, balletic figure standing on her left leg, the right held high and crooked at the knee, her right foot arched inwards. Then, seemingly without thought, she would begin to dance barefoot over the tiles and between the chimney stacks, skipping and jumping, effortlessly gliding over the rooftop to some secret tune in her head.

Sometimes her sister and brother would appear on the manicured lawn below and, craning their necks, stare mesmerized at this daring performance. They wished they could do the same. Once Frances waved to them to come up, but as she did so, their mother's voice rang out and the two spectators scampered back inside. The young girl on the rooftop glimpsed the gold of the setting sun reflected in a nearby lake as she made her way down into the house. She felt a certain sadness as her moment of freedom ended, knowing that whatever her secret desires, it was her destiny to be a lady, bred to take her place in a class-ridden world, and to follow a code of behaviour and a system of rules that were both extremely rigid and, in so many ways, anachronistic.

'It is very hard to harness Frances's energy,' reads her first school report. And while her parents and tutors tried to pull her into line, her independent, and often wilful, nature would never be denied. Not even the threat of being kept indoors, or the wrath of her parents, was enough to curb her spirit. In fact, Frances admits that she revelled in the challenge. 'I never minded my punishments and adored the delicious joy of my triumphs when I wasn't found out.'

Sometimes she would be spotted at the back of the garden at Park House, gazing up at a tall cypress tree and its strong thick boughs. With almost no thought for her own safety, she would shimmy up to the top, sliding effortlessly through the tangle of branches. There, to the alarm of her protective father, she would wrap both legs tightly round a branch, locking them together until she hung upside-down like a bat, laughing out loud at her own fearlessness.

As a girl, and unaccountably for a child brought up in the entrenched and conventional ways of the British aristocracy, Frances refused to be confined to the mores of upper-class society, as it existed in the years before the Second World War. Surrounded by wealth and privilege as the younger daughter of the fourth Baron Fermoy, Frances still would be Frances, no matter what. Yet despite her wilfulness it was not to be many years before she was to suffer the dark side of privilege. Before long, she would find herself being used in the obsessive pursuit of a male heir in order to continue a blood line, maintain the continuance of another title, and assure the inheritance of a great estate.

By the time she was twenty-one, Frances had borne two healthy children. Sarah was born in the spring of 1955, a fraction over nine months after a spectacular Westminster Abbey wedding to Johnnie Spencer, Viscount Althorp, heir to the Spencer earldom and a scion of one of the country's most noble families. Then, two years later, in February 1957, Jane arrived. It was soon clear to Frances that the birth of another girl was regarded as a disappointment, and the quest for a male heir took on the aspect of a race against time.

True to her nature, she remained optimistic that she would eventually bear a son, although she was increasingly and acutely aware that the price of failure was high. All too soon, however, the obligation to fulfil the dreams and expectations of a rich, powerful and influential aristocracy began to create intolerable strain in her marriage and her life. She tried to carry on as normal, knowing that her role was, self-evidently, pivotal, but her husband sank into dark moods that said more than he could ever articulate. Having made his bed by marrying Frances, however, he now had to toss and turn on it. While no male heir was forthcoming, he was in danger of suffering the ignominy of losing the Althorp seat, on his own death, to another branch of the Spencer family, since the estate would pass to the closest male heir. Althorp was presently occupied by Johnnie's father, the seventh Earl Spencer, and he would undoubtedly inherit it and the earldom on his father's death; whether he could secure it for his own descendants, however, depended upon his having a male heir.

To make matters worse, the swift arrival of the two Spencer girls had made Johnnie's financial situation dire, for he was now trying to support a family on the meagre allowance his father gave him. Frances was haunted by the fact that she had not yet fulfilled her obligation in the male-dominated era that followed, in upper-class circles at least, the end of the Second World War. Love was one thing, an heir quite another. 'There was this amazing pressure to have sons. When I was born it was a different era where boys were important – rather like china,' she has said, adding wryly, 'You used to throw the girls back in the river.'

In this atmosphere, Frances announced that she was pregnant again in the late spring of 1959. It should have been a happy time. Instead, an oppressive atmosphere of collusion between her husband and her mother, to which she was not party, prevailed, and she seemed to sense underhand forces at work that frightened her. As her pregnancy progressed she became increasingly weary, and, living on her wits, prayed that her husband and mother would be pleased, whatever the outcome. She lived each day in the knowledge that if things did go wrong – either with the pregnancy, or if the baby should be another girl – the responsibility lay solely at her door. Her own mother, the formidable and royally connected Ruth, Lady Fermoy, appeared to be losing patience with the succession of girl babies. 'It will be a boy this time,' she asserted to Johnnie, in an effort to placate him, while he, desperately clinging to such prophecies, tended to believe everything she said. As a close friend of the Queen Mother, Ruth Fermoy gave Johnnie influence at Court. And to Ruth, the daughter of an army colonel from Aberdeen who had married into the aristocracy, the Spencers were a rung up the aristocratic ladder. Their relationship was, from her side, both parasitical and sycophantic.

Throughout the months of the pregnancy, Johnnie Althorp's anxiety intensified. He was often to be seen broodily pacing the grounds of Park House, Frances's childhood home, to which they had come to live at Ruth's suggestion after the death of Frances's father in 1955. The house stood, facing north, at the end of a long sweeping drive overlooking an expanse of parkland. They moved in on the understanding that it would be a convenient and well-positioned stopgap (since it was rented from the Sandringham Estate) for Johnnie until his father died and he inherited Althorp. For Frances, however, the house she had loved as a child was quickly turning into a gilded cage.

At some time early in January 1960, Frances decided to give birth in the familiar surroundings of her home, rather than in hospital. This was not an uncommon occurrence at the time, especially since her previous two children had been born without major complications. When her baby was almost due, she persuaded doctors at the Queen Elizabeth Maternity Hospital in King's Lynn to allow her request; the midwife who would attend the birth nodded in agreement.

A few days later, on 12 January, John Spencer was born in the master bedroom at Park House. Here at last was the long-awaited heir to Althorp, and all that went with it. Frances, overwhelmed with joy, longed to tell Johnnie the wonderful news of the birth of their son, for it was not the custom then for fathers to be present at the births of their children.

Then her world turned dark. Within seconds, the calm in the room evaporated, becoming a frenzy of activity, a blur of doctors and nurses working away on the baby's limp body. Johnnie was summoned from somewhere in the house to be with his by now panic-stricken wife, while the baby was whisked away to undergo secret treatment in the nursery. Left alone, Frances tried to stay calm but was further distracted by the sound of muffled voices outside her bedroom. Although exhausted by hours of childbirth, she recognized the disquietingly hushed voices of both her husband and her mother. She was unable to hear actual words, but she could make out their sombre tone and knew immediately that something had gone drastically wrong. Left on her own for hours, she felt bereft, confused and terrified.

As she lay recovering, the last sound Frances heard, before the dreadful truth was explained to her, was the scraping noise of the baby's crib being wheeled away. Despite the best medical efforts, John Spencer's life had lasted just ten short hours.

Frances admits that she will never forget the well-meaning, if misguided advice, given to her by the family, and cannot help but wonder what their reaction would have been if John had indeed been another girl:

> I was told to forget him, [as if] he was nothing, but he was [something] for me. My husband, my mother and my mother-in-law expressed their grief in a trio of empathy. They were angry it had happened, but it was the era of the Establishment 'males only', so it may sound a little harsh but I think probably if I'd had another daughter at that stage perhaps their grief wouldn't have been so profound.

For Frances, her natural instinct to hold and to love her dead child, and then to grieve for him, was suppressed and then denied. Yet despite her personal anguish, she did as she was asked. Looking back to those difficult days more than forty years later, she still feels a sense of guilt about the sudden and unexpected death of her first-born son. She acknowledges that many decisions were made behind her back, something that did little to lessen her pain and her longing for her lost child.

Occasionally the door [of the bedroom] would shut and I'd think, 'I know what they're up to, they're putting all the baby's clothes away, they're putting the pram away, they're doing all kinds of things like that.' And they were. It was like he'd never happened, but I'd had him on board for nine months. He was mine. As a mother I felt hugely responsible and very possessive of whom I was carrying and what I did, how I ate and exercised. Only I was responsible. Two people made that baby, but I was responsible from the beginning to birth. That is a mother's part, and only hers.

The trauma of John's death, and his funeral a few days later, were almost too much for Frances. The loss of her son brought back awful memories of the death of her true confidant and guide, her father. Their relationship had been an especially close one, and his death from cancer five years earlier had deprived Frances of a sounding board for her lively opinions as well as the reassurance of knowing that she was loved unconditionally. 'He was everything to me. He was and is the most caring, lovely, sensitive person I've ever met.'

Her father and her son were buried just a few yards apart in the west corner of Sandringham churchyard, the baby's headstone bearing the plain yet poignant epitaph, 'In loving memory'. Together, these two graves became a constant and tragic reminder of life's arbitrariness. What was supposed to have been the happiest period of Frances's life had become one of tragedy and failure.

She yearned for her father but she had only her distant and undemonstrative mother for comfort. Ruth Fermoy expected Frances to rely upon aristocratic resilience, stoically playing on with the cards she had been dealt. There was little understanding, and no access to – or particular desire for – counselling.

To add to Frances's woes, she began to hear rumours that her baby, John, had been born terribly deformed. Several commentators have suggested that a genetic condition must have been responsible for the newborn's premature death. And indeed the death certificate, issued on 13 January 1960 and certified by one J. L. B. Ansell MRCS, reads: 'John Spencer, son of Edward John Spencer, the Viscount Althorp, a Landowner, died from extensive malformation.'

While the facts were clear, it would have been terribly upsetting for Frances to be confronted with such news. There was another factor, however. To lose a child is one thing; to be saddled with the stigma of genetic deformity in such circles is quite another. The family would be marked for ever. Together, therefore, Johnnie and Ruth Fermoy made a decision: to preserve the family's reputation as a pure and healthy line, they told Frances that John had been born with unformed lungs.

From Johnnie Althorp's perspective, it was not unreasonable to soften the truth a little. An act of kindness, to conceal from his wife the full extent of their son's disabilities, was thoughtful. It was also self-interested. Knowing the brutal truth might well have deterred Frances from trying for another child – at a time when the pursuit of an heir had become more pressing than ever. The deception had been carried out by the simplest of means, by never allowing Frances to see her child. In trying to be kind, however, her husband and mother had in fact unwittingly colluded in an act of great cruelty. Speaking of her long-dead son, Frances admits:

> I never held him. Of course nowadays you very often give birth under an epidural and immediately leap out of bed. But in those days you stayed in your bunk and somehow it was in your mind that if you got out of bed you'd keel over. So although he was in the next room to me, I didn't feel equipped to [follow] my biggest urge and hold him.

Any sympathy for the bereaved mother was not to last long, however. While at her lowest ebb, Frances faced the humiliation of being reminded of her failures yet again. Both her mother and her husband, united in their quest to find an answer not only to what had brought about John's death, but also to Frances's apparent inability to bear male children, arranged for her to be sent for medical tests in London. There she was subjected to intimate examinations and tests by Harley Street specialists, principally to uncover why she was so singularly failing to produce healthy boys. 'They believed something was wrong with me, that some sort of pill or minor operation would straighten me out. So they paraded me and went to enormous trouble to send me to specialists in London to be examined.'

The awful irony of these tests was their complete pointlessness. As is now well known, it is the father's genes that determine the sex of a child, not the mother's. In 1960, however, such information was little known and certainly

REGISTRATION DISTRICT					King's Lynn			
1960 DEATH in the Sub-district of ...King's Lynn............					...in the ...County of Norfolk........			
Columns:– 1	2	3	4	5	6	7	8	9
No.	When and where died	Name and surname	Sex	Age	Occupation	Cause of death	Signature, description and residence of informant	When registered	Signature of registrar
56	Twelfth January 1960. Park House, Sandringham.	John SPENCER	Male	10 hours	Son of Edward John Spencer, The Viscount Althorp, A Landowner.	1(a)Extensive Malformation. Certified by J.L.B.Ansell M.R.C.S.	Althorp, Father, Park House, Sandringham, King's Lynn.	Thirteenth January 1960	J.H. Wilson Registrar

John Spencer's death certificate, issued on 13 January 1960

would not have been considered important by dominant, and sometimes domineering, males.

The medical tests proved to be such an unpleasant experience for the young and bereaved mother that she retreated into a kind of half-life. Unable properly to understand why she was being treated in such an apparently callous manner, deeply offended by what amounted to a public acknowledgement of her failure, and degraded by the examinations she had to undergo, Frances withdrew into herself. When she next found herself pregnant, a few months later in the summer, she did not tell anyone, neither her doctor nor anyone in her family. The fear of having to prove herself and meet the high expectations of those around her was simply more than she could cope with. So she stayed silent, keeping to herself the knowledge of her pregnancy as protection from her husband's growing impatience. Johnnie questioned her about the state of her health and watched her every move until her natural confidence and stamina dwindled to almost nothing. As she herself says, 'It was obvious that I was considered the reason why John was not able to survive. So when I became pregnant the next time I was fiercely aware what was expected of me. I suppose it was a form of protection, [but] I decided I would keep this pregnancy to myself until I was a bit further on.'

Disheartened, exhausted, worried and deeply saddened, Frances needed to get away. So later that summer she took the two children to the seaside in Devon for a few days to get some sun and sea air and to try to find the courage to announce the news of another potential Spencer heir.

At first the holiday went well. She built sandcastles on the beach with the girls, cooked, read and, in the evenings, listened to music alone while Sarah and Jane slept. She began to relax and to feel better about herself. Then one night she awoke in terrible pain. She knew immediately that something had gone horribly wrong. Walking gingerly to the bathroom, not wanting to wake her daughters, she sat on the cold floor and quietly sobbed. There, alone and afraid, she miscarried the child that only she knew about. The one blessing in this dreadful event was Johnnie's absence, and thus the lack of his reproaches and admonishment. He went to his grave without ever knowing that he had fathered another child. 'Away on holiday in Devon with Sarah and Jane I miscarried that baby during one night, totally alone and without anyone's knowledge. I actually didn't tell my children until after their father died; he never knew.'

By the autumn of 1960, once more at her husband's insistence, she was pregnant again. This was her fifth conception within five years, and Frances was by now so emotionally fragile that she made the conscious decision not to mention this pregnancy either. 'I then had a double dilemma: I'd given birth to a baby who hadn't survived and had a secret miscarriage. But I honestly felt keeping this to myself was the only way for me to survive.'

By the time she dared acknowledge to herself that the baby was viable, and announced her pregnancy to her husband and family, she refused to have the baby anywhere other than at home at Park House, her mistrust of the medical profession still raw. That the doctors agreed, given her recent obstetric history, seems remarkable. Frances, however, was hiding one part of that history, something that made her decision to give birth at home even more typically headstrong: 'All through the pregnancy I worried that I hadn't seen a doctor after my miscarriage to make sure all was well. I was anxious but determined no one should discover the truth.'

Despite enduring a forty-seven-hour labour with her first child and suffering the death of her last, Frances went ahead and she and Johnnie once again prepared Park House for the arrival of their new baby. This time there were no problems. On 1 July 1961, the child slipped easily into the world. Only then did it sink in that this baby, although beautiful, was yet another girl. Frances was immediately and hugely relieved at seeing a healthy, very handsome baby, long-limbed and saucer eyed. She remembers the moment vividly:

> Diana was born and she was everything I wanted, hoped and prayed for – a healthy child. She was born at home in the evening just as a great cheer resounded around Sandringham Cricket Club as the local speed cop scored a century. I thought that was really rather nice that she came into the world with a clap of hands.

Perhaps inevitably, Johnnie's initial reaction was one of disappointment, although he tried hard to hide such thoughts from his wife, who was clearly besotted with the baby. Nevertheless, Frances could see a familiar look, almost of exasperation, in her husband's eyes. The long-term future of Althorp, his family home, still remained in jeopardy.

The atmosphere at Park House, as Frances recalls, was one of mixed emotions: relief at the birth of a healthy child, coupled with frustration that Lord Althorp still had no male heir. Again feeling that she was somehow, however obscurely, to blame for the child's sex, Frances knew that she had become the focal point for everyone's displeasure within the immediate family. Nor was it only her mother and her husband who minded the birth of yet another girl. Her father-in-law, Jack, the seventh Earl Spencer, was bitterly disappointed, and did not hold back from making his feelings abundantly clear to his son within earshot of Frances. 'Jack Spencer built bonfires to be lit when a son and heir was born. While outwardly there was tremendous joy at Diana's birth, I couldn't help thinking, rather wryly, that there was going to be a bonfire lit at Althorp and if I'd been there, I might have been on top!'

Johnnie, when asked to comment on his new child, perfunctorily declared that she was a 'perfect physical specimen', and would not be drawn further. It may be, however, that given the unhappy circumstances of the last birth in Park House, this was as much as he was able to say without feeling too distraught. Yet after all, what good was another girl to a man in his position? As a father, no doubt he was as delighted as most, but as a potential landowner and heir to an historic title and a great estate and fortune, he had a problem. Frances later put her husband's aspirations into perspective when she remarked, 'I do wonder if the quantity in your wallet equates to the quality of living.'

Frances immersed herself in caring for her new baby who, two months later, was christened Diana Frances at the Church of St Mary Magdalen, Sandringham. She became the only one of the Spencer children to have commoners for godparents rather than at least one member of royalty, a telling sign of her lack of hierarchical importance, but also perhaps an indication that Frances had rebelled against her mother's social aspirations, her glittering connections to high society and the Crown. To Frances, Ruth and Johnnie had become a little too close to each other for her liking – or comfort – since together they could exert considerable pressure on her. (It is an intriguing thought that the difference in ages between Johnnie and his wife, and Johnnie and Ruth, was almost the same.)

More worryingly, and despite the arrival of Diana, cracks had also now started to appear in the relationship between Frances and Johnnie. Frances, headstrong and vivacious, finally refused any longer to play the submissive little woman or give way before Johnnie's demands. Rows, often alcohol fuelled, became commonplace; worse, they were noticed both by the children and the staff. Johnnie was fast approaching forty and the onset of middle age, whereas Frances, still in her twenties, was at the peak of her physical and emotional powers. Having gone through periods of great personal turmoil she needed a good deal of love and consideration, but in her marriage both were in short supply. There was a coldness between the couple that was fast becoming impenetrable. Diana later had vivid memories of her parents' rows, and one of the staff at Park House recalled that 'She [Diana] thought she had seen her father hitting her mother. It was possible. Their rows had led to violence before.'

Even so, the Althorps resolved between them to weather their marital storm, and out of a shared sense of duty and of responsibility to their children, struggled to maintain an outward appearance of stability. Three years after Diana's birth – a larger age gap than with any of her other children, itself perhaps an indicator of the decline in the closeness between her and Johnnie – Frances was pregnant again. Given the deterioration of her relationship with Johnnie, this was to be her final attempt at producing an heir, and every necessary precaution was taken. Park House and local doctors were spurned in favour of a more advanced medical unit at the London Clinic. Frances was booked in to a room, while Johnnie spent much time pacing outside. Frances, nervously superstitious, put paid to her father-in-law's eccentric plans for a pyrotechnic celebration of the imminent new arrival. 'I did say, "Don't plan a bonfire – [then] I might have a boy!" He didn't. Then I did.'

On 20 May 1964 the Spencers' dream was at last realized. Frances was safely delivered of a baby boy, Charles Edward Maurice, a child born to inherit all of his father's property, and most of his ambitions. Althorp was secure in the hands of Johnnie's descendants for another generation.

The birth of a healthy male heir to the Spencer title and estates was much exalted, despite one small but significant historical catch. Sadly, Charles could not follow in the Spencer tradition of being christened John. Frances explains how she later consoled her second son about the family name. 'Charles is the first Spencer [i.e. the first heir to the earldom] who's not called John. He's called Charles Edward ([the latter being] his father's name) and Maurice (my father's name). He did say to me when he was old enough to realize, "I'm the only one highlighted," and I said, "Well, you weren't the oldest son."'

That small disappointment aside, Charles's arrival and subsequent christening far outshone the relatively sober reception for his sister, Diana. Johnnie ordered flags to be flown at Althorp to mark the joyous occasion of his son's birth, and the majestic setting of Westminster Abbey was chosen for his christening, which was held with the appropriate degree of regal pomp. To cap it all, the Queen agreed to act in the honorary role of godmother. It is easy to sense the hand of Ruth, Lady Fermoy in all this.

Yet these grandiose celebrations only served to mask for a while what Frances now knew. The birth of Charles was the beginning of the end of her marriage. Frances had fulfilled her part of the marital bargain. Young, lively and interested in everything around her, she wanted to start enjoying life after almost a decade of pregnancies.

The remaining years of their marriage – and there were not to be many of them – saw Frances and Johnnie lose for ever the mutual respect that lies at the core of all healthy, loving relationships. Her free spirit and love of people were confined and clipped amid the limited circle of rural, if not royal, Norfolk society. Still only twenty-eight when Charles was born, she longed for the stimulation of London. The fixation on producing an heir, coupled with the loss of their first-born son, had suffocated the marriage.

Charles Spencer was later to tell Diana's biographer, Andrew Morton, of his father's sadness at the death of John, something that confirms its damaging effect: 'It was a dreadful time for my parents and probably the root of their divorce because I don't think they ever got over it.'

In securing the Spencer line, however, Frances had become perilously exposed. In a sense, she had outlived her usefulness. Now she was to be betrayed in a manner that her father, had he still been alive, would never have allowed, and which, even today, seems scarcely credible.

CHAPTER TWO

Kings, Queens and Royal Circles

T HE HON. FRANCES ROCHE grew up a daddy's girl. Completely at ease in her father's presence, she loved his calm, gentle manner and ready wit. As a nine-year-old she would sit on his knee, staring up wide-eyed up at his kindly face. Lord Fermoy would smile down, in no way distracted from getting on with the important business of being the Unionist MP for King's Lynn, which he represented for a total of thirteen years, from 1924 to 1935 and again during the austerity of the last two years of the Second World War.*

Maurice Fermoy was an active man, a genuine champion of the people, with a powerful sense of duty that led him to involve himself with his constituents' hopes, fears and aspirations. He was a world away from the peer who pontificates from the grandeur of a drawing room. His popular and populist attitudes endeared him to ordinary men and women, while his title allowed him access to politics. Troubled constituents would file into his office to ask for advice and help, and Frances would watch the proceedings without a hint of awkwardness from her busy father. The same naturalness made him popular with people of all classes and all ages. Frances proudly sums up his feeling for people: 'My father had no interest whether you lived in a castle, a croft or a caravan; he was only interested in the person.'

Physically, Maurice Fermoy was a great bear of a man, with an oval face and a receding hairline, which gave him a slightly daunting appearance belied

---

* Normally, an hereditary (or a life) peer is not able to be elected to Parliament, since he had (until recently) a seat in the House of Lords by right. The Fermoy barony belongs to the Irish peerage, however; when the Irish Free State (now the Republic of Ireland) was established in 1922, peers of the Irish creation lost the right to sit in the House of Lords, which in turn permitted them, if they had chosen to become British subjects, to stand for Parliament and, if elected, to sit in the House of Commons.

by his kindly manner. Having spent almost forty years in America, he was an untypical father among the English upper class in the harsh 1930s. Maurice placed far less accent on tradition than did more conventional members of the British aristocracy, who were largely brought up to believe that children should be seen and not heard. Upper-class children were rarely allowed to see their fathers during working hours (when their fathers did work, that is), never mind encouraged to spend time with them. Yet Maurice Fermoy managed to straddle happily the fine line between position and informality, without in any way diminishing his authority. Frances recalls that, 'He was a great teacher who expected you to be alert, interested, looking the person in the eye, shaking hands. Yet he also recognized the limited attention span of children [when they were with him at work] and let you off the hook after about twenty minutes.'

He had married late and was almost fifty years old before his first child was born, something that perhaps made him a more patient parent. Himself an identical twin, he also had an instinctive understanding that comes from close sibling contact. He genuinely liked people and had a gift for making them feel included, at however brief a meeting. A fellow MP described him as,

> not an orator nor even much of a politician, though he worked very hard to try to be both. His surpassing popularity was instantly won by his strangely attractive personality. He was indefatigable in his rounds of the constituency. He had an uncanny memory for faces and names and could always recall previous conversations with individuals. His humour was . . . a cross between native Irish wit and Broadway wisecracks. The mixture was unique.

He enjoyed community life in Norfolk enough to accept, in 1931, the honorary position, albeit an added responsibility, of Mayor of King's Lynn, and during his year in office became something of a local celebrity. His popularity in the county grew, as also did his influence. This was in no small measure helped by his love of traditional country pursuits, for these kept him involved in local life, and over the years he became a regular companion of royalty, especially during the grouse-shooting season, or when they were in Fermoy's constituency at Sandringham, which maintains a large sporting estate.

He was often to be found tramping over royal estates in company with two of his most illustrious friends, Prince Albert and his wife, the former Lady Elizabeth Bowes-Lyon – the couple known more formally as Their Royal Highnesses the Duke and Duchess of York.

Maurice's unwavering friendship with these and other members of the royal family of the day proved to be exceptionally fruitful, and he was rewarded with the lease of the magnificent Park House on the Sandringham Estate, which had been bought by the then Prince of Wales (later King

Edward VII) as a royal holiday residence. This was seen as a favour granted to the Duke of York by his father, King George V, who owned the entire property and spent a good deal of his time in the nearby York Cottage. Although Park House, which has ten bedrooms, had originally been built to accommodate guests and their servants during the busy shooting season, by the 1920s it was considered better that it should be used as a full-time home. Set at a small distance from the main house at Sandringham, it offered considerable privacy. Letting the property to Lord Fermoy and, from 1931, his wife Ruth, had the added benefit of providing the estate with extra income, and the royal family with discreet, sympathetic and trustworthy neighbours.

The arrangement was no doubt helped by the genuine warmth between the two men's wives, who had struck up a firm friendship that was to last a lifetime. Lady Fermoy and the Duchess of York shared a Scottish heritage, a fierce pride, an intense self-discipline and an unbending sense of duty; both had worked industriously behind the scenes to ensure that they became neighbours.

Ruth Sylvia Gill, a beautiful and talented concert pianist, was just twenty and studying at the Paris Conservatoire when she first set eyes upon the distinguished Maurice Fermoy, a man more than twice her age. He found her beauty – a fellow musician recalls her 'perfectly symmetrical face and huge eyes' – and overwhelming confidence entrancing, and in return beguiled her with his charm and easy laughter. Born on 2 October 1908, the daughter of Colonel William Smith Gill, she was raised in the sober Aberdeenshire town of Dalhebity, Bieldside. From childhood, Ruth was to acquire a steely determination, considerable social ambition and a commoner's view of bettering oneself through a good marriage and excellent connections. Given these, it is hardly surprising that she found Maurice Fermoy a sound marriage prospect. She also knew her place in what was then still a heavily male-oriented society, and immediately agreed to abandon any professional musical aspirations in order to support wholeheartedly her future husband's political career, it being true then, as it is still often true today, that an MP's wife can make or break his career.

Despite the considerable age difference (which was to become something of a family trait, mirrored in the marriages of both her daughter Frances and her granddaughter Diana), they wed in Bieldside on 17 September 1931, when Ruth was twenty-two and Maurice forty-six.

The Fermoys settled into life on the Sandringham Estate secure in the knowledge that they were now a part of the royal family's inner circle. Outwardly mild-mannered and painfully shy, the Duke of York placed great store upon personal friendship and loyalty, and Maurice's discretion was always unquestioned. A good listener by nature, and naturally courteous, Maurice never once showed embarrassment or impatience at the Duke's stammer, which was at once both a cause and a symptom of his marked lack of self-confidence and self-esteem. When King George V died in 1935, and was succeeded by his son David as Edward VIII, it seemed that the Yorks would enjoy a royal life away from the spotlight, performing such duties as they were required to but otherwise living a peaceful family life among friends and neighbours.

This relatively relaxed and informal lifestyle away from the cares and responsibilities of the throne was suddenly shattered, however, when the Duke's older brother, Edward VIII, glamorous but weak to a fault, declared that he was in love with an American divorcée, Mrs Wallis Simpson. A constitutional crisis loomed: the King could not possibly marry someone who was divorced. To conservative elements – indeed, to most of the country and the Commonwealth – it was unthinkable; Edward VIII must either do his duty and give up Mrs Simpson, or abdicate the throne in favour of his younger brother, the Duke of York. It was a time of great upheaval during which the Duke and Duchess sought the advice and support of Maurice and Ruth Fermoy.

The Duchess, anxious at the strain placed upon her nervous husband, almost certainly confided her hatred of Mrs Simpson to Lady Fermoy. Both Elizabeth and Ruth prided themselves on being loyal, faithful, family-oriented, and wedded to notions of tradition, duty and service, in stark contrast to the behaviour of the King and his paramour. This resentment was intensifying even before the Abdication crisis reached its height. Indeed, the two friends would mull over Mrs Simpson with almost obsessive regularity, ensuring that any antagonism which came their way was returned with equal vitriol.

In his book *Royal Feud*, Michael Thornton commented:

> The Duchess of York took an instant dislike to the sleek, chic, epigrammatic Mrs Simpson. And Wallis, quickly aware of the coolness of this influential member of the royal family, unwisely took to mimicking Elizabeth's mannerisms and to deriding her ultra-feminine, sometimes baroque style in fashion. 'The Dowdy Duchess' was how Wallis liked to describe her.

The Yorks, and the Fermoys, clung to the hope that the King would at last display some strength of character and abide by his duty and his birthright, rather than give up everything to follow his personal desires. Ruth listened as the Duchess expressed her deep hurt at speculation suggesting that her emotionally and physically fragile husband (he had been sickly as a child, and since then had undergone operations for appendicitis and a duodenal ulcer) would be incapable of ruling in the event of abdication. It was even suggested that the crown should pass to the Duke's younger brother, the Duke of Kent, who already had a son and heir (the Yorks had two daughters), an idea the Duchess regarded as an insult.

Ruth and Maurice had no doubt that the Duke would do his duty if he had to, and his best by his country. Like the rest of the nation, they listened to the momentous broadcast on 11 December 1936 as Edward VIII expressed his decision in public, telling the nation that he was unable to 'carry the heavy burden of responsibility . . . without the help and support of the woman I love'. Maurice squeezed Ruth's hand when the King said enviously of the younger brother who was to succeed him, 'He has one matchless blessing, enjoyed by so many of you and not bestowed on me, a happy home with his wife and children.' On the following day, 12 December, Prince Albert, Duke of York, was proclaimed king as George VI.

In the light of all that has befallen the royal family in the past thirty years or so, it is easy to forget that it has suffered serious crises of public opinion before, and weathered them. In 1936, the behaviour of Edward VIII led to massive slippage of public support for, and confidence in, the monarchy. In private the Duchess of York expressed to the Fermoys her disgust at the King's selfishness, and all of them watched impotently as the public's good opinion of the monarchy ebbed away. Even so, Maurice advised the Duke to hold fast and wait for the shock of Edward's abdication to diminish.

A kind of angry disbelief had indeed gripped the country, and in government and royal circles there was growing fear of a constitutional crisis. The public outrage was so great that there was even speculation – regarded as almost treasonous in those days – as to whether the monarchy could survive. In this atmosphere, perhaps more than at any other moment, the Duke had valued the calm outlook of his quiet friend, Maurice, who, older than him by ten years, and wiser and more experienced after his years spent in America, seemed only to have his best interests at heart. The two men had discussed the pros and cons of the situation while walking over the estate, away from prying eyes and whispering tongues, and Maurice had slowly instilled in the Duke a growing conviction that he could succeed as king, even as the Abdication crisis drew to a head.

Now, after the months spent waiting in the wings, and buoyed up by family and friends, the shy, unprepared, frail and stuttering Duke of York was thrust unceremoniously into the limelight. To the public, 'It was as if they expected Clarke Gable, and instead they got George Formby,' as one historian put it (referring to a popular English comedian and entertainer of the time). Yet despite his reluctance, his initial reticence and timidity, and his almost paralysing lack of self-confidence (he had burst into tears upon his mother's shoulder on hearing the news that he was to be crowned king), the Duke brought himself to the role with passionate resolve. In doing so, he shored up the wavering public support for the monarchy, ably supported by his devoted wife, Elizabeth, who showed herself to be not only the backbone of the marriage, but also of the Crown itself. Queen Mary's understated assessment of the new King and Queen had proved to be correct: 'The Yorks will do it very well.'

The Duke and Duchess did not forget that throughout the tempestuous abdication affair the Fermoys had remained the epitome of tact and diplomacy, and an oasis of calm and good sense. Their sound, intelligent approach and heartfelt belief in their friends' abilities never swayed. None the less, the dynamics of the friendship had now changed: the Duke and Duchess of York had become King George VI and Queen Elizabeth, standing at the head of an empire in a world on the brink of war.

Elizabeth never forgave her brother-in-law or Mrs Simpson for inflicting such crippling responsibility on her beloved husband, which she was convinced shortened his life (he died in 1952, aged fifty-six). Privately, however, the new Queen's hostility towards the American 'with two husbands living'* may have been coloured by jealousy. While Elizabeth ended up as Queen, she was, in a sense, married to the wrong man. She had taken nearly three years in coming to her decision to marry Prince Albert of York (as he then was), turning him down on more than one occasion. True love in another couple can be hard to swallow if you yourself have settled for compromise and companionship. It was an issue with which Ruth Fermoy would be faced in relation to her daughter, Frances, many years later.

Other speculation follows a different line. When they discussed their husbands Lady Fermoy detected in her friend a hint of unrequited love. Members of the royal family, according to at least one commentator, also had their own theory, as Michael Thornton has written: 'The Windsors would confide to friends that they believed Queen Elizabeth's hostility [towards Mrs Simpson] to be of a more personal kind; that it was not so much jealousy of the Duke, as of the Duchess, for having married him.'

With all the principals now dead, such speculation is fruitless. Of more use, however, is the view of the infighting and power play within royal circles once the catastrophic decline in popular support for the monarchy had become apparent. It offers a prophetic vision of future events at Court nearly

---

* Wallis Simpson divorced her first husband, Earl Winfield Spencer Jr, in America in 1927, after eleven years of marriage; a year later she married Ernest Aldrich Simpson, an American businessman who had become a naturalized British subject, in England, and divorced him, also in England, in 1936, as the Abdication crisis deepened.

sixty years later, as Ruth Fermoy's granddaughter, Diana, Prince Charles and the Queen all vied, albeit with more sophistication and media savvy than had been evident at the time of the Abdication, first to retain and then to increase public support. Back in 1936, control within the royal family was based on Victorian values – principally the maintenance of a dignified silence and a refusal to admit anything publicly. Echoes of this exist to this day in the Queen's 'never explain, never complain' philosophy.

It was a code that Diana, like her mother before her, found antiquated and stultifying.

In 1936, too, as in 1992, the festering resentment between the different factions spilled over into the public arena. Attempts to close ranks proved hopelessly inadequate when King George VI effectively ostracized his older brother from court circles by refusing to attend his wedding when, in June 1937, he and Wallis were married in France. Most telling of all, the King, who had appointed Edward and his wife Duke and Duchess of Windsor after their marriage, spitefully withheld the courtesy title 'Her Royal Highness' from Wallis, even though her husband was so designated, thereby reducing to nothing any claim she may have had to royal status and treatment. The brothers never really regained the trust, love or respect they had once felt for one another, and the animosity between the two women continued long after the Duke of Windsor died from cancer in 1972. The Duchess died in Paris in 1986; she and her husband had not lived in England since the Abdication, but they are buried side by side in the royal burial ground at Frogmore, close to Windsor Castle. It is true to say that the royal family bears the scars of the Abdication to this day. It is a scandal that is never far beneath the surface – indeed, in 2002 papers were released that showed that Wallis Simpson had been kept under surveillance by the security services, and had apparently been unfaithful to Edward even before the crisis came to a head – and Edward and Wallis are still regarded as the black sheep of Britain's first family.

For the new Queen, this experience of divorce, even though at second hand, shaped her view, as it did Ruth Fermoy's, for ever. She came to see divorce as wrong in every respect, a selfish act to be avoided at all costs. She believed absolutely in the sanctity of her wedding vows, and, devastated by the premature loss of her husband, blamed Wallis and Edward's illicit relationship for his death. Nor did time diminish her intolerance. Overpowering in her role as matriarch after George VI's death, she refused to relent when her younger daughter, Princess Margaret, fell in love with, and sought permission to marry, a divorced man, Peter Townsend. And she was even more vociferous in her condemnation of Prince Charles – her favourite grandchild – when he and his wife, Diana, separated, later to divorce. The Prince's long-standing, if sporadic, relationship with Camilla Parker Bowles served only to bring back harsh memories of Edward VIII's fall from grace – something hardly calculated to commend the relationship to his grandmother.

Absolute and unstinting loyalty was at the core of Queen Elizabeth's code. It was a quality that Maurice and Ruth Fermoy had demonstrated to the full, which in turn meant that they found themselves swept along on a tide of good fortune, since they were now at the very core of British society. Although their friends' elevation to King and Queen was not one of choice, it nevertheless brought very attractive benefits to the Fermoys, a couple who had, in every other respect, all that they could materially desire.

The ability to communicate – and, as we would say, 'network' – was a family trait put to great effect by Maurice's American grandfather, Franklin H. Work. A self-made millionaire, he used his connections to live the American dream, rising from abject poverty to become a successful stockbroker, retained by some of America's richest families. It was this gift of gritty determination that was passed down through the generations, from Maurice to Frances to Diana.

Born in 1819, Franklin was raised in Chillicothe, Ohio and, apart from a passion for riding and swimming, he was desperate to earn enough money to make his mother proud. According to Anne Edwards:

> As a young boy, he would gallop naked astride a gaunt grey horse the length of the main street of Chillicothe, on his way home from swimming in the river. As he passed the market house, people would throw fruit and vegetables at him, but the barrage never slowed him down. When a teacher at his school whipped him for his behaviour, Frank took his small savings and ran away from school. He never saw his mother again – she died before he made his fortune.

He went to New York where he found a job in a gas-fitting store and ended up owning the company. Within five years he'd switched to playing the stock market and his fortune was estimated at $15 million (£10 million).

But with money comes power, not always in a very edifying form. After marrying Ellen Wood, she bore him Frances Eleanor on 27 October 1857. Franklin became obsessed with protecting both his heritage and the American way of life. Anne Edwards maintains that this was compounded by the fact that Ellen was descended from Nathan Hale, one of the heroes of the American Revolutionary War. The result was that 'the American flag flew proudly over the Work Mansion on Fifth Avenue and his daughters were warned they must marry American men or lose their rights to inheritance.'

Of the children of Frank Work's marriage, one daughter, Frances, known as Fanny, always knew her own mind and was inclined to be dismissive of such threats. 'She was like me, wild and independent,' says her granddaughter and namesake, Frances Shand Kydd. 'Her heart ruled her head.' As a young woman, Fanny decided that she would marry for love, with or without her father's blessing. It was not long before her romantic ambitions were realized. In 1879, while on holiday in London with her mother, Fanny was introduced by Winston Churchill's mother, Jennie, Lady Randolph Churchill, herself an American, to the Hon. James Boothby Burke Roche, the flamboyant heir to the Fermoy title. Despite (or perhaps because of) her father's strictures, Fanny could not help falling madly in love with the dashing though relatively impoverished Irish aristocrat, and accepted his proposal of marriage before setting sail back to New York. Her father's fury erupted. That Roche would inherit a title counted for nothing with Franklin Work, the by now highly successful New York stockbroker. He insisted that 'international marriages should be a hanging offence' and impetuously cut his twenty-two-year-old daughter out of his will. Fanny, however, always her own woman, refused to take any notice, and after marrying 'Jim' Roche at Christ Church, New York City, on 22 September 1880, returned with him to England.

Cynics were inclined to say that Jim had proposed to Fanny in the nick of time, for she conveniently arrived with considerable personal wealth – since her father had settled a considerable sum on her before he struck her from his will – which bolstered the depleted Fermoy coffers. The family had breeding and a title, and properties in Ireland, but not an income to match, and Jim Roche's love of gambling and socializing frittered away his wife's fortune to the point of ruin.

The early days of the alliance were happy enough, however, and three children were born to the couple in a mere thirteen months. On 10 April 1884, while they were living in Pont Street, Knightsbridge, Fanny bore a daughter, Cynthia, followed, on 15 May 1885, by twin boys. The first-born, Edmund Maurice Burke Roche, pushed his way determinedly into the world only a few minutes before his identical brother, Francis, but those minutes were enough to assure him of the title. The arrival of two healthy sons was greeted with traditional aristocratic relief – the vulgar phrase 'an heir and a spare' was not then current, but no doubt that was how the twins were regarded. While they may have been physically identical, in personality the two boys could not have been more different, Maurice being forthright and relaxed where Francis was timid and anxious. It was a difference that perhaps explains Maurice's later considerable understanding of the shy Duke of York's character.

Having made the grand gesture, Fanny found herself less than enamoured of sedate motherhood, and became quickly disillusioned, desperately missing both her home country and the high life. She had done her duty, having produced a son to secure the Fermoy line; now she was ready to defy convention once more. Boldly – for in late-nineteenth-century England such a desertion by a wife was a matter for widespread disapproval, at the very least, in upper-class circles – she gathered up her young family, abandoned her profligate husband and returned to New York, prepared to weather the hostile reception awaiting her at her father's house.

It was indeed a strained homecoming, though tempered by Franklin agreeing to reverse his will and provide for Fanny and the children, on two conditions. First, she was to bury her former identity by dropping both her courtesy title and her married name. Second, and here he twisted the knife, she must never again set foot in Europe.

Relieved to be back in America but reeling from a failed marriage and with severely depleted funds, Fanny's usual hot-headedness rapidly cooled and she reluctantly complied with the substance of her father's edict. With his help, she divorced Jim in the Superior Court at Wilmington, Delaware on 3 March 1891. It was not long, however, before her wild spirit reasserted itself and, having regained her former zest for living, on 4 August 1905 she married a Hungarian stableman called Aurel Batonyi and promptly found herself disinherited once again.

Franklin died in 1911, aged ninety-two, but he had ensured that his grandchildren wanted for nothing. They enjoyed a privileged lifestyle, the boys both receiving an elitist and, even then, very expensive Harvard education. Any thoughts that their grandfather might have loosened his grip on the purse strings while on his deathbed proved to be ill founded, however. Instead, such was his dislike for foreigners, he insisted that not a cent would go to his daughter or grandchildren if they attempted to live outside America, a provision that formed a significant part of his will.

Faced with this, Maurice and Francis joined forces to contest what they saw as the xenophobic and unreasonable conditions of their grandfather's wishes, and battled through the courts to have the will overturned. At stake was a little under £600,000 ($900,000) each, an enormous sum then, equivalent to many millions in today's money. As none of the other beneficiaries of Franklin's will complained at this action, the judge sided with the boys, a stroke of fate that was eventually to bind Maurice to Britain and to one of the institutions on which that country is founded – the monarchy. Fanny kicked up her heels and, taking full advantage of the new-found freedom her sons had won for her, disappeared to Europe to enjoy the high life; she died in 1947, aged eighty-nine.

James Roche, third Baron Fermoy, died in 1920, aged sixty-eight. At the age of thirty-six, his oldest son, Maurice, inherited the title (having, so it is said, graciously offered it to his identical but fractionally younger twin brother first). He arrived in England a wealthy man, erudite, outgoing, handsome, titled and single. As a result he was immediately welcomed into the highest circles of society, not least because he was considered a fine catch for any young girl, and that society has always been something of a marriage market. Yet he took his time in choosing a wife, waiting another ten years before he decided to settle down and raise a family.

His maternal grandfather would have turned in his grave had he known that his will had been quashed with such devastating consequences. Not only had his grandson gone to live outside the United States, but he later married outside the United States; worse still, his American heritage was about to be absorbed by the British. Yet no one could have foretold that Maurice's second daughter was destined to play a vital part in the continuation of the British monarchy.

The Hon. Frances Ruth Roche was born on 20 January 1936, in her parents' bedroom at Park House. On the same day just a short distance away, King George V died in the main house at Sandringham. Frances can therefore claim to have lived in two reigns within twenty-four hours of her arrival. She was the second of three children. Her elder sister, Mary Cynthia, had been born two years earlier, and her brother, Edmund James Burke, who would one day become the fifth Lord Fermoy, would arrive on 20 March 1939, a little under six months before the start of the Second World War.

Maurice regarded each successive birth with a proper fatherly pride, although Frances believes that the timing of her arrival meant that she became something of a favourite with her father. 'I'll probably be hit by my sister but I think I was his favourite. I think initially he felt sorry for me as everyone was mooning around as I was born . . . the night King George V was dying, less than a mile away.' It is, too, a measure of the close and friendly manner with which the royal family viewed their near neighbours, that the late King's widow, Queen Mary, despite her own grief, sent a congratulatory note to Park House in which she enquired after the health of the Fermoy's newborn baby.

As was usual in upper-class families, the real joy was reserved for the birth of the son and heir three years later. If Frances was at first put out, she soon found that there were advantages to having a younger brother:

When Edmund my brother appeared in this world – and it was rather like when my son was born – he was greeted as a messiah. There was immense joy, relief and an amazing united feeling which seemed very odd to me. My elder sister Mary was really a good child, she sat and read books and ate sweets and was generally very undemanding, unlike me who was always being a daredevil. I failed to muster my sister as a partner in crime, but with my brother I thought here was a little treasure who might well fill the role. So I trained him up, and he was brilliant. And although I was always accused – and rightly so – of being a bad influence, my brother and I had enormous fun. I don't mean doing evil things in any way; just high spirits and we knew every prank. I enjoyed chancing my arm.

The young Roches' early childhood was more or less typical of an aristocratic country upbringing at the time. War had broken out in the year Edmund was born, and during the early 1940s the children were kept busy with work around the estate, ensuring that they did their bit for the war effort, since so many men had volunteered or been called up for the services. They collected metal scrap for ammunition and chestnuts to be made into toothpaste, and, having commandeered a pony and trap, trotted round the estate to look after the menagerie of hens, ducks, geese and turkeys which, under rationing, had become an important source of food. Despite the worldwide turmoil and the many inconveniences and restrictions of wartime, they found it an idyllic life. Their parents went to work during the dark days of conflict. In 1944, Ruth was appointed a magistrate on the King's Lynn bench, while Maurice, who took over as MP for King's Lynn in 1943, spent much of his time in the heart of government at Westminster, where he brushed shoulders with the Prime Minister, Winston Churchill, and other cabinet ministers.

Again like many upper-class children of that era, especially girls, Frances's early education was at home under a succession of governesses. Her own favourite was a Scotswoman, Gertrude Allen. 'Ally', as she was fondly known, was devoted to a life of service, and seemed to relish her part in bringing up other people's children. Lessons, which included knitting socks and scarves for the troops, would be held, with other children from around the Sandringham Estate, at Park House, in a schoolroom next to the dining room.

It was here that Frances came face to face for the first time with a young boy who later, as a fully fledged courtier, was to play an important part in her own and two of her daughters' futures. The dark-haired, rather studious child sitting beside her in the schoolroom was destined to become her son-in-law and a member of the royal family's most exclusive inner circle. His name was Robert Fellowes – as a future Private Secretary to the Queen, he was to be closely involved with the troubled life of Diana within the royal family. Of his time in the schoolroom, Frances remembers: 'We shared a governess for a while and I watched him learn his ABC – he doesn't like me reminding him of that though!'

If Frances's weekdays were relatively carefree – work on the estate interspersed with lessons and mischief-making – the weekends were dominated by worship. As a child Frances complied – but then, as a child she would not, in any case, have been allowed to default – only finding much later in life that her faith would ultimately sustain her through some terrible times. 'Sandringham church was next to our house and it wasn't an option, you went to church [on Sundays], usually twice, and to Sunday school. That early discipline and reasoning makes me feel that the seed of faith is in everyone but it needs to germinate.'

By her own admission, Frances adored her father, but her relationship with her mother was never as easy. Ruth Fermoy was an unbending perfectionist with exacting standards and impeccable manners, an uncomfortable combination for a young child overflowing with spirit and energy. Ruth's austere Scottish upbringing and near obsession with her family's position in the world left her unable to deviate from protocol. True, she had found in music an escape from the austerity and discipline of life at home in Aberdeenshire, but she never lost the decorum, the sense of what was or was not appropriate, that had been drilled into her from an early age. Once, while accompanying a member of the royal family along a street in some Norfolk town, she saw a friend standing at the side of the road, eating an ice cream. Yet rather than attempt what, to her, could only be an unseemly introduction, or even acknowledge her friend, Ruth chose instead to walk straight past. At the last moment, however, she did manage a majestic 'steely flicker of an eyelid'. Frances concedes that her mother was 'a woman of enormous confidence, unswerving in believing she was always right, which was very daunting'.

At the age of eleven Frances left the security of Park House and followed her sister Mary to boarding school, first to Downham and then to West Heath in Kent. One of her closest schoolfriends at West Heath was a slim dark-haired girl, Susan Wright, later Ferguson (and later still, Barrantes), the mother of Sarah Ferguson, who was to marry Prince Andrew. Frances and Susie shared the same sense of humour and liking for mischief, and remained friends for more than forty years, until the latter's early death in a car crash in Argentina in September 1998. Upon Sarah's engagement to Prince Andrew in 1986, Frances sent Susie a witty warning note: 'So glad there's another rotten apple at the bottom of the barrel with me.' Her friend telephoned her and remarked, laughing, 'It's so you – only you could write that.'

At school, Frances excelled at sports, and especially tennis, at which she became so accomplished that she was selected to play at Junior Wimbledon in 1952. Unfortunately, a couple of days before the event she was struck down with appendicitis and forced to withdraw. Her energy and sociability made her a good team player, and her teachers were sufficiently impressed by her leadership qualities to make her head girl.

Academic studies were a different matter, however. Although she had, and has, a quick, enquiring mind, Frances showed no interest in her lessons. Nor was it necessary for an upper-class girl to do so in those days, for the marriage market beckoned. So after finishing school, the Hon. Frances Roche prepared for life as a debutante, dancing and partying in the most desirable country homes, being introduced to potential – and, it was hoped, well-bred, well-connected and well-off – suitors. Debutantes were still presented at Court then, but no one was under any illusion that 'doing the Season' was anything other than a concerted effort to find a suitable husband.

The Fermoy's diligence and hard work in ensuring that Frances's spirited nature was properly directed seemed to pay off. Her disciplinarian Scottish mother and astute, largely American-raised father instilled in her the idea that there could be no excuses, emphasizing over and over again the importance of first impressions and the inordinate value of good manners. Moreover, during her teenage years Frances seemed to lose something of her wildness. Then again, perhaps she had a plan – a show of initial compliance in order to get her own way when a suitable young man presented himself as a possible husband?

Whatever the motive, the timing was perfect. In upper-class circles there were, and to a certain extent still are, two unwritten rules concerning a young woman's function: first and foremost, she must marry in the blossom of youth. Then she has to produce – and preferably at the first attempt – a son and heir. Faced with these duties, it was never going to be easy for a free spirit like Frances to suppress her true nature. Unless she fell deeply in love, something about which she felt passionately: 'I think you should only marry because it is the only thing you want to do, never for the popular vote, ever!'

Reflecting upon her eighteen-year-old younger daughter, her mother considered the kind of man who might best harness Frances's spirit, for there seemed to be no one of her daughter's age capable of dealing with such animated self-assurance. Ruth Fermoy discussed the problem with her neighbour and friend, Queen Elizabeth who had become the Queen Mother, intimating her concerns. More than once during their discussions the same name was mentioned.

CHAPTER THREE

Perfect Love

To any scheming mother's eye, Johnnie Spencer, Viscount Althorp, was a fine catch. Scion of one of Britain's leading aristocratic families, he was heir to an earldom and to the family's country seat at Althorp in Northamptonshire. Bought in 1508 for £800 ($1,200), the Althorp estate provided both riches and prestige for its owner. The present house, which dates from the early eighteenth century, contained an irreplaceable collection of paintings, among them works by Vandyke, Gainsborough and Rubens, together worth millions of pounds. Behind the grand, white-brick frontage, its 110 rooms displayed cascading chandeliers, the finest furniture built by master craftsmen, and a wealth of intricate plasterwork. It is set in 13,000 acres of some of the most valuable farmland, deep in the heart of England. Perhaps more importantly, however, the house and its estate spoke for the historical power and status of the Spencer family. Their name can be traced back to 1082 and derives from the Norman name DeSpenser, meaning steward or head of the household, a royal appointment at a period when the favour of the newly arrived Norman king meant inevitable advancement. The impeccable Spencer heritage claimed blood ties back to Charles II and the Dukes of Marlborough, Devonshire and Abercorn; Johnnie's great-uncle, the fifth earl (known as the 'Red Earl' because of his sandy-coloured beard), had served under Gladstone in various posts, including those of Viceroy of Ireland and First Lord of the Admiralty, and had been Gladstone's choice as his successor.

Not everything about Lord Althorp was quite as glittering as it seemed, however. He was already approaching thirty, and aspired only to the relatively simple life of a rich landowner and country gentleman. This was a great source of irritation to his father, Jack, the seventh Earl Spencer, who by the 1950s was becoming increasingly anxious about the lack of interest in marriage evinced by his son. Jack lived and breathed Althorp; it was his *raison d'être*, and he was desperate to secure its future within his branch of the family. He was unable to fathom why Johnnie – who served as an equerry to the King from 1950 to 1952, and was an equerry to Queen Elizabeth II from

1952 to 1954, had been educated at Eton, had trained as an army officer at Sandhurst and had been commissioned into the Royal Scots Greys, with which he had seen active service as a captain and tank commander in France during the war – seemed incapable of choosing a decent, childbearing wife. His opinion of his son's intellectual capabilities, never high, began to sink even lower, leaving an uncomfortable atmosphere of strain between the two men.

The impasse appeared to resolve itself when Johnnie met the seventeen-year-old Lady Anne Coke during a house party at Windsor Castle for the annual royal meeting at Ascot. Despite the difference in their ages, Johnnie and Anne were genuinely attracted to one another, with the result that after her coming-out ball, they settled into a period of informal engagement. When Lord Spencer, as domineering as ever, found out about the liaison, however, he bullied his son into submission and stopped the romance from going any further.

Lady Anne, the daughter of the Earl of Leicester of Holkham Hall in Norfolk, was distraught, although she now gracefully describes Johnnie's bachelor days in a rosier light, looking back fondly at their relationship: 'Although he already had lots of girlfriends, I fell very much in love with him. We saw each other a lot over the Season and I went to stay at Althorp. It was a wonderful time. There were weekend parties and two or three dances a night. We used to go from one to the other. It was incredible.' Lord Leicester's views are not known.

It was as Johnnie was stalling over Lady Anne that Frances appeared, another beautiful seventeen-year-old barely out of school. She had the advantage of having previously met the eligible viscount at Sandringham when she was a precocious fourteen-year-old, but it was at her and her sister Mary's joint coming-out ball in Park Lane in May 1953, that, for her, Johnnie came into full focus. For his part, seeing Frances's father open the event by dancing with the Queen Mother assured Johnnie that she had just the right royal associations. For Lord Althorp harboured a private ambition – he did not just want a wife, he wanted a woman close to the Crown.

Whatever his ambitions, however, he and Frances quickly became besotted with each other. Johnnie's connections, as an equerry to the late King and the present Queen, thrilled Ruth Fermoy, and although she felt some concern about the age difference, she remained sanguine, remembering that she had been less than half the age of Frances's father when they had married. How then could she object to the match?

Yet although Johnnie was good-looking, possessed of considerable charm and a relaxed manner, others saw a different side. His former commanding officer in the Greys described him as 'very nice but very stupid, very slow and lacking in go. He was never the brightest of people. It was all squashed out of him by a domineering father. He had beautiful manners and was always very correct.'

To his credit, he showed enough energy to capture the heart of the young and robust Frances, twelve years his junior, while he was himself entranced by the teenager's zest for life and idiosyncratic humour. She had also mentioned her love for children, and it seemed clear that she would be a willing mother – something viewed as a prerequisite to a successful union. To the young couple, it appeared from the outset to be an excellent love match. Relations and friends told Frances how lucky she was, although the pace of events barely gave time for thought – or doubt. Aged only seventeen and not long out of school, woefully inexperienced in the ways of the world, Frances now found herself poised to become Viscountess Althorp. The Fermoys and Spencers were delighted, the royal family, in the person of the Queen Mother, expressed its approval, and it would take only the birth of a son to complete the fairy tale.

The British aristocracy, under laws of primogeniture that date back to feudal times, still largely follows the rule that land and titles pass automatically to the first-born son on the death of the father. Frances, naive at seventeen, saw no threat in this. Johnnie's calm, uncomplicated nature must have appeared similar to that of her own much loved father, besides being a perfect foil to her impetuous nature. He provided a stillness to her lively character, and an anchor for her potential waywardness. Furthermore, and perhaps surprisingly, Frances was also seen by Jack Spencer as an ideal choice, someone who would provide an energy and enthusiasm that his son seemed to lack.

To Lord Spencer's added pleasure, Johnnie speedily called off his unofficial engagement to Anne Coke and started seriously to woo Frances. Five months into their courtship they played tennis at Park House, and at some point during the game, he got down on one knee and asked her to marry him. She accepted without hesitation, and their engagement was announced on 16 October 1953. As to whether she was in love, Frances candidly admits, 'Yes, but frankly when you meet someone at the age of fourteen and get engaged just five months out of school at seventeen, you can look back and ask "Was I an adult?" I sure thought I was at the time.'

Jack was relieved that his son was settling down at long last and that the continuation of the Spencer line through his own descendants would be assured. From the very beginning, he had made his son only too aware that the Spencer lineage was both a blessing and a burden. He himself had been a godson of King Edward VII, but his own upbringing had suffered from the lack of a mother's touch, for his mother, Margaret, had died in childbirth when he was only fourteen. Jack's father, Bobby, the sixth Earl Spencer, never recovered; overtaken with grief, he withdrew into himself, handing the raising of his five children to Delia, the elder daughter. As a consequence the poor girl missed out on her own childhood. The present Lord Spencer has said of his great-aunt, 'She filled the gap left by her mother's death as best she could, both with regard to the other children and frequently acting as companion to her father on official functions.'

Like his mother by nature, Jack was shy, while the trauma of his early teen years had left him with an obsessive streak and a mistrust of other people. He was sent away to school at Harrow and then went up to Trinity College, Cambridge, where he felt an outsider. During the First World War he served as a captain in the 1st Life Guards and was badly wounded, the legacy of which was chronic pain and a foul temper, possibly exacerbated by all that he had been through during the war. At thirty he inherited the earldom and Althorp on the death of his father. He was a charmless and irascible man who, perhaps because of his father's comparative lack of interest in the house and inability to talk about his mother's early death, sought to prove himself by showing off his knowledge. As a habit, it brought him a kind of emotional security, while also indulging his taste for talking down to other people.

He married the pretty Lady Cynthia Hamilton two years before he inherited Althorp, and once they had moved in she brought a much needed light and softness to the house. Cynthia was very fond of children and hated sending her son and daughter, Lady Anne Spencer, away to boarding school. She regularly visited them at school, whereas Jack could never bring himself to bother with such trifling duties. Kindly, patient, trusting and loving, she was the antithesis of her husband.

Cynthia tried to maintain Althorp as a home rather than a museum, but Jack's fixation with the house and its contents was such that she fought a losing battle. He even knocked a lit cigar out of the mouth of the then Prime Minister, Winston Churchill, to stop the ash falling near a collection of rare books. A pragmatist to the core, he had neither interest in nor regard for other people's opinions, or feelings. Showing a remarkable lack of sensitivity and absolutely no subtlety, he ordered that the remains of his dead ancestors should be brought from the family vault in Great Brington church and cremated. The vault, he said, needed a good clear-out, adding that his predecessors were not in a position to care. His blunt indifference caused profound shock, as well as the disapproval of the local people.

Johnnie found communicating with his father difficult at the best of times, but having snared a future bride upon whose suitability they agreed, he was anxious not to rock the boat. A small but difficult distraction loomed, however. Johnnie's position as an equerry required him to accompany the relatively inexperienced Queen on a long tour of the Commonwealth. This meant that he would be out of the country from February to April, just before his wedding, which had been set for June 1954. Johnnie showed his devotion by commissioning a portrait of Frances, which had to be painted at just twenty-four hours' notice. In stepped artist Nicholas Egon, who completed the life-size painting in record speed, and even helped to stow it on board the royal tour liner *Gothic* before the ship left dock. It was a quixotic decision, given that photographs were readily available (for their engagement was one of the society events of the 1950s, as was their wedding, and countless photographs of Frances were published in the *Tatler* and elsewhere), but it showed a more impulsive and frivolous side to Johnnie which Frances found captivating. To a teenage girl, this flamboyant act must have seemed incredibly sophisticated and romantic.

Before the *Gothic* sailed, Frances was chaperoned on board by her mother, Lady Fermoy, to bid Johnnie farewell. He was in dress uniform, complete with sword, and he was later to complain, having been entrusted with the Queen's cine camera, that it was impossible to cope with both sword and camera at the same time.

During his absence, Frances attended finishing school in Florence and Paris, where she took advantage of the haute-couture designers and added to her wedding trousseau. She also bought cocktail dresses and replenished her wardrobe of smartly casual clothes. Johnnie wrote to her every day and telephoned as often as he could. They both missed each other, and longed to be reunited.

The Queen, who could well remember the absences of her fiancé, Prince Philip, on active service with the Royal Navy, did Johnnie a kindness by granting him special leave to disembark at Tobruk in Libya and fly directly home to his fiancée. This was an act of some compassion as there was no particular closeness between the Queen and Frances, although they had often met at Sandringham and elsewhere. The bond between Johnnie and the Queen went back even further, however, and was more relaxed than simply that between monarch and equerry. Prior to her marriage, Princess Elizabeth had occasionally written to Johnnie while he was on active service with his regiment during the war. There are, too, suggestions that he was at one time considered as a potential suitor. If that is true, then having once been close to being a royal consort may have ignited his ambition to marry as close to the monarchy as he could. It might also explain why the Queen kept her distance from Frances, considering her too much of a loose cannon for own taste, the differences in their personalities clouding the relationship. Loyalty was always seen to be rewarded, however, and the Queen felt indebted to Johnnie, who returned home a hero, happily aware that the tour had been judged a great success. His schoolfriend, Sir Roger Cary, described Johnnie as 'a brilliant equerry at the key time'.

Lady Fermoy directed wedding operations with military precision from her London home in Wilton Street, Belgravia. The Queen had personally agreed to the Fermoys' request for the ceremony to be held in Westminster Abbey, a rare privilege. The day was set for exactly one day under a year after the Queen's coronation, and Frances would be the youngest bride to be married in the Abbey since the turn of the century.

Seventeen hundred people received invitations to the ceremony, although the number of guests had to be scaled back for the reception. Three days before the wedding one newspaper carried an article detailing the preparations:

> Although there will be 1,700 guests at the Abbey ceremony, only 900 can be asked to St James's Palace for the occasion by the Queen. Delicately weeding out the unlucky 800 caused the brows of everyone concerned to be furrowed for many a day. Finally it was decided that only personal friends of the bride and bridegroom should be asked to the reception – including of course the nine 'Royals'.
>
> Then there is the catering – there can be no ham sandwiches at the wedding of the year. At the Fermoy town house activity was in high gear. Tradesmen taking and delivering orders knocked constantly. Messengers and postmen called laden with parcels. The telephone scarcely stopped ringing. 'It's been like this for three months,' remarked Lady Fermoy. 'The preparation for a large wedding is fantastic – we shall be busy right up to the day.'

At the arduous, hour-long wedding rehearsal on the day before, Johnnie, amid sniggers, tempted fate by introducing Frances to two regimental friends with the words, 'I would like you to meet my wife.' He also made sure that his regimental sergeant-major, who would be on duty at the reception, was aware of how things stood. 'Now don't forget,' he said, 'there's champagne for the toasts, and the other stuff for the rest of the time.' No doubt the 'other stuff' was of sufficiently good quality.

Newspapers called the affair on Tuesday, 1 June 1954 'the wedding of the year', and it was indeed a spectacular society event clouded only by the early-morning drizzle. An abbey verger helped to control the mass of sightseers – for in those days a high-society wedding, especially one at which royalty would be present, attracted large crowds of people hoping for a glimpse of the good and the great, and especially the bride – by the strange act of sniffing the air. It was his idiosyncratic way of separating genuine guests from sightseers: if he caught just a gentle hint of scent as a woman entered the West Door he waved her through since she was obviously a guest. If, however he could detect her scent from twenty yards away then she obviously had no claim to a seat and was quickly shown the exit. 'I've only been wrong once today,' he claimed.

The guest list included the cream of British royalty. The Queen Mother, wearing a smoky blue lace dress and matching jacket, arrived alongside her younger daughter, Princess Margaret. The Duke of Kent, one of the ushers, showed guests to their purple-cushioned pews; his wife the Duchess wore white and cinnamon, their daughter Princess Alexandra was in slate blue and the Duchess of Gloucester in royal blue.

Snarled in the crowds and traffic, the Queen's car arrived at the abbey four minutes late. A message had to be relayed to Frances and her father to slow their own car down to ensure that monarch and bride did not enter at the same time. The delay meant that Johnnie was left anxiously glancing at his watch, wondering, as do all bridegrooms on their wedding day, if he was to suffer the most awful humiliation imaginable. Several minutes later, however, he could almost be heard sighing with relief as his bride walked tentatively into the abbey, her father at her side and her bridesmaids and pages stepping carefully behind.

For Frances, the delays all added to her being 'hugely nervous', although she concealed her feelings with a sweet smile. A sea of faces turned towards her as she glided down the aisle on the arm of her devoted father like a princess, in a swishing ribbed woven-silk wedding dress embroidered with crystals, rhinestones and hand-cut diamond-encrusted flowers, her veil crowned by a beautiful diamond-tipped tiara. In her hands, which were trembling slightly, she held tightly on to the bouquet of stephanotis, lilies-of-the-valley and white roses. 'The nave was filled with hundreds of tenants and employees of the Althorp estate and I found it quite daunting walking past all those people, some of whom I'd never met. And this was my wedding day!'

As the bride's party had assembled at the West Door, she had glanced at the trio of page boys, thinking that she and Johnnie had chosen well. David Wake-Walker (Johnnie's nephew), Viscount Raynham and James Dawnay wore white satin suits with stiff collars and powder-blue moire sashes, in imitation of a Reynolds portrait at Althorp. The three young bridesmaids skipping lightly behind her were Elizabeth Wake-Walker (Johnnie's niece), Lady Margaret Cholmondeley and Bridget Astor. Frances caught the eye of her older sister, Mary, who was one of four older bridesmaids with Sylvia Fogg-Eliot, Fiona Douglas-Home and Rowena Combe. Their dresses were white spotted muslin with a fichu neckline and full skirts, and all wore long white gloves and the same blue moire sashes as the pages. Frances had also insisted that their posies and headdresses should be composed of the same flowers as her bridal bouquet.

At the head of the aisle stood her future husband with, beside him, his best man, Captain John Dawes of the Royal Scots Greys. As Frances arrived before the altar, Maurice released his daughter's arm and tenderly urged her towards Johnnie, who broke into a huge smile and reassuringly squeezed her cold hand in his as the first hymn resounded through the abbey. Facing the Bishop of Norwich, the couple listened carefully as his words rang out: 'You are making an addition to the home life of your country on which, above all others, our national life depends.' In later years, they would be seen to have had an almost prophetic significance.

After the marriage ceremony, the Queen, Prince Philip, the Queen Mother and Princess Margaret stood up from their seats and walked through to witness the signing of the register. Marriage certificate number 223 reads: '1954 Marriage solemnized at City of Westminster in the Close of St Peter Westminster, in the County of London. Edward John Spencer, aged 30, a bachelor, living at 56 Curzon Street, London W1. Rank – Viscount Althorp, Captain Royal Scots Greys. Father – Albert Edward John Spencer the 7th Earl Spencer.' Frances has no profession listed, the line for her reading: 'Frances Ruth Burke Roche, aged 18 a spinster, 10 Wilton Crescent, London SW1. Father Edmund Maurice Roche, the 4th Baron Fermoy.'

The certificate shows that the couple 'Married in the Westminster Abbey according to the rites and ceremonies of the Established Church by Special Licence'. Then, reinforcing the aristocracy's predilection for single names, it states that the marriage between Althorp and Frances Roche was solemnized in the presence of 'Elizabeth R, Philip, Elizabeth R, Margaret, Spencer, Fermoy', as well as 'Cynthia Spencer and Ruth Fermoy'.

Relieved that the ceremony had gone without a hitch in front of such an august audience, the smiling couple emerged from the abbey, walking arm in arm beneath swords held aloft by the guard of honour, eight members of the groom's regiment. The photographs show Johnnie, grinning broadly as he

No.	When married	Name and surname	Age	Condition	Rank or profession	Residence at the time of marriage	Father's name and surname	Rank or profession of father
223	1st. June 1954	Edward John Spencer	30	Bachelor	Viscount Althorp Captain R.W.2 Royal Scots Greys	56 Curzon Street W.1.	Albert Edward John Spencer	7th Earl Spencer
		Frances Ruth Burke Roche	18	Spinster		10 Wilton Crescent S.W.1	Edmund Maurice Roche	4th Baron Fermoy

Lord and Lady Althorp's marriage certificate, issued on 1 June 1954

steps forth, and Frances, slightly more tight-lipped and now a viscountess, making their way out into the light.

After the reception the couple left for their honeymoon – a leisurely tour of Europe in a Bentley. Frances, supremely happy, conceived their first child before they returned to Britain. They were beginning married life with a baby on the way, and everything seemed perfect. It was the sort of future of which dreams are made.

What could possibly go wrong?

CHAPTER FOUR

Secret Desires

IN AUGUST 1954, as Frances was driving home with Johnnie from their idyllic two-month honeymoon, she found herself dwelling on the doubts going through her mind. Not about her husband – for she was very much in love – but about what would happen next. As they motored from the ferry along the quiet roads towards London, and from there on to the Gloucestershire village of Rodmarton, she found herself at something of a loss.

In truth, Johnnie was himself a little adrift, having that summer given up his post with the royal household. Now aged thirty, and about to become a father, he needed to find a new direction. Life in the service of others was beginning to lose its appeal. While travelling had its attractions (it also allowed him to indulge his love of photography), being at the monarch's beck and call as an equerry required enormous self-restraint. Such personal demands had started to pall for Johnnie Althorp long before he met Frances, and their three-month separation while he had accompanied the Queen on her royal tour of the Commonwealth had confirmed in his mind that he wanted to get out. The cost now outweighed any benefits.

There was the question of money, however, and of how he proposed to earn a living to supplement the meagre trust fund his father had settled on him. As the couple pulled up in front of their modest rented house in Rodmarton, half an hour's drive from Cirencester, Frances, although exhausted by the long drive, was eager to get inside and unpack. Johnnie had wanted to buy a house in the area, but had been unable to find anything suitable in his price range. Not wanting to be humiliated at the hands of estate agents, and needing a roof over his head, he chose to rent.

The truth was that Johnnie's allowance had fallen short of what he needed even during his bachelor days, and he frequently resented his father's meanness. Now newly married, he realized that he had to act promptly to provide for his wife and what would soon be an expanding family. To an observer, these financial pressures might not seem to have been particularly pressing, but also at stake was his inordinate sense of pride.

Quite simply, the heir to the Spencer fortunes did not wish to go cap in hand to his wealthy wife to solve an immediate financial problem. Frances in turn did not question his decision to embark on a career change at an age when most men were beginning to reap the rewards of their working lives. She deferred to Johnnie because he was older, ostensibly wiser, and seemingly in control; he was also her husband, in an age and of a class that invariably placed wives in a subservient role. Quite naturally, therefore, she was more than happy to play the caring, supportive wife, nurturing his dreams and ambitions.

At first, he considered becoming a stockbroker. Hearing from Frances about her rich American great-grandfather, Franklin Work, no doubt influenced him, making him aware of the considerable profits that could be made from successfully playing the markets. He approached a schoolfriend, Lord Wardington, for advice. To no avail: 'Johnnie came to me and asked if I thought he could join Hoare and Co., the stockbrokers I was working for, but I said no, partly because there wasn't a vacancy and partly because mathematics was never his strong suit.'

However kindly the refusal, it was a severe blow to Johnnie's ego and further reduced his already weak confidence. He therefore decided upon a career closer to home, one with which he was already familiar, and an uncontroversial choice, given the Spencer family tradition – he would become a gentleman farmer. After all, he would one day inherit Althorp, which, quite apart from the house and its contents, boasted 13,000 acres, numerous farms and workers' cottages, and an immense wealth founded on sheep farming.

Johnnie enrolled at the Royal Agricultural College in Cirencester three months after his wedding. There he would study farming and estate management while Frances made a home for them and prepared for the birth of their baby. With great tact for someone of her age, she recognized her husband's delicate position and went out of her way to protect his pride, waiting patiently to see how he would improve their situation. Her faith in him never wavered, and once he had started his studies, she generously encouraged him by promising to release some of her personal fortune to buy farming land.

Financial worries aside, the couple settled easily into marriage, delighted in being together and content with the simple pleasures of domesticity. Frances loved cooking for Johnnie after he came home each evening from the college. They would eat supper and discuss their day and the minutiae of imminent parenthood – the nursery, names and where the baby would be born. Having always loved children, Frances wanted a large family, and was eagerly looking forward to being a mother for the first time.

Yet as her pregnancy progressed, she became increasingly concerned about having a healthy child. She took good care of herself by walking, swimming and playing tennis to keep fit. Although still very young, and often naive, she approached motherhood with great seriousness, regularly seeking the advice of her elder sister, Mary, who tried to reassure her younger sister about her growing fear of the pain of giving birth.

These were not Frances's only worries, by any means. Even before the end of the year, the carefree early months of her marriage had evaporated as the pressure on her increased. Johnnie's father, unable, if not unwilling, to contain his natural tendency to gruffness, and never a model of subtlety, made his feelings very apparent: 'I waited, miserably aware that my father-in-law was expecting a son and heir, and not anything else.'

As time went on, Frances's relationship with Jack Spencer, the surly seventh earl, became more arduous. To the detriment of his relations with the people around him, he was completely obsessed with Althorp, a man who meticulously listed every item within the house, and one who wore the sobriquet 'the Curator Earl' with some pride. Solitary and introspective both by nature and inclination, he was an almost completely unapproachable yet demanding father who became increasingly frustrated at his son's relaxed indifference to the details of his beloved Althorp. The two were like chalk and cheese – a father obsessively knowledgeable about his ancestry, and a son only cursorily so. Despite the pleasure his marriage had brought him, and others, Johnnie was now in a hopeless situation – his commitment to Althorp would never match that of his austere father, with the result that he existed in a kind of guilt-ridden limbo where his difficult parent was concerned, torn between his sense of duty and his desire for an easy life.

One day in March 1955, Frances recognized the early signs of labour. She was barely nineteen years old. With that mixture of excitement and apprehension familiar to all prospective parents, she and Johnnie, who were at Althorp, checked into Northampton General Hospital, the father relegated to the corridors to await what he hoped would be an heir. It proved to be a long and difficult delivery, one that Frances would never forget. 'I was terribly nervous and shy about the whole labour, which lasted forty-seven hours. The sister was rather brusque – she seemed to be ancient, [but] she was probably thirty.'

Elizabeth Sarah Lavinia Spencer, to be known as Sarah, was born on 19 March. Frances was relieved above all that the baby was healthy and that the ordeal of giving birth to her was over. Her father-in-law's reaction was not quite so easy to read, for to Frances, although his mouth smiled, his eyes seemed to betray a different emotion. 'He was thrilled when Sarah was born, but it was not his first thought,' Frances reflects. He had, of course, hoped for a grandson. Johnnie was cheerfully delighted with his daughter, but knew immediately from the look on his father's face that this baby must have a brother. And soon. Jack Spencer would not be content until the succession to the title and Althorp had been secured for at least two generations of his descendants.

Frances, however, fell in love at first sight with her beautiful sandy-haired baby, and the bond between mother and daughter has endured – even today, she and Sarah are very close. After a while, Sarah was taken to the nursery and Frances tried to rest. It was customary then for women who had recently given birth to stay in bed as if recovering from a severe illness. They quickly settled into a routine as she got to know her new child. It was not to last long, however, for the midwife swept into the room and issued a bizarre instruction, which Frances felt unable to challenge. 'She came into me afterwards and pronounced, "You've got a lot of milk." I thought "Hurrah! I've done something right." Then she said, "You don't need it all, there are illegitimate triplets to feed." So I fed Sarah and two boys and another girl for a week. I was exhausted. It was slave labour.'

By a bitter irony, just as Frances became a parent, she found herself at the point of losing her own father. A few short months and many tears later, on 8 July 1955, Maurice, Lord Fermoy, died from cancer. 'My father died at seventy when I was nineteen – it was still too young to lose him.' His death left a gap in her life that she has never completely filled.

Maurice Fermoy had lived a colourfully abundant life. As is almost inevitable with such a charismatic and wealthy man, many stories have emerged, some with substance, many others the result of idle gossip. It has been suggested, for instance, that he had an illicit affair with a 'commoner' on the Sandringham Estate which resulted in what the newspapers of the day delighted in calling a 'love-child'. Such was the power of money and rank, however, that the alleged mother, Evelyn Rudderforth, was paid in cash and packed off to a foreign country, on the understanding that she and the child would be provided for in return for her discretion. There has been at least one unsuccessful attempt by the supposed child of this affair, a Canadian named Ann Ukrainetz, to establish that she is the half-sister of Frances.

Many years earlier, before Maurice came to England and married, he was travelling alone on a crowded train from San Francisco to New York, dressed, as befits a wealthy man who would one day inherit a barony, in a silk tie, wing collar and gold watch chain. As the train thundered over the Great Salt Lake in Utah, he noticed a pretty American woman in the carriage. Edith Travis, her long hair neatly pinned in a bun, a divorcée in her mid twenties, seemed to be fully occupied in keeping her boisterous twin boys amused. Nevertheless, she did not fail to notice the distinguished-looking gentleman sitting opposite, watching her, and she smiled quietly to herself.

They began talking and then found that they could not stop, time racing as the train carried them on to New York. At journey's end, they exchanged addresses. She did not expect to hear from the soon-to-be Lord Fermoy – why would he bother with someone like her? But he wrote to her immediately, a polite, friendly letter, and they arranged to see each other again. She found him charming, easy and tremendous fun to be with, and, although from another class, not in the slightest bit aloof. It was not long before their delight in each other's company led to a passionate affair. They continued writing to each other, and over the weeks and months Edith fell in love. Their relationship was destined to remain an affair, however, for Maurice explained gently to Edith that they could never marry – the stigma of taking a wife who was a divorcée was too great at that time. He did, however, offer her a way of continuing their love affair and allowing her a degree of financial security. He wanted her to sign an agreement whereby she would become his mistress in America and have his children, and he would provide a regular allowance. She felt unable to accept, but they continued to express their love for each other in a torrent of letters across the Atlantic for over forty years until Maurice's death in 1955. Edith's daughter, Edith Hodgins, still retains much of the correspondence.

There were other scandals or near-scandals. In 1952, his character was tested to the full when the car he was driving was involved in a head-on collision, tragically causing the death of the thirty-one-year-old driver of the other car. Maurice refused to comment at the inquest for fear that he might incriminate himself, although he need not have worried: the coroner felt that his moral character and forty-seven years' driving experience were sufficient to exempt him from blame.

Whatever his shortcomings as a husband (or as a driver), Lord Fermoy was a clever, kind and dutiful man, and one of the few aristocrats of whom it could truly be said that he could 'walk with Kings – nor lose the common touch'. Possessed of great sympathy, making people feel comfortable and keeping them amused was his stock in trade, a natural gift, perhaps honed by his American upbringing, that he passed on to Frances.

After his death the family gathered around Ruth Fermoy who, at the age of just forty-four, now faced life alone. As resourceful as ever, she made her plans and then announced them: she would stay on at Park House. In this decision, her new post as an extra Woman of the Bedchamber to Queen Elizabeth the Queen Mother (an honorary position that belies its title, her duties including writing letters and acting as a companion on tour) proved a blessing, for it allowed her to keep busy while she came to terms with her loss.

By now Johnnie had completed his course at the agricultural college, and he waited eagerly to begin life as a farmer. Jack, rather out of character but no doubt prompted by a desire to further the next generation at Althorp, offered the couple Orchard Cottage on the estate. This rather quaint but fairly basic dwelling stood some way from the great house and its ever-present master.

None the less, both loomed forebodingly in the background; their presence felt, even when not seen.

It was, however, a new start for Johnnie, although he had mixed feelings about being thrust into the Althorp domain once again where, beholden to his father, he would be obliged to take an interest in his birthright that he scarcely felt. Although uncomfortable for him, however, it augured well for Althorp.

The prospect of a grandson in the near future encouraged Lord Spencer, while the trim figure and long legs of his daughter-in-law wandering the grounds did not go unremarked by him either. Frances's arrival on the estate proved timely and she began to take her role as Viscountess Althorp very seriously, anxious to help in the community, especially with the local children.

In the summer of 1956, Ruth Fermoy called with a proposition. Since her husband's death she had begun to find Park House rather hard to manage by herself, while the size of the property lent itself to use as a family home. Would the young couple, she wondered, be interested in taking over the lease? Frances, although openly excited at returning to her childhood home, was nevertheless hesitant about going back to live there. The house held a special place in her heart, yet her memories of it were also tinged with sadness at her father's recent death. She felt his presence in every room, just as later she was to see his expressions in the faces of her young children. Johnnie, of course, was delighted at the prospect both of getting away from his father's ill-natured and demanding ways and of attaining the space provided by a house, and one so closely tied to royalty, at that. Only now did he realize how much he had missed the glamour and status that mixing with the royal family had brought him.

Johnnie and Frances awaited the arrival of their second child while settling into Park House. On 11 February 1957, less than a month after her twenty-first birthday, Frances gave birth to another daughter. Cynthia Jane – named after Johnnie's kindly mother and to be known as Jane – was born at the Queen Elizabeth Maternity Hospital in King's Lynn six weeks prematurely. Yet again, however, pleasure at the birth of a healthy child was tempered by the knowledge that the elusive son and heir had still to be born.

Frances, always positive in her outlook, and perhaps wanting to mollify her husband for the absence of a son, immediately invested £20,000 ($30,000) of her own money in 600 acres of land at nearby Snettisham for Johnnie to farm. He had never been happier, settling quickly into the 'Sandringham set' and indulging his love of cricket on the royal lawns. He also relished the opportunity to get to know his mother-in-law, whose intimacy with the Queen Mother fascinated him. Johnnie and Ruth grew to have an understanding: he was amiable male company at a time when she missed her relaxed yet much respected husband. To her, Johnnie was both companion and confidant; as unchallenging as she was formidable, his compliance pleased her. The fact that he was also a Spencer, a name now allied with the Fermoy line, also gave her tremendous satisfaction. To her, Johnnie Spencer was an important link in her bid to rise to the upper echelons of aristocratic society.

Quite naturally, Frances was pleased to have gained her mother's approval by marrying well, and expected her full support, especially as Ruth had been through similar pressures, having given birth to two daughters before her own son arrived. By now, however, Ruth had priorities rather different from her daughter's. Having fought strenuously to achieve her social position from an ordinary childhood in Aberdeen she could not and would not stand by and watch her hard-won gains being undermined. Not surprisingly, the more she probed Frances, the less her daughter co-operated. Tension between mother and daughter escalated. Their relationship, always complex and often distant, now began to unravel.

Ruth, Lady Fermoy possessed extraordinary self-discipline, and like her friend the Queen Mother, an unquestioning adherence to duty and protocol. Frances's *laissez-faire* attitude both irritated and perplexed her. She identified more closely with Johnnie, older and a former soldier like her own father, rather than her flighty daughter who seemed steeped in frivolity. Ruth Fermoy would come to stake her reputation on her principles born of empire and class. Resolute in her values, she placed them above all else, as Frances would later discover, to her great cost.

Ruth's position as a trusted friend of the royal family had been further enhanced when she was appointed to the OBE in 1952 for her part in founding the King's Lynn Festival. The honour was a genuine measure of her achievements, but it was also, to her, an endorsement of her traditional, predictable world, and as such made her even less responsive to her daughter's emotional outpourings.

Frances, not for the first time, felt her mother's disapproval with every sideways look, and heard it in her dismissive tone. By late 1960, shattered by the death of her son and her secret miscarriage, and traumatized by her treatment at the hands of specialists, she reacted by withdrawing into herself, keeping her own counsel, and turning away from her mother, rather than towards her. Unable to discuss her worries rationally with anyone close to her, and nervous in any case at the alliance between her husband and her mother, she found that they magnified until she became an increasingly isolated, fearful and unhappy figure. Once Charles Edward Maurice Spencer, the much wanted male heir, finally entered the world in May 1964, Frances although still only twenty-eight, was mentally and physically exhausted.

The demands of duty – and in particular the obsession with a male heir – had made her marriage increasingly fragile until it began to spiral into deep trouble. There were fierce arguments with Johnnie, and suggestions of violence on his part filtered out into local society. Diana's early recollections illustrate the marked difference between her parents at that time, telling Andrew Morton, 'It was an unhappy childhood. Parents were busy sorting themselves out. Always seeing my mother crying. Daddy never spoke to us about it.' What was certain was that there was now an increasing distance between a sedate, uninspiring and older husband and a young, bored and emotionally frail wife. Lord Wardington recalls, 'Frances caught the other side to gentle Johnnie. He had a bit of a cruel streak as he got older.'

Frances herself admits, diplomatically, that:

> The last three years we spent together we just drifted apart and there was nothing either of us could do about it. There was no single circumstance which served as a moment of realization that we were hitting marital rocks. Little things seemed to creep up which didn't appear to be threatening. But this happened relentlessly and in the end overwhelmed us.

As Johnnie approached middle age, Frances recognized that he no longer held any fascination for her. She saw him as staid and, increasingly, in a similar mould to her father-in-law. With the two older children, Sarah and Jane, already boarding at West Heath School in Kent, and the two younger still in the nursery, Frances coped by taking frequent trips to London to visit galleries, to shop, and to have lunch with girlfriends. Although surrounded by people, she had never felt more lonely in her life – trapped with the Queen as a neighbour and a lady-in-waiting to the Queen Mother for a mother.

Her children dominated her thoughts. Diana and Charles were still young and Frances entrusted their care and early education to her own governess, the delightful Ally. During the hours they were in the schoolroom Frances had time on her hands. Travelling to London provided distance from Johnnie and the atmosphere in the house, and gave her time to think clearly. It became a necessary – indeed, an addictive – release.

She thought many times of leaving Johnnie and of taking the children to start a new life somewhere. But this was the mid-1960s, when divorce was still a rarity, and marked one for life. Women's rights were still in their infancy, and men generally held positions of power at work and at home. Frances certainly could not confide in her mother, who believed that marriage was for life, no matter what, and who in any case saw no wrong in Johnnie. As a result, Frances confided in no one; 'Only two people are in a marriage and everyone else is on the outside,' she said many years later. She would certainly not be the first abused wife to have kept her counsel, or to have blamed herself for her husband's rages. Indeed, the respected battered-women's rights campaigner, Erin Pizzey, based her novel, *In the Shadow of the Castle*, with its themes of domestic violence, alcohol abuse and mental instability, on information gleaned from Frances and Johnnie's relationship.

Frances sought solace in the capital, where she felt energized and alive again. After shopping she would go to the hairdresser and pamper herself in an effort to bolster her diminishing self-esteem. Inevitably, however, her regular visits to London meant that local gossip about her motives grew as the months passed. Of this tendency of outsiders to comment, albeit behind their hands, she has forthright views:

> People's judgement as to where to lay the blame doesn't help one bit since it is a time of wholesale sadness, a time of aching for space and peace and compassion. It is a bereavement, a hard-hitting human one, where the marriage has died. All one's resources are needed to support your children – praying that you can honestly answer their needs and questions. The rug is quite literally pulled out from under each member of the family. We all suffered enormously. Johnnie and I shared the blame and we were the only people in a position to do so.

Frances was a beautiful, young, vivacious and wealthy young woman who needed an outlet for her repressed spirit. Even though she was married, it was only a matter of time before she caught the eye of another man. Peter Shand Kydd, the heir to a wallpaper fortune and a brother-in-law of the infamous Lord Lucan,* proved a relaxed, debonair, witty companion. Although he had been married since 1952 to an artist, Janet Munro Kerr, their relationship, like the Althorps', was troubled.

Peter had been educated at Marlborough and Edinburgh University before embarking on a successful career as a naval officer. On leaving the navy at the end of the war he reluctantly joined the family business, which he found rather dull in comparison to life on a warship. In 1963 he resigned from the board and took his family halfway across the world to the Australian outback. There, with considerable enterprise, he started a sheep farm, which he ran with great enthusiasm. But the new home was also miles from the nearest town, which could be reached only by dirt tracks, and they had only a local hardware store for supplies. In this wilderness, and cut off from any

---

* Richard John Bingham, seventh Earl of Lucan, known to his friends as 'Lucky' Lucan, disappeared in November 1975 after his wife, her face covered in blood, ran into a London pub; investigating police found the body of their children's nanny hidden in a mailbag in the Lucans' house. The case was a *cause célèbre* of its day; Lucan was charged in his absence with murder, but his whereabouts has never been discovered.

sort of social or artistic life, Janet, unsurprisingly, became disillusioned and depressed. An acquaintance described Peter as 'a bit of a gypsy, never happy in one place for long, dabbling in different adventures'. This adventure presumably suited him, but its attraction for his wife rapidly wore off.

They stuck it out for three years, until Janet forced the return to England with their three children, Adam, Angela and John. Unfortunately, however, this move only highlighted the differences in their emotional needs, and the rift between the couple began to widen.

During her many trips to London, Frances would often receive invitations to dinner, and being highly sociable she went to many, sometimes with Johnnie. The first time she met Peter Shand Kydd was at just such an occasion in the summer of 1966, when in fact both their partners were also there. The two men got on well and there was a good deal of innocent joking between courses. The real spark was between Frances and Peter, however. Frances recalls, 'It wasn't love at first sight, but I do remember we made each other laugh. We were both married so there was never a thought of anything except enjoying each other's company.'

The two couples kept in regular contact, and before long arranged to go on holiday together. In early 1967, on a skiing trip in Courchevel some six months after their first meeting, Frances and Peter became suddenly and acutely aware that the attraction between them was mutual and irresistible. There is no question in Frances's mind that the exact moment they fell in love can be pinpointed to that week in the French mountains. 'That's when we realized there was a strong attraction.'

From then on other forces took over, and although Frances had no wish to stray, the inattentiveness of Johnnie made her feel not only that he did not respect her, but that he did not care what she did. She adamantly maintains that Peter was not responsible for the final breakdown in her relationship: 'If Johnnie and I had had a strong marriage it wouldn't have happened.' Besides, the marriage had already been under strain for some considerable time.

The affair was passionate, intense and consuming. Frances fell deeply in love; starved of affection for so long, she was intoxicated by Peter's thoughtfulness and good humour; life with him seemed easy, and tremendous fun. Despite being a similar age to Johnnie, Peter had a different, lighter outlook, and a worldly wisdom and experience that made him both fascinating and a wonderful raconteur. He rented a flat in South Eaton Place in Belgravia and he and Frances would arrange to meet there for secret liaisons.

These were thrilling, impetuous times, and inevitably Peter and Frances became a little reckless. By September 1967, whether by design or accident, or the agency of some supposedly well-meaning 'friend', Johnnie had discovered the affair. The knowledge left him incredulous, and deeply embittered at the public humiliation that news of the affair would bring to the family. Never for a moment, however, did he believe that Frances would leave him. To find his wife in the throes of an adulterous affair with a man he considered a friend was shocking enough, but to think that she would walk out on their marriage was beyond his comprehension. Arrogantly, he believed that she had neither the courage nor the audacity to begin a life away from him and his impressive connections.

On her part, however, Frances felt that she had no choice. If she stayed she would become embittered and depressed, and the already turbulent, and deteriorating, relationship with Johnnie would sink to unbearable depths. It was not a decision she made either lightly or suddenly. In many ways, it would have been easier to stay and hush up the affair, and thus avoid offending so many sensibilities. She had sufficient money to buy a London flat if needed, and enough freedom to carry on a discreet liaison, though the emphasis would have to be on the 'discreet'. She might thereby have retained her lifestyle, her home and her position, but being desperately unhappy drove her forward. Screwing up her courage, she told her husband that she believed that they should separate.

Johnnie, understandably furious, took her suggestion as a personal insult to his manhood. Nevertheless, he agreed to a trial separation as he had no wish for his wife's affair to become public, fearing humiliating gossip. Events were about to take another turn, however.

Peter, unable to maintain the deception any longer, left Janet and moved into the flat in South Eaton Place. Outraged, Janet petitioned for divorce and cited Frances as the 'other woman'. From then on there would be no turning back for Johnnie. Frances was a liability. She would have to go.

In the face of overwhelming social condemnation and family disapproval, Frances left Park House for a flat in Cadogan Place in London. Since the two older children were away at boarding school, she only needed to pack for Diana and Charles. Schools were arranged for both children, and Johnnie (who until then had had little to do with the children's upbringing) arranged to see them at weekends.

To begin with, considering the disruption, things went relatively well, as Frances told Gordon Honeycombe:

> In the summer of 1967 Johnnie and I agreed to a trial separation. It was decided I should take Diana and Charles with me to London. A furnished house was rented and Diana, then aged six, and Charles, who was four, were enrolled at a girls' day school and a kindergarten respectively, both of which were seen and approved by Johnnie.

At weekends, Diana and Charles returned to Norfolk to be with their father, and he would sometimes journey up to London to take them on an outing. In October, the family were reunited at Park House for half-term, when the two older children came home from school, and a similar plan was agreed for part of the Christmas break. These cordial arrangements seemed to be mutually convenient, but complications, exacerbated by resentment, were already emerging, further doomed by the involvement of lawyers.

> Johnnie and I would decide an arrangement for the children, our respective lawyers always advised this should be documented and, by the time they'd used their professional language, a friendly arrangement seemed to be complicated beyond all measure. And this would invariably result in argument. Not surprisingly, it would then be the children who suffered.

It was always a strain for Frances to be back inside Park House, but she and Johnnie tried hard to minimize their differences for the sake of the children. It was during the Christmas holiday that Frances asked for a divorce. Her request had a dramatic effect, and one that was the reverse of what she had expected.

All Johnnie Althorp's hurt and resentment bubbled over. Having had time to reflect, he worried that it would appear that Frances's actions were being condoned if he meekly allowed his children to be taken away. He knew that far more was at stake than just the marriage. With his close ties – and physical proximity – to royalty, he wanted neither his social standing to be affected, nor his adulterous wife to get what she wanted. Adopting the view that possession is nine-tenths of the law, he issued an ultimatum. As Frances revealed to the broadcaster Gordon Honeycombe, 'Johnnie now insisted that Diana and Charles should be sent to school in King's Lynn, not far from Park House, and that they should thenceforth stay at the house with him. He refused to let them return in the New Year to London.'

Shocked and confused, Frances later confessed to being 'devastated' by Johnnie's action but, alone with him in Park House that Christmas, she felt powerless and physically afraid of defying him. Upon returning to London, however, she did what any mother would do – she fought for her children.

In a petition to the High Court, separate from the later divorce proceedings, she applied to be granted custody of the children during the separation, assuming that, as their mother, she would shortly be reunited with them at the order of the court. As she put it rather formally, 'In a court action in June 1968, [I] sought that the children be allowed to live with and be cared for by their mother.'

Enraged, Johnnie, like many a cuckolded husband before and since, used the children as weapons in the war with his wife. He wanted revenge for the rejection, and for the humiliation poured upon his family name. He wanted

Frances to pay personally for the suffering she had caused both him and their children by falling in love with another man. Most of all, he wanted to teach her a lesson: that she could not win.

He mustered his network of well-connected friends and began to build a case against his wife using the most hurtful and patently untrue allegation imaginable – that Frances was an unfit mother. From now on, her character would be vilified, and no one would be left in any doubt of Lord Althorp's absolute determination to raise his own children in his own way. He no longer needed or wanted Frances, and he now decided that the same was true of their children. It was a deceitful act of immense cruelty that would have considerable repercussions in the future.

In another act of sheer spite, Johnnie and his friends came up with the demeaning epithet 'the Bolter' for Frances (a nickname taken from Nancy Mitford's 1945 novel of upper-class life, *The Pursuit of Love*), applying it whenever her name was raised as a means of describing, in as derogatory and humiliating a way as possible, how she had left the family home with no consideration for her husband or children. It was also a label which, Frances knew, she would have to live with for the rest of her life.

CHAPTER FIVE

Discarded and Divorced

A LONE IN LONDON, Frances felt the weight of the Establishment against her. It was a very desolate position. Without her children, she threw herself into her relationship with Peter Shand Kydd, but although he was a tremendous emotional support, she still felt bereft. She saw the children at most weekends, but was being forced further and further out of their lives as Johnnie hired a succession of unsuitable, if pretty, nannies.

It was a time of intense emotion. Years later, Frances's third daughter, Diana, was to say: 'We all have our own interpretation of what happened. People took sides. Various people didn't speak to each other. For my brother and I it was a very wishy-washy and painful experience.' Sometimes at night, at Park House, she would hear her younger brother Charles crying, 'I want my Mummy,' but was too afraid of the dark to go to him. 'I just couldn't bear it. I could never pluck up enough courage to get out of bed.'

Throughout this time, Frances worked tirelessly to regain custody of her children, even as she grieved at losing them. The day of reckoning arrived in June 1968, and Frances was so convinced that the court's verdict would go her way that she booked Diana and Charles back into their London schools. It was commonly accepted that the mother was the best person to bring up children, and Frances had been given no reason to doubt the advice of her lawyers, who believed that the court would uphold this view. These were not 'common' circumstances, however. As the heir to an earldom, Johnnie was to deploy his rank and connections to devastating effect, forcefully arguing his case from a moral standpoint, portraying Frances as an uncaring, selfish and untrustworthy woman who put herself first and her children last.

As the day of the hearing drew nearer, Frances could think of nothing else but the impending case. Sleeping became difficult, eating almost impossible, and she felt mentally and physically drained. Yet she remained determined to give everything she had to bring her children home. Dressing in simple elegant suits, her hair loose but neat, she entered the London court, unable to hide the look of anguish on her face.

Inside the chambers, Frances pleaded with the judge to order the return of her four children to her care. She argued passionately, as an involved and loving mother who knew the children better than their father, and who genuinely understood their needs.

Johnnie, however, proved to be a more formidable opponent than she had expected. He fought back resolutely, undermining her statement and targeting flaws in her personality. He had, too, a stroke of luck when, just days before the hearing ended, Janet Shand Kydd was granted a divorce on the grounds of her husband's adultery, naming Frances as the co-respondent. It was a serious blow to Frances's good character at a crucial moment in the case.

Johnnie was almost home and dry, but he was then offered one more clinching piece of evidence to swing the verdict. Astonishingly, it came in the form of evidence hostile to Frances from her own mother. Ruth Fermoy, showing more respect for titles than blood ties, and perhaps fearing that her grandchildren would be raised in the shadow of the tawdry wallpaper industry – with its awful taint of 'trade' – rather than royalty and aristocracy, supported her son-in-law. Johnnie could not believe his good fortune.

The reasoning behind Ruth's decision to testify against Frances remains an enigma, although it was undoubtedly due in part to her own sternly moral views. Perhaps she wanted to teach her daughter a lesson for her scandalous indiscretion and the shame that it had brought upon their families. Or perhaps pure self-interest was at the heart of the matter – Ruth simply wanted to keep a royal roof over her grandchildren's heads. Most probably her decision was an amalgamation of raw emotion, careful persuasion by her son-in-law, and moral outrage backed by snobbery. Adulterous affairs were no more unusual among the aristocracy than in any other class, but Frances had made the mistake first of being found out, and then of admitting that her marriage was unhappy. The airing of such dirty washing was considered undignified and demeaning; her mother's action was a way of bringing Frances into line. It is also hard not to imagine Ruth being influenced by her closest friend, the Queen Mother, who abhorred divorce.

Curiously, however, the court case was not without personal ramifications for Ruth Fermoy. Park House staff noticed a marked change in her demeanour when she visited Johnnie and the children; 'She did not seem at all like her old self,' said one. 'She was a woman in crisis. She would hurry in and out and spend very little time with the children, and several times I could see that she had been crying.'

Whatever the reasons for her betrayal, Ruth's devastating testimony meant that Frances's appeal lay in tatters. Although she was granted weekly access to the children, the custody she craved was, most unfairly, denied. Furthermore, little thought appears to have been given to the effect that losing their mother would have on the children. Instead, they were used by their father as pawns in a bitter battle. Frances collapsed in court on hearing the judge's decision.

Ruth Fermoy's contempt for her own daughter undoubtedly lost Frances the case, and neither woman ever fully recovered from this act of treachery. At this point, too, any residual feelings of respect or affection between Johnnie and Frances evaporated and it became open season as they vented their spleen upon each other. Lashing out, Frances demanded a divorce, citing Johnnie's cruelty as grounds. Rumours of violence within the relationship had often been heard, but this was the first time she had made them public. Johnnie reacted angrily by counter-suing, using the already proven adultery of Frances with Peter Shand Kydd as the basis for his petition. Once more Johnnie could not lose – the Shand Kydd divorce had been uncontested, and the acceptance of its findings created a precedent. Frances was forced into a humiliating retreat. Mr Geoffrey Crispin, QC, representing Johnnie, told Mr Justice Wrangham, 'Lord Althorp entered upon this course with hesitation and reluctance. He would much rather have his wife back, but he recognizes now that this marriage has broken down completely.' Heaping disgrace upon frustration, the judge ordered Frances and Peter jointly to pay £3,000 ($4,500) towards costs.

On 15 April 1969, in the High Court of Justice in the Strand, London, the decree nisi was issued in front of the Honourable Sir Geoffrey Wrangham. It stated:

> The Judge decreed that the marriage solemnized on 1st day of June 1954 at the City of Westminster in the Close of Saint Peter, Westminster, in the county of London between Edward John Spencer, Viscount Althorp and Frances Ruth Burke, Viscountess Althorp (then Roche) be dissolved by reason that since the celebration thereof the petitioner Frances Ruth Burke, Viscountess Althorp has committed adultery with the party cited Peter Shand Kydd.

The decree was made absolute at the Divorce Registry, Somerset House, in London on 29 April 1969.

Three days later, Frances and Peter were married at Westminster Register Office. They began married life in Frances's flat at 69 Cadogan Place, just off the King's Road, before moving to 'Appleshore', an unexceptional suburban house in Itchenor, close to the coast in West Sussex. There Peter could indulge his love of sailing. They were happy to be together, but both were shattered by the fall-out from their illicit love affair. A close friend of hers said that Frances 'suddenly seemed to have aged. She was far more serious, almost sombre. She walked with an air of recent sorrow.'

The same friend, a member of the Norfolk county set upon which Johnnie put such store, revealed the swell of opinion against Frances.

Divorce was quite traumatic in county life at the time, particularly among the Viscount's gossipy hunting friends. Everyone knew Frances and Shand Kydd were involved in a major love affair . . . We all took sides. People have never forgotten it. Although a lot of people felt sorry for Johnnie at the time, many also liked Frances.

Yet the opinions of, and gossip about, the declining state of the Althorp marriage had been limited to their social circles and to town folk. Contrary to popular belief, for it is often referred to as a 'scandalous divorce', there were no salacious newspaper reports. Far from being the stuff of front-page headlines, the event was managed without causing a furore across the nation. That did not stop it from becoming the talk of King's Lynn, however. In the late 1960s the Althorps were of some local importance, though the Spencers were not a family of any great public renown. That was to be saved for later, and would be owed to Frances's daughter, Diana.

After the divorce, Johnnie and Ruth made no secret of their closeness, and would openly greet each other with a kiss on the cheek when they met in public. One prominent contributor to the King's Lynn Festival, in which both Ruth and Johnnie were active, commented:

> Outwardly she was very gracious and well mannered, as was Johnnie. But you wouldn't trust them, it seemed like a veneer. Underneath there was an arrogance and snobbery about them both. The affection seemed to be for show, for others as well as themselves. They say if you sup with the Devil use a long spoon and that was certainly the case. His wife never stood a chance.
>
> Ruth once chastised Lady Margaret Douglas-Home for having dinner with the town's solicitor. She said, 'How can you eat with that common, vulgar little man?' That sums up her attitude.
>
> The townspeople were very creepy towards Johnnie as he lived on the Sandringham Estate, so nobody said anything to his face. But the stories about drunken fights and unpleasant behaviour [at Park House] came from the staff and spread throughout the town. And after Frances left that's when they [Johnnie and his friends] stopped using her name and always referred to her as 'the Bolter'.

In a sense, Johnnie's was a hollow victory. He had Sarah, Jane, Diana and Charles firmly entrenched at Park House, but having almost no practical experience as a parent – for his wife had handled that side of things, aided by nannies and governesses – did not quite know what to do with four young children. He decided that the best way forward was to adopt overt and visible means of making life fun for them, and set out to make the place child friendly. He organized the building of an outdoor swimming pool, imported specially from America, arranged regular sporting events, including tennis and cricket matches, and tended to turn a blind eye when the children tormented a succession of nannies.

The children all coped differently. Diana kept a menagerie of pets, and involved herself in activities such as ballet, swimming and being mischievous, while Charles, three years her junior, padded round after her. The older girls, already in boarding school, distracted themselves more easily. For Sarah, horses were a passion, and she would make the most of the freedom permitted an older child and ride whenever she could. Warning bells should have started to ring, however, when she began to show an undue interest in alcohol and her weight started to drop, but Johnnie did not recognize the signals. Her younger sister Jane was an easier child, being both more introspective and more practical, given to reading or other thoughtful activities.

That his efforts as a single parent were not therefore wholly successful was largely because Johnnie did not adapt at all well to living alone. He became morose, drank more than was good for him, and was often either uninterested in, or testy with, the children. He seemed to be becoming more like his own father, ruling rather than raising. Charles Spencer later said of his father, 'He was really miserable after the divorce, basically shell-shocked. He used to sit in his study the whole time. I remember occasionally, very occasionally, he used to play cricket with me on the lawn. That was a great treat.'

Johnnie's frustration was not helped by his inability to find a new wife. True, he had many women friends, but no one particularly special. One woman who knew him at the time explained why:

> He was not the most fascinating company. Travel, the world, even gossip did not seem to interest him much. No wonder when he was once mentioned as a possible husband for the Princess Elizabeth she crossed him off her list. He was good-looking and from a great family, but he lacked charisma. And after Frances left him he also had four children who were not that easy to deal with. Johnnie was a man of high and low moods. I was wary, and I guess not as hungry for the splendours and responsibility of an estate like Althorp as some women might have been.

The children, too, suffered from the local gossip. They were regulars at Sandringham church, where the unsubstantiated suggestions of Frances's 'bolt' (for she had not, of course, 'bolted', but had agreed a trial separation with her husband, taking the two younger children with her) had been cruelly turned from idle gossip into hard fact. One church staff member recalled, 'It was a shocking thing. We all felt sorry for the father but much more saddened for the little ones.'

In the aftermath of the divorce, they were frequently visited by their grandmother, Ruth Fermoy, whose influence on the children did not go unnoticed either. She would take them to Ladyman's, an old-fashioned tea room in King's Lynn, while Johnnie went off to do his shopping. One shopkeeper mentioned the effect this had on locals:

> We all knew who the children were and about the scandal. It was a sad thing. What in God's name is the father to do with all those little ones, was the question most asked. The boy was one thing, but three girls? We expected he would remarry. Who, was the mystery everyone wanted to see solved. He used to come in my store alone, do his shopping himself about once a week. He was all alone in that big house once the children went off to boarding schools. Must have been pretty lonely in that rattling old Victorian place they lived in.

Despite having the weight of the Establishment and of local Norfolk opinion against her, Frances made great efforts to maintain a constant presence in the children's lives. 'I may not have been physically there all the time but I knew what was happening in their lives down the phone. They continue that to this day. And Diana always did.'

She gently introduced the children to her new husband, and Diana affectionately remembered their first encounter with Peter: 'Charles and I went up to London and I said to Mummy, "Where is he? Where is your new husband?" "He's at the ticket barrier," and there was this very good-looking, handsome man and we were longing to love him and we accepted him and he was great to us and spoilt us rotten.'

There was, of course, a world of difference between Park House and the Shand Kydds' new home in Sussex. Accepting their mother's new circumstances meant that they never got above themselves, as Charles Spencer explained: 'It wasn't all stately homes and butlers. My mother's home was an ordinary set-up and every holiday we spent half the holiday with our mother so we were in an environment of relative normality for much of our time.'

With the custody battle and the divorce over, their lives began to settle into a routine of school and holidays and access visits by or to their mother. Frances quickly recognized, however, the impact that the upheaval was having on the children: 'Of course there were tears, on both sides, from all my children. It would be ridiculous to suggest that it was anything other than traumatic.'

Even so, they were all beginning to accept a kind of *modus vivendi*, so that before too long there did not seem to be anything very out of the ordinary about the lives they now led.

In 1971, however, there came a sea change when a nanny, Mary Clarke, joined the Althorp household to look after the children. Mary testifies that she found Johnnie an amenable and concerned parent whose interests were wholeheartedly directed towards the children. Nevertheless, the introduction of a more permanent nanny at Park House did nothing to dilute Frances's anxieties. She still remained acutely concerned for her children's welfare, and was irked by the thought of this young woman taking charge of them.

For her part, Mary Clarke was nervously aware of Frances's tensions and hated the times when they met, usually when Mary brought them to London to see their mother, handing them over at King's Cross station. Sometimes Frances would become so overwrought with emotion that she could barely bring herself to look at Mary, often choosing to speak through the children. The pain of watching another woman bring up her children was one that she had never expected to endure; furthermore, she did not trust Johnnie's judgement.

Her suspicions of the new arrangement had been further aroused during one such handover at King's Cross, when Mary brought the children to join their mother and Peter, who were taking them on a skiing trip. It was the first time the two women had met. Frances noticed Diana holding her arm, and assumed she had bumped it in some way. There was an awkward silence between the two women, and nothing was mentioned about the injury. But Frances's disquiet was greatly increased during the holiday, when it was discovered that her daughter's arm was broken. She was furious. Of this incident, Mary commented:

> Like all children with their inherent ability to switch from one situation to another, they had already shut Park House from their minds and were looking forward to the next chain of events. I was told their mother would meet me at the barrier at King's Cross. This was to be the first time we had met. A polite smile on her face did not reach beyond her mouth. Her eyes were cold as she formally shook my hand. It was no more or less what I expected so I was not disappointed.
>
> The two weeks went so quickly and in no time it seemed I was back at Liverpool Street waiting to collect the children. To my surprise I saw that Diana had her arm in a sling. Her mother indicated that Diana had been brought to London with her arm unattended when all the time it was fractured.

Not only did this incident distress Frances greatly, but it prompted her to return to court to try once again to secure custody. She believed that it was only the routine check on the ski slopes that had allowed the fracture to be discovered; without it, Diana might have been left in considerable pain, and with the possibility of her arm not setting properly. It is an irony that having been catechized as an unfit mother, Frances now had to make her case against

Johnnie as an unfit father. She was desperate, however, terrified that worse might befall one or other of her adored children.

Mary Clarke continues:

> In June the solicitors paid another visit to Park House. Later that evening when Charles was in bed, Lord Althorp called me to his study. He proceeded to read a statement to me, constantly breaking the dialogue as he tried to excuse his ex-wife's comments. I was rather taken back by the attack on me. At every level my competence was called into question and thus my ability to care properly for the children. I felt wronged, misquoted, but intertwined with these emotions I felt sadness and compassion for a woman whose only natural wish was to gain custody of her children.

At the beginning of July, just before the schools broke up for the summer holidays, the case began, again heard at the Queen's Buildings in London. It lasted for five days and, with so much at stake, was aggressively and deviously fought on both sides. Johnnie instructed Mary to wear a quiet and unassuming dress instead of her more usual jeans and sweater. On the penultimate day of the hearing, the nanny was called to give evidence:

> I was asked to take the stand. In front of me at the far end of the room sat the judge. On either side of the aisle sat each aggrieved party with their lawyers and secretaries and witnesses who had already stated their case. In one of the front seats sat the children's mother and across the aisle sat the father, my employer.
>
> The questions began. Lord Althorp's QC led me through a series of questions relating to comments made in my statement to get my confirmation and to highlight the relevant points that would strengthen his client's case. Then it was the turn of the other side. Questions were fired at me. I was hardly allowed to finish one before attacked by another and before I could give the complete, balanced answer a further one would be barked. The judge was always sympathetic when I insisted upon answering an earlier question in full. My brain immediately went into overdrive . . .
>
> Both parents were entitled to their children, but naturally my loyalties lay with the father and it was necessary for me to defend my character and capabilities. I wanted no share of the despair of the mother or the jubilation of the father. I just wanted my job honestly and without hassle. The next day the case closed and as predicted, Lord Althorp retained custody of the children.

Legal documents from the time have languished unseen for over thirty years. After extensive enquiries in December 2002, all the files for the divorce and the two custody actions were removed, on application, from storage in Hayes, Middlesex, and brought to the Principal Registry of the Family Division in High Holborn, London. The papers for the entire case, number

8257/1968, are still complete and set out within copious legal notes. A special application was made to access these records; after all, the three surviving children are now approaching middle age, Johnnie and Diana are dead, and Frances is no longer married. But on 13 January 2003, Judge Robinson refused to release the papers, citing family proceeding law:

> No document lodged in open office, other than a decree or order made in open court should be open to inspection by any person without the leave of the district judge and no copy of any such document or extract from such document be taken by or issued to such person without leave.

Public access to these documents is still denied. This secrecy prevents the disclosure of information that might well provide answers to a number of questions, including about how Frances was treated by the wealthy and powerful elite of the day, as well as providing an invaluable insight into Diana's unusual upbringing. The case file is likely to remain locked in a vault, however, given the obviously sensitive, and possibly sensational, nature of its contents.

Yet whatever was said at the time in the various court actions, the fact was that Frances had failed again. She was being punished by the Establishment for her mistake in falling in love with a married man after years in a loveless, and sometimes abusive, marriage. She could not believe the callousness of her treatment. Nor could she understand it, much less forgive it. In an obvious reference to her first husband, she said: 'Once trust has gone it's for the rest of your life, it doesn't come back whatever the behaviour of the person who has broken it.'

Day by day the truth sank in deeper – Frances would never regain custody of her children. This was one of the lowest points of her life. For her own self-preservation, as she saw it, she had to escape the claustrophobic grip of the Establishment that had demeaned her, and then revenged itself upon her. Driven to a point beyond endurance, she and Peter decided to leave England.

CHAPTER SIX

Heirs and Grace

INEVITABLY, FRANCES WAS DENOUNCED for moving out of London and away from her children. After their upbringing had been taken out of their mother's hands, Johnnie put Charles and Diana into boarding schools. Both children hated their father's intransigence about this decision, crying and throwing tantrums, but he refused to listen. On one occasion Diana screamed from the doorway of her school, 'If you love me, you won't leave me here.' Charles was to say later:

> I have always questioned the wisdom of forcing boarding-school education on to children. I can always remember the agony of the six months before I was sent away to my prep. school, my sleep punctuated by the unknown nightmare of this place I had to go to, where I would know no one and where I would, despite being surrounded by other people, doubtless feel alone. I have always found it slightly disappointing that he [Johnnie] subscribed to the view that 'your school days are the best time of your life,' since this has never been a philosophy I could share.

Johnnie then courted sympathy by declaring how much he missed his children. In reality, however, he believed such educational establishments to be character-building, and they allowed him greater freedom and time away from the constant demands of young children. As Mary Clarke observed, 'I didn't see much of Lord Althorp, he was often away or caught up in his own affairs. In the early days he wasn't very relaxed with them [the children]. He tried to communicate but they only answered his questions – they never started a conversation.'

Frances knew that once all the children were in boarding schools, contact with them would become more spasmodic. Wherever she lived, keeping in touch would to a considerable extent have to be by telephone and letter. In essence, therefore, it made little difference where she lived. When, as a result of the second custody case, access rights were eventually agreed – the children were expected to divide their time equally between both parents during the holidays – Frances started looking for a place not only where she and Peter could be happy, but where the children would feel at home.

Since both loved the outdoor life, they wanted to buy a working farm. After many enquiries they discovered the Isle of Seil on Scotland's west coast, a picture of wild beauty, with its heather-covered hills and steep rocks against which, on the seaward side, the Atlantic Ocean crashes. The Shand Kydds were, not surprisingly, completely entranced.

The island is reached from the mainland by the tiny stone Clachan Bridge, built in 1792 and known – either rather grandly, or ironically – as 'The bridge over the Atlantic'. Although 500 miles from London, a two-hour drive from Glasgow and half an hour from the nearest town, Oban, Seil is not as difficult to get to from southern England as its remoteness might suggest. The area attracts thousands of people, being a popular tourist stop-off. Reached by driving down windy roads to the bridge, the island has a quaint pub called Innish, a gift shop and, at the most southerly point, an oyster farm and an art studio. Most of the rest of Seil is put to farmland or crofts. With its dramatic scenery and small population, it remains a haven even in an age of mass tourism.

Frances and Peter Shand Kydd discovered a place called Ardencaple for sale. Set on a hillside, it was an attractive eighteenth-century farmhouse with spectacular views, capable of sleeping up to twelve people and surrounded by 1,000 acres of wild farmland. The house was large enough to allow the children to bring friends to stay, but suitably remote from prying eyes. They bought it at first sight.

Moving to Seil would play to Peter's love of sailing and wildlife, while Frances would make a home for them and put her mind to commercial ventures. It promised a new way of life, a fresh start, and a chance to escape society's condemnation after the court cases. For Frances, it was also something of a homecoming, for her mother had been born and raised in Scotland, and the Roche family had often taken holidays in the area. A sense of peace dawned on the couple when they first saw the property. As Frances was later to explain: 'Peter has a passion for the sea and the Isle of Seil provided the perfect outlet. Part of my love of Scotland is because the people have characteristics that are hugely attractive to me, the total innate respect for everyone's privacy and the total lack of class structure – we're all the same.' The comment about 'class structure' is an interesting one, not simply because of the condemnation she had suffered as a result of upper-class gossip, but because Frances takes after her father in having time for anyone, regardless of their supposed status.

Once on Seil, the Shand Kydds were swiftly accepted into the local community. The Spencer children regularly made the long journey to the island, where they would go sailing, fishing or lobster-potting, and indulge themselves at Frances's beach barbecues. Diana kept a Shetland pony called Soufflé at the farm and fell in love not so much with the island, as with the freedom it brought her. At her boarding school, West Heath in Sevenoaks, she tried to counter her homesickness by keeping a poster of the island above her bed. As for her brother Charles, he remarked simply, 'Ardencaple was a magical place which Diana and I adored.'

During their years together, Frances and Peter came to love the freedom and peace they had won, for on Seil they were surrounded by the wild Atlantic, and by acres of undulating land. Life there provided them with everything they wanted. On the farm they settled down to a happy domesticity, preferring to get on quietly with their lives rather than trumpet their wealth and position. Seil provided privacy, beauty and a community that respected their chosen way of life. In fact, until Diana became engaged to Prince Charles, very few people in Oban made the connection between Frances and the aristocratic world into which she had been born and had first married.

Both Peter and Frances saw the potential of farming on Seil, and used government grants that became available for diversification. This simple existence, with no particular frills and adornments, was quietly disrupted only when they discovered that the soil at Ardencaple was far from good enough for crop farming. One local farmer understood their predicament only too well, remarking: 'You can grow grass for silage, turnips for animals to eat and even potatoes for your own use, but nothing for commercial purposes. There is not a lot of depth in the soil, it's something we live with. That's the way it's always been in the west of Scotland.' Instead they looked to sheep, cattle and Shetland ponies to provide an income and as a way of maintaining the land. This suited them well, as it was a way of life that both of them had known – Peter in Australia, and Frances in Norfolk.

Even so, as a way of expanding her interests, Frances turned to the seas after learning that the area was ripe with oysters. This set her thinking, for she knew that such delicacies were in high demand in the cities, not least because of their supposedly aphrodisiac qualities, and she therefore decided to establish an oyster farm. It proved to be labour-intensive work, since after laying down packs in suitable areas of the sea, oysters have to be regularly and skilfully turned so that they can be harvested later.

Their time on Seil also allowed Peter to get to know Frances's children, and the quiet remoteness of the place helped to heal some of the damage that the divorce had brought in its wake. Much of this was due to Peter, as Frances acknowledges: 'There was a great mutuality because my children liked Peter. He was a permanent surprise to them, great fun, masses of integrity and always self-effacing.' In turn, the children liked and respected him; 'Peter (was) humorous, generous, spontaneous and exciting,' said Charles.

Peter's own children were included in this family scene. Frances took on the role of stepmother to Adam, Angela and John, although, concerned that she had been portrayed as the woman who had stolen their father and broken up a family, she approached the situation carefully.

> I really had enormous fun with my stepchildren. Even before I met them I had my own ideas which haven't changed. Firstly, a step-parent is never asked to turn up in their arena. Secondly, their mother should be respected in every possible way – and I would not encroach on that. A step-parent should tiptoe around the scenery. Never assume or try and organize a family outing just so they can be included. Find something else to do and if you're asked, turn up. I was lucky, I was always asked. You want to be a friend to them out of love for your partner.

What struck most people who knew the Shand Kydds was what good friends they were. There was an obvious attraction between the couple, but also a deep bond as well as a similar sense of humour. Neither of them stood on ceremony, but they loved to laugh, and to look at the wry side of life. They shared similar views, notably a dedication to their children and a love of simple pleasures – music, sailing, walking, dinner with friends. After the complications of life in London and the custody battle, they wanted to lead as quiet a life as possible, despite, in later years, Diana's fame. One islander commented, 'Diana didn't have much impact in Seil because Frances was there before Di married Charles. She wasn't going to change just because her daughter married into the monarchy.'

When Peter and Frances visited London, however, they lived rather differently. There they were more sociable, visiting the theatre, opera and ballet as well as entertaining in an elegant flat they had taken in a mansion block near Victoria Station. Always generous with pre-dinner drinks before their guests arrived, Peter would mix whisky for himself and a gin a tonic for Frances. Gordon Honeycombe, who dined with them in London and on Seil, recalled one evening: 'Peter picked me up from the station and took me to their top-floor flat in the middle of the square. We had dinner. They were very generous, excellent hosts and very entertaining . . . I can't remember getting home!'

Honeycombe, who first met Frances while he was researching his book about Diana's first year as a princess, which included reference to her parents' acromonious separation, also recalls:

> She [Frances] wanted me to have an account of her divorce from Earl Spencer.

It was quite sudden. She phoned me up and I got the overnight train to Glasgow and then another on to Oban where Peter picked me up at the station. It was all so unusual and strange – an overnight dash to Scotland to have breakfast with Frances at home on the Isle of Seil . . . which of course was Diana's holiday home as well.

Ardencaple was a rather large home but it felt all so homely, not at all grand or chintzy, just a homely, functional place. It was like somewhere from the south counties with a reasonable comfortable drawing room. It seemed a little like Dummer – Sarah Ferguson's former home in Hampshire – with similarities in that southern-counties style of furnishings – comfortable for hunting and fishing types. There were lots of pictures and good-quality furniture. It was all very tasteful.

I walked in and Frances was making breakfast and having a cup of tea. She offered me tea and breakfast in the kitchen and she showed me what she had written out. There was nothing wrong with it whatsoever, it was very factual. She was straight to the point, no fuss, it answered all the questions clearly and directly. She didn't behave like a grand lady by any means, she was a very helpful intelligent woman. I remember her being amazingly attractive, I was bowled over by the eyes and whole persona and at how beautifully dressed she was.

Frances and Peter also bought 2,000 acres of farmland near Yass, south-west of Sydney in New South Wales, and the children started spending their summers in the clean air and wide-open spaces of Australia. It was a way for Peter to return to a country he loved with a new wife who was as enthusiastic as he for all his 'gypsy' adventures. The large farm was situated miles from the nearest town, although it bordered on a property owned by the press baron Rupert Murdoch, something at which, had she been able to see into the future, Frances might well have baulked.

For six weeks each summer, she and Peter would head off to their ranch in Yass, partly to take a break from life at Ardencaple, but also to enjoy the glorious weather of the region at that time of year, which is winter in Australia, but a very far cry from winter in Scotland. Frances never wanted to live in Australia, certainly not at the ranch, but she enjoyed the vast open space, saying, 'Yass was wonderful. You talk to sheep – they don't ask questions or answer back.'

In the autumn of 1972, Johnnie's mother, Cynthia, Countess Spencer, died of a brain tumour. Her loss was felt deeply by all her grandchildren, who had loved her for her gentle and sympathetic nature, in such stark contrast to her husband's. After her memorial service, which was held at the Chapel Royal in St James's Palace, Ardencaple became a haven for them as they mourned her.

Frances understood that Diana had loved her grandmother and needed time away from the strained atmosphere of Park House and Althorp. In the aftermath, Johnnie cut a lonely figure – alienated from his father, his mother dead, his wife gone and his children at boarding school. Increasingly he turned to Ruth Fermoy for moral support and companionship.

The following year Sarah – Frances and Johnnie's first-born – came of age. A memorable eighteenth-birthday party was held for her at Castle Rising, a Norman castle in Norfolk. Sarah and her then boyfriend, Gerald, Earl Grosvenor, heir to the dukedom of Westminster and the fabulous wealth that went with it, danced together for most of the night. To most people who saw them, it seemed that the announcement of their engagement could not be long in coming.

In the event, however, their relationship ended, leaving Sarah inconsolable. Although extremely bright and, like her grandmother, a talented pianist, she had already been expelled from West Heath for drinking. Much of her time at Park House was unsupervised, and she became disruptive, more than happy to show off, often with Diana at her heels. On one occasion she rode her horse straight into the drawing room in front of her grandmother – inordinately funny if you were a child, but deeply disrespectful if you happened to be Ruth, Lady Fermoy.

Although the collapse of her parents' marriage has often been blamed for the type of youthful rebelliousness she was displaying, Sarah has a far simpler explanation. Of her expulsion from school she said: 'I was bored, that's why I drank. I would drink anything, whisky, Cointreau, gin, sherry or, most often vodka because staff couldn't smell that. I was not the only sinner. Group boredom was the reason. Twenty of us were involved, with two of us being made the scapegoats.'

Packed off to a finishing school in Switzerland, Sarah's rebellious nature led her into a spiral of decline. She developed anorexia and refused to eat, surviving on a diet of cigarettes and Coca-Cola. She became pitifully – indeed, dangerously – thin, as she herself has admitted. While Frances has no doubt that 'it was relationship stress that triggered Sarah's illness,' it is unlikely that breaking up with a boyfriend was the sole cause of the disease, for there are many different theories about this complex problem. Frances, although extremely worried, refused to panic. Instead, she devoted herself to Sarah, and proved to be instrumental in setting her daughter on the road to recovery. It was, however, an onerous task. At the height of her illness Sarah, at 5 feet 7 inches tall, weighed an alarming 5 stone 10 pounds (80 pounds). She was reduced to buying her clothes from the children's department of Marks and Spencer. 'I ended up believing I was beautiful looking so thin,' she was to admit later.

I believed that if a man said I should put on weight, he just preferred fatter women. And that if women said the same, they were just jealous. One behaves like an alcoholic. You just don't admit there's a problem.

I would toy with a couple of pieces of lettuce and if I forced a meal down I would just bring it up again. Naturally I was worried to begin with but after being taken into hospital in May 1975 things got worse. Instead of losing weight slowly I lost half a stone [7 pounds] in two weeks.'

Bizarrely, it was while she was battling anorexia that she met Prince Charles and began to go out with him. He has been widely credited with having persuaded her to check into the Regent's Park Nursing Home; in fact, as Sarah explains, 'It was my mother.'

It was as confusing a time for Sarah as it was for her family and friends. When Prince Charles and Sarah were seen together at both Ascot and then during a polo match at Smith's Lawn in Windsor, there was speculation in the newspapers about the intensity of the couple's romantic attachment. With scant regard for tact but with typically headstrong honesty, Sarah dismissed the rumours – as well as any chances she might have had of marrying the future King – when she said, 'He's a fabulous person, but I am not in love with him. I won't marry anyone I didn't love whether he's the dustman or the King of England. If Charles proposed I would turn him down. I think of him as the big brother I never had. Our relationship is totally platonic.'

Sarah recognized that marrying without love was a recipe for disaster, even if one day it made you Queen. Despite her problems she knew her own mind, and her eventual recuperation, though slow, was successful. Her mother's dedication and concern throughout her illness left a lasting impression on her oldest daughter.

By the time Sarah had finished school, there was another woman in her life and her family's – Raine, Countess of Dartmouth. Johnnie had first met Raine before he married Frances, and she had changed little since, almost the spitting image of her famous mother, the romantic novelist Dame Barbara Cartland. Despite her bouffant hairstyle, heavy make-up, and tendency to gush, Raine was not a person to be underestimated, being highly intelligent and absolutely dedicated to her own personal crusades.

She was among the four hundred guests at the party Johnnie gave for Sarah's eighteenth birthday. The event had been planned as a fancy-dress party and Raine managed to ingratiate herself with both daughter and father by arranging a costume for Johnnie as King Henry VIII, and for Sarah one of the dresses worn by Geneviève Bujold, as Anne Boleyn, in the 1969 film *Anne of the Thousand Days*. The celebration was a huge success, and Sarah drove ecstatically away in her father's birthday present to her, a green MG sports car. At the time, however, she had no idea that the woman who had dressed her was to become her stepmother. Had she done so, her smile might have been less carefree.

For if their first encounter the previous year was anything to go by, it is clear that none of the children ever wanted anything to do with Raine. Their nanny, Mary Clarke, recalls that this first formal introduction over luncheon at Park House was peppered with bad behaviour and resentment:

> The butler had placed Lady Dartmouth on Lord Althorp's right and Sarah opposite her on his left. Charles sat next to Sarah with Jane on his left. I sat opposite Jane with Diana between me and Lady Dartmouth, the sight of whom had already proved a source of astonished amusement to Diana. I knew her mother was Barbara Cartland, the romantic novelist who always dressed in pink, so I suspected her daughter might also be a bit different. However, nothing prepared me for the woman who appeared in the dining room.

The meal was an unmitigated disaster from beginning to end. Far from providing a gentle introduction to welcome their father's new woman into the bosom of the family, there was uproar. Raine sat a picture of silent, icy reserve, unable to connect with the children on anything other than the most superficial level. Sarah resorted to shock tactics by acting as obnoxiously as possible, at one moment letting out a loud belch. Diana thought this hilarious and could barely suppress her sniggers. Johnnie, recognizing that it had all gone horribly wrong, lost his temper and, throwing aside all attempts at decorum, demanded that Sarah leave the table immediately. In this, he showed his true colours by taking sides with his new love against his children. As Mary Clarke noted, 'None of us had ever heard him speak so sternly, it was quite a shock for all.'

Raine McCorquodale had married Gerald Legge, Viscount Lewisham, the future Earl of Dartmouth, at St Margaret's, Westminster, on 21 July 1948, when she was only nineteen. The couple had four children, William in 1949 and Rupert in 1951, before, in effect, a second family arrived with Charlotte in 1963 and Henry in 1968. Yet early on Raine grew tired of her husband – who has been rather unkindly portrayed as a chinless wonder with money and a title – and lamented the fact that he had a title but no great house to go with it. They had to make do with a nine-bedroom, five-bathroom house in Chester Street, Belgravia, staffed by a mere five servants.

Raine found an outlet for her unexploited energies by becoming involved in local government, making her maiden speech at a church in Herne Hill, south London. She enjoyed the feeling of power that came from having a captive audience to hear her views, and decided to embark on a political career. In the course of her journey to civic influence she became well known not only for her often outspoken views but for the way in which she presented herself, a kind of make-believe figure, dripping jewellery and a perma-smile, beneath a mass of carefully coiffed and rigidly controlled hair.

Her career took off when she was elected to represent West Lewisham on the London County Council, later followed by Richmond-on-Thames. A tireless committee woman, she was involved with the Historic Buildings Board and made regular appearances on television and on the lecture circuit. Yet as her career flourished and her fame grew, so her marriage floundered. Gerald was pushed further into the background, rarely making an appearance, despite inheriting the earldom on his father's death in 1962, thereby making Raine the Countess of Dartmouth.

By the time she had reacquainted herself with Johnnie in the early 1970s, barely an eyebrow was raised if she appeared on her own at social gatherings. From early 1974, she openly pursued him, and he fell completely under her spell. She had, said a colleague, 'an iron hand in an iron glove, which is so beautifully wrought people don't realize that even the glove is made of iron until it hits them.'

Perhaps curiously, the one thing that Jack Spencer and his son agreed on was their admiration for Raine Dartmouth. In 1975 she was commissioned to write a book, *What Is Heritage?*, for which Johnnie agreed to take the photographs. Raine, to her credit, brushed aside the ill feeling between Johnnie and his father, ploughing gamely on with the grouchy earl and doing her best to repair the damaged relationship by always appearing friendly and amenable. She found a way into the old man's heart by buying him a selection of walking sticks, which rather touched Jack. In the course of her research for the book she visited Althorp, and listened attentively while she and the old man wandered together around the rooms and corridors and stairways of the great house. Jack could never resist an opportunity to talk at length about his favourite subject, and Raine proved to be an admirable listener, nodding as he waxed lyrical about the building's wealth of paintings, artefacts and antiques. Thereafter they met many times and Jack grew to trust her, enjoying the respect she displayed for the house. He encouraged her relationship with his son, believing – ironically, as it turned out – that Raine could be trusted to continue his work when Johnnie inherited the earldom.

On 9 June 1975, in the midst of her flirtation with Johnnie, Jack Spencer, the seventh Earl Spencer, died in a nursing home after a bout of pneumonia, aged eighty-three. Although he had been unwell, it was assumed that he would make a full recovery, and the family were genuinely shocked by his death. His passion for Althorp reduced him in his last few years to the life of a caretaker, meticulously polishing silver knives and forks and constantly checking the state of the building and its contents. Unfortunately, his gruff, uncompromising and charmless manner had worsened with the passage of time, and there was little warmth towards him among the rest of the family.

According to Charles Spencer, he died 'cold and lonely in a nursing home'. His enslavement to the past and ill-concealed contempt for most other people ensured that he created a lonely and loveless life for himself. Charles cynically observed that his grandfather was 'the first Spencer for at least nine generations to make no political mark whatsoever in England's history'.

Jack's death at last gave Johnnie the freedom to become his own man. At fifty-two, he had finally come into his inheritance. He was now the eighth Earl Spencer, and his son and heir, Charles, aged eleven, dropped the courtesy title 'the Honourable' for the mantle of Viscount Althorp. His sisters, too, could dispense with the prefix 'the Honourable' and were to be known by the altogether grander title of 'Lady', coupled with their first name and surname.* More disruptively, the family was to leave Park House, close to the Norfolk coast, to take up residence at brooding Althorp in landlocked Northamptonshire. It was not a place to which Frances would have chosen to go. 'In my late father-in-law's time it was essentially a beautiful museum. It wasn't cosy, comfy.'

Johnnie, however, could not wait and left for Althorp in a rush, giving his butler of many years' standing, Bertie Betts, then two years from retirement, only a month's notice. Johnnie's solicitor informed Betts that he would be taken to court if he did not leave immediately he had served out his notice. In an echo of what had been said of his employer by some of those who had known him in Norfolk, Betts wrote in his diary:

> While this was going on it was very hard to pack up his lordship's pictures, silver and two cellars full of wine . . . I feel very bitter now after giving my whole life to private service. I was treated very badly by this great lord. Everyone thinks he is so charming, but there is another side to him that the public don't see.

The move also proved a tremendous upheaval for the four children. None of them wanted to go. Charles went round the house and mournfully waved goodbye to each room, and Diana later vividly, and somewhat acidly, recalled the turmoil for her appointed biographer:

---

* The late Diana, Princess of Wales, is still often referred to as 'Lady Di', especially in the United States. This is because before her marriage to Prince Charles she was styled 'Lady Diana Spencer'.

When I was thirteen we moved to Althorp in Northampton and that was a terrible wrench, leaving Norfolk, because that's where everybody who I'd grown up with lived. We had to move because Grandfather died and life took a very big turn because my stepmother, Raine, appeared on the scene, supposedly incognito.

Raine Dartmouth supervised a major part of the relocation, although Johnnie tried to placate the children, whose dislike of her had, if anything, deepened, by telling them that she was only around to help with the organization. The children, in the throes of such an enormous change in their lives, and having already conceived a considerable mistrust of this new woman, were now being lied to. Johnnie simply could not bring himself to explain the real reason for Raine's presence in his life.

During his illicit relationship with Raine, he also hypocritically chose to forget the legal stand he had taken against Frances when they separated. Having condemned his former wife as a 'bolter' and an unfit mother in court, he was now happily conducting a sexual affair with a married mother of four children. If he felt any remorse, it was well hidden.

Mary Clarke believed that Diana's attitude towards Raine was complicated by her love for Frances:

> Diana felt . . . a rather confusing sense of loyalty to her mother. Now and again, she asked me if it was possible that her father might marry again. I told her I had no idea. Diana was reassured by the natural surprise I expressed and went on to add that she was pleased as it would not really be fair to her mother.
>
> When I pointed out that her mother was already married again, Diana regarded this as an irrelevant issue. Basically, the children wanted no competition in the affections of their father.

As Raine became more of a fixture at Althorp, the children found ever more artful ways of venting their frustration at Johnnie's choice of escort. They walked through the house chanting, 'Raine, Raine go away!', while behind her back they took to calling her 'Acid Raine'. Dinner was always a tense time, when the girls would assert their own authority by refusing to change out of their jeans. A relation of the Spencers remarks that 'Raine hadn't been brought up that way and didn't understand. She resented the jeans and they resented being told to dress up.'

Sarah remained the most outspoken of the four. When the press, which had found out about the incipient scandal, called about Raine's constant presence in Johnnie's life, she saw no reason for discretion, telling reporters that her father could not be disturbed as he was still in bed . . . with Lady Dartmouth. 'Since my grandfather died,' she told one journalist, 'and we moved from Sandringham to Althorp, Lady Dartmouth has been an all too frequent visitor.'

Raine continued to deceive her husband and her children, something to which Johnnie turned a blind eye, besotted with this woman after so many years alone. Their relationship was noticeably libidinous, their driver instructed to wait for an hour or two at hotels while they enjoyed what might be called 'passion stops'. As a family friend confirmed, 'The children didn't stand a chance. Raine can be ruthless. If she makes a beeline for a man she's difficult to resist.'

His pleasure, and relief, at inheriting Althorp was tainted for Johnnie by the realization that he was now responsible for an astronomical inheritance tax bill of more than £2 million ($3 million). Raine offered to use all her considerable energy and business acumen to help, but first Johnnie felt that he should make an honest woman of her. Her marriage to another man complicated the situation, however.

'What can you do?' asked her mother, Barbara Cartland. 'You've got to stand by your daughter. There was nothing wrong with Gerald. He was a sweet person and very gentle. He hadn't done anything wrong at all. She just fell madly in love with Johnnie and that was her happiness.' It would have been interesting to know what Ruth, Lady Fermoy, might have thought of this opinion.

The problem was solved when Gerald Dartmouth, angered and exasperated at being publicly humiliated by his wife, consulted lawyers and demanded a divorce. Like Frances before him, Johnnie was named in the petition, but because Raine admitted adultery (though without admitting with whom), she spared Johnnie further condemnation. Judge Everett, after reading Raine's statement, granted Gerald his wish, citing as grounds her adultery with a man 'against whom the charge has not been proved'. Gerald, like Johnnie, was given custody of the two younger children, since the two older were no longer minors; all four kept their own counsel. A member of the family recalls, 'They never said a word about what was happening . . . Gerald was a nice, decent man, who certainly got the rough end of the deal.'

On 14 July 1976, two months after her divorce had been made absolute, Raine and Johnnie sneaked off and were married at Caxton Hall, London. They told no one until after the event, and even then Johnnie, aware of his children's disapproval, turned coy again and allotted the job of informing his son to the boy's headmaster. Barbara Cartland said of the wedding, 'It was such a quiet wedding that even I didn't go. They rang me immediately afterwards and just said, "Hello. We're married." When it's your second marriage, I don't think you should have a reception.' Raine later confessed that her mother had been shocked by the news, but added icily, 'She is not allowed to interfere.' Diana astutely remarked of Raine many years later, 'She wanted to marry Daddy, that was her target and that was it.'

Johnnie summed up his new relationship as the attraction of opposites:

> We are both very different but we compromise. My wife is a very forceful personality, but easy to get on with once you know her . . . She's a town woman. I'm a country man. She's a saver, I'm a spender – I suppose good champagne, brandy and port are my biggest extravagances. She has beauty and brains and she came to me an older and wiser woman.

His opinion was not one that was universally shared, and other people adopted a less then glowing view of Raine when she persuaded Johnnie to open Althorp to the public in order to help pay the tax bill. She then went one stage further by bringing in her own designers and painters to impose her individual 'style' upon the house, a style that was at variance with Althorp's classical atmosphere and appearance. The 'Curator Earl' must have turned in his grave.

Raine wallowed in being mistress of a great house. A colleague of Johnnie's, Rupert Hambro, said, 'She had a way of making people who [had] played a part in his family life before she arrived feel small. She was totally insensitive to Johnnie's family, his life and his interests. Everything became "ours" and "mine". When you did see him she became his mouthpiece.'

During long telephone calls, Frances would listen patiently to her children's conversations, full of complaints about their new stepmother. As someone who knew the pitfalls of the role, she tried to be neutral; after all, the children disliked Raine enough without her adding to the debate. She angrily dismissed newspaper suggestions to the contrary: 'They say I turned my son Charles and Diana against their stepmother. That is very damning stuff.' The fact was that she had no need, or wish, to do anything that might make matters even worse for her children.

Indeed, Frances actually welcomed the fact that Johnnie now had a wife who might give point and purpose to his life. Always protective of her children, she naturally worried when they were upset, and became frustrated by Johnnie's inaction. Yet she knew that Raine had no particular interest in her children – all she wanted was Althorp, a place that Frances had always disliked.

In 1977, Jane, who was still only twenty, also had marriage on her mind. Always quieter than her siblings, she became engaged to Robert Fellowes, then thirty-six (and a near-contemporary of Frances's from her childhood days at Park House), the arrival of Raine perhaps encouraging her into Robert's arms sooner rather than later. Jane, who at that time was working as a fashion assistant at *Vogue*, said, without any great sense of occasion, 'We have known each other all our lives and have gradually grown closer,' although her sister Sarah gushed, 'We had been trying to trap him for years.'

Their marriage in April 1978, however, went straight to the heart of the royal court, where Robert had been Secretary to Prince Charles and was now Assistant Private Secretary to the Queen. Described by an American friend as 'a consummate company man,' he was regarded as steady, clever if somewhat staid, but immensely discreet and utterly trustworthy. Having been brought up on the Sandringham Estate, he was also an 'insider' who knew the ropes where both the Spencer and royal families were concerned.

In what was perhaps a statement of her complete independence from Johnnie, Frances paid for the wedding at the Guards Chapel, Wellington Barracks, in London, and the reception at St James's Palace. The Queen Mother arrived with Ruth, Lady Fermoy; the Duchess of Kent and the Duke and Duchess of Gloucester all attended, thereby putting the royal seal of approval on the match. Diana was chief bridesmaid.

Although both tried to put a brave face on it, tension between Johnnie and Frances was obvious throughout the wedding. The years of conflict and resentment went too deep even for civility. Even then, Raine managed to inflame the atmosphere by insisting on being in all the family photographs, refusing to bow to etiquette and allow the natural family their place together, until a photographer directed her to stand aside 'as Peter Shand Kydd had gracefully done'. Frances managed a secret smile at the respectfulness of the man she loved so dearly.

Diana empathized with her mother's resentment, and her own ill will towards Raine exploded just a few months later when the family suffered another crisis. Johnnie, by now fifty-four, overweight, unfit and known to quaff a few too many bottles of champagne, collapsed at Althorp while Raine was away in London at a lunch at Claridge's. He was taken to Northampton General Hospital with a suspected stroke, and the doctors did not expect him to live through the night. Diana had vivid memories of that day:

> He had a brain haemorrhage. He [had] suffered headaches, took Disprins, told nobody. I had a strange premonition he was going to be ill whilst staying with some friends in Norfolk . . . Next day the telephone rang and I said to the lady, That will be about Daddy. It was. He'd collapsed. I was frightfully calm, went back up to London, went to the hospital, saw Daddy was gravely ill. They said, 'He's going to die.' The brain had ruptured.

Johnnie was fighting for his life, but Raine, determined that he would survive, insisted on his being transferred to the National Hospital in London, where there were specialist facilities for treating his condition. For Johnnie, in a coma and suffering from pneumonia, the two-hour journey by ambulance was extremely risky and might have killed him.

By now, his only chance of survival lay with brain surgery. Against all the odds, he pulled through the four-hour operation and after three weeks on a ventilator in intensive care at the Brompton Hospital, South Kensington, at last opened his eyes again. Raine never left his side 'hour after hour, week after week,' Johnnie remembered,

> holding my hand and talking about our holidays and my photography, things she knew I liked . . . She used to shout at me sometimes, bless her. 'Can you hear me?' she'd yell. I nodded because I couldn't answer. She was always there at my side and I felt her great strength, her determination that I should live even when the doctors said she must lose me. Raine won.

Whatever people may have thought – or may still think – of Raine, sometime Countess Spencer, it cannot be taken from her that by sheer force of will she saved her husband and won him many more years of life. In a sense, however, it was a pyrrhic victory. Johnnie's illness had taken a terrible toll on the family. Raine, her raw character exposed, alienated the children by refusing to allow them to see their critically ill father while she was by his bedside. 'There's pure steel up my backbone. Nobody destroys me,' she said, significantly. They hated her absolute self-interest, and several times there were fierce arguments in the hospital corridors as Raine blocked their way. Later she was to claim that, 'Nobody was going to destroy Johnnie so long as I could sit by his bed,' before going on to identify the enemy: 'some of his family tried to stop me.' The idea that any of Lord Spencer's children would have wished to 'destroy' him was both preposterous and insulting.

Diana's interpretation is somewhat different from her stepmother's: 'We saw another side of Raine which we hadn't anticipated as she basically blocked us out of the hospital, she wouldn't let us see Daddy. My eldest sister took charge . . . He couldn't talk [to Sarah] because he had a tracheotomy so he wasn't able to ask where his other children were.'

The fear, frustration and anger felt by his children after Johnnie's brush with death was directed entirely at Raine. If Johnnie's new wife was intent upon tearing the family apart, Frances knew better than to become involved.

CHAPTER SEVEN

Love Changes Everything

FRANCES HAS NEVER been someone to be intimidated, by wealth, rank, position or anything else, and it is a trait that each of her children inherited. Diana meant it when she said that having the royal family as neighbours, 'was no big deal'. As a child living on the Sandringham Estate, she complied without either nervousness or embarrassment when invited one Christmas to watch the film *Chitty Chitty Bang Bang* with Princes Andrew and Edward. She was relaxed in their company – even if a little bored by their antics.

As she grew older, however, the one member of the royal family who continually fascinated and attracted her was the princes' elder brother, Prince Charles, the seemingly unattainable heir to the throne. His charisma and maturity made the idea of him as a boyfriend extremely alluring, and, surrounded as he was by all the trappings of royalty, Diana felt drawn to the man even before she came to know him well.

It is not altogether surprising that as a sixteen- and seventeen-year-old she idolized a man who was then widely regarded as the country's Prince Charming, and became determined to know him better. Aided by the cooling of the relationship between Charles and Sarah, Diana became more resolute, and the competition between the oldest and youngest sisters stepped up a gear. Diana could feel the power base shifting – and it was a feeling she liked. She had always deferred to her oldest sister – until now, when she determinedly struck out on her own. As Sarah's debilitating eating disorder left her thinner and weaker, so Diana was filling out and growing into an eye-catching beauty.

Diana had met Charles at Althorp with Sarah in November 1977. Almost a year later, in the autumn of 1978, an invitation arrived at Althorp that surprised everyone. Diana was to be a guest at Prince Charles's thirtieth birthday party at Buckingham Palace in November. Not wishing to offend her sometimes temperamental sister (who, although no longer his girlfriend, was still friendly with the Prince), Diana thought it best to ask her permission. Sarah would gladly have told her to refuse, but the invitation was addressed to Diana and to turn it down would have been impolite.

By now, Prince Charles's inability to commit himself to a suitably marriageable woman was becoming an embarrassment to the Queen and Prince Philip, not least because it was a subject for comment in the press. Having been allowed the latitude to sow his wild oats, as had been recommended by his great-uncle and mentor, Lord Mountbatten, he was now being pressurized into settling down to produce an heir. Manipulative as ever, Ruth Fermoy spoke at length with the Queen Mother. Prince Charles was the latter's favourite grandchild, and she made Ruth privy to her thoughts about potential brides. Her friend was well aware of the anxiety in the Windsor camp, and of the fact that acceptable girlfriends were becoming harder to find. This was especially so because, to the Palace, a suitable bride for the heir to the throne would, for preference, be royalty herself or, failing that, at least of 'good family'. She must be younger, healthy, Protestant, and a virgin with no hint of a past to uncover. In the liberated era that had followed the 'sexual revolution' of the 1960s, the last was not unlike finding a needle in a haystack.

Sarah, a Spencer and a good match, had shown herself to be too outspoken, while other girlfriends such as Sabrina Guinness had no wish to take on the daunting role of being the future Queen of England. The latest woman to turn the Prince's head, and the one who was at his side during his thirtieth-birthday party, the film actress Susan George, would not, it was thought, be suited to the rigours of a royal way of life; she was not only a commoner but an outsider, and the Queen would never agree to the union of her son with an actress. Her Majesty wanted a woman who was pure, untainted and biddable – after the scarring experience with her uncle, Edward VIII, there must be no more skeletons in the Windsor cupboard.

At his party, Charles was very pleasantly surprised by Diana's appearance and greeted her warmly, saying, 'You've grown up.' She, after two weeks of dieting, replied flirtatiously, 'Oh, I hope not, sir.' Later she reflected, 'Had a very nice time at the dance – fascinating. I wasn't at all intimidated by the surroundings.'

Like Frances, she had charmed an older man with her natural unaffected manner, beauty and sense of fun. A friend described Diana as 'very bubbly and giggly but not in a vacuous way', and she had, too, the gift of being able to make anyone, however important or ordinary, feel the centre of her world. It was a powerful skill which worked wonders on the Prince of Wales. He would not forget her. (Coincidentally, Frances had been exactly the same age, and with the same moon face and compelling eyes, as her youngest daughter when she had fallen in love with Johnnie Spencer, who, like the Prince, had also been thirty.)

In the following January, Diana went to stay with her sister Jane and husband, Robert, on the Sandringham Estate for a weekend shooting party. Prince Charles was there, and Diana talked with the Queen, who inquired after Johnnie's health and took trouble to find out more about her young guest. Her Majesty politely said what a good thing it was that Diana had completed a cookery course, perhaps implying that she would make a good wife. Diana pointed out that the course had been her mother's idea but that she had enjoyed it. The Queen gave her a royal nod of approval and moved away, having no desire to become involved in a conversation about Frances, but delighted by her daughter.

As it turned out, Sarah airily dismissed Diana's first encounter with 'her' prince as she had a new love herself, Neil McCorquodale, a distant cousin of the much-hated Raine. Theirs was a quick courtship; 'I am a whirlwind kind of lady,' Sarah admitted, although she had, in fact, known the twenty-eight-year-old former Guards officer for two years. After only five weeks of going out together, however, they decided to marry without delay. The engagement was announced in August, when Sarah was twenty-four. She told her father while he was distracted during a game of cricket at Althorp, and he absent-mindedly gave his blessing.

Then, almost immediately, in a characteristic show of Spencer impetuosity, the couple split up and Neil flew off to Australia to think things over. Upon his return they came together again, agreeing to change the venue for their wedding from London to a smaller country church, and set a date for the following 17 May at St Mary's Church, Great Brington, hard by the gates of Althorp. Frances was quoted as saying, 'I am very very happy for them. They were very worried and uncertain. They seemed to have got landed with a big London wedding and I think they both felt they wanted more time to think and were a bit nervous about the whole thing.'

Diana, as – yet again – one of the bridesmaids, watched Johnnie walk his eldest daughter unsteadily up the aisle; not without envy, for marriage was all she had ever wanted, and yet she remained single. Frances once again paid for the reception, this time at Althorp, during which she spent much of her time avoiding Raine and her mother, Barbara Cartland. Neither of her parents had any inkling of Diana's determination to marry into such heady circles. Johnnie had always hoped that his girls would marry well, in his terms, and had quietly considered the pairing of Diana with Prince Andrew, who was of a similar age, and single. He never dreamed of the bigger prize that, unbeknown to him, was now falling within his grasp, and especially so since Sarah had now put herself out of the running.

Academically average, prone to being a bit of a dreamer but extremely good with people, Diana had left school without any qualifications, after which Frances had arranged for her to attend finishing school abroad, at the exclusive Institut Alpin Videmanette, near Gstaad in Switzerland.

Diana was dreadfully unhappy there, however, homesick, bored and struggling unsuccessfully to master a foreign language. She returned home early, and within days her father collapsed, hovering for weeks on the brink of death. This, coupled with Raine's behaviour while Johnnie was ill, was a great deal for a seventeen-year-old to cope with, but worse was to follow. It is impossible to gauge the anguish Raine subsequently caused as Althorp's treasures were sold off, supposedly to pay Johnnie's inheritance taxes. Masterpiece after masterpiece was shipped down to London to be sold for quick cash, many paintings failing to recover their full value due to the lack of forethought and planning behind the sales, and the haste with which they were effected.

The whole family had become much more insular since Raine's arrival but Johnnie, weak from illness, which had left him impaired both in speech and movement, and indebted to her for having saved his life, meekly agreed to this mass trade in fine art. There was overwhelming anger and frustration among his children, and at home on Seil Frances received many late-night calls from them, listening to their outpourings when they were at their lowest ebb. Unable to persuade their father to resist his wife's suggestions, they discovered the truculent side to him that Frances knew only too well.

Once back from Switzerland, Diana found work. She moved in with family friends in Hampshire and earned a small allowance looking after their children and doing a certain amount of cleaning. Her spare time was largely taken up with driving lessons and making frantic calls to her mother begging to be allowed to live in London. Frances, cautious but willing to compromise, suggested that her headstrong daughter might move into her Cadogan Square flat, wanting to keep Diana's natural spiritedness under her own wing for as long as possible. Perhaps too, like many mothers, she was trying to savour those precious few months before her daughter, the last of her little girls to grow up, became truly independent.

Frances arranged for Diana to earn her keep by cleaning the Cadogan Square flat as well as those of her sisters. Luckily Diana was not averse to 'getting stuck in'. Frances, never too proud herself to do her own chores (to this day her name appears regularly on Oban Cathedral's cleaning roster), was pleased to see her daughter doing likewise. Despite the privilege to which they had been born, Frances was determined that none of her children should think themselves above such tasks.

Beyond these relatively simple arrangements, however, Frances had a plan for Diana. Mother and daughter shared a passion for dance, and although

Diana had grown too tall to pursue a professional career in ballet, Frances knew that she would make a committed teacher, and that children adored her. Dance would also allow Diana to express her natural flamboyance. Frances contacted Miss Betty Vacani, a dance teacher of great renown who had taught ballet to three generations of royal children, writing to ask if there was a vacancy for a teacher at the Vacani dance studio on London's Brompton Road. Since this was close to Sarah's flat, it would allow the older girl to keep a protective eye on her sister. Diana was hired as a grade-two student ballet teacher and found herself in her element. She was not in the post for long, however, for her interests were rapidly expanding, as was soon apparent to Madame Vacani, who said of her, 'She realized that you've got to be absolutely dedicated – and she had rather a full social life.'

When, in March, Diana damaged the tendons in her left leg during a skiing holiday (for which Frances had paid), her days as a dance teacher were truly over. Returning to England with her leg in plaster, she busied herself with a succession of part-time nannying jobs.

In order to rein her in a little, Frances made it clear that she would not settle any money on Diana until she turned eighteen. The pleading calls continued: Diana was desperate to have her own place like Sarah, whom she was still secretly emulating. She did everything she could to persuade her mother that she was both grown up and responsible. Impressed by her capacity for hard work and her fortitude, and with her eighteenth birthday due that year, Frances began enquiring at London estate agents for a suitable flat for her youngest daughter.

On 1 July 1979, Frances presented her daughter with the keys to 60 Coleherne Court, a £50,000 ($75,000) flat in a traditional mansion block in Earls Court. A delighted Diana immediately dashed round to her new home and then called her best friend from school, Carolyn Bartholomew, asking her to move in. Two other girls joined them as room-mates: Anne Bolton, and Virginia Pitman, the oldest of the four. Diana loved being at Coleherne Court, saying '[I] laughed my head off there,' and she was fiercely house-proud. 'She always had the rubber gloves on as she clucked about the place,' recalled Carolyn. 'But it was her house and when it is your own you are incredibly proud of it.' As part of the deal with her mother, and partly to make sure life was not too easy, Diana held down two jobs, at the Young England Kindergarten in St Saviour's Church Hall, Pimlico, and looking after Patrick Robertson, the baby son of an oil executive from America. She was at last truly in her element, and this period proved to be one of the happiest and most stable times of her life.

With Diana more settled, Frances turned her attention to her son, Charles. Although still boarding at Eton, to which he had gone in 1977, during the holidays he returned to Althorp, and he found these times a perpetual trial. He just could not get on with Raine, while she in turn was growing acutely aware that her time as lady of the house was limited. Once Johnnie died, Charles would succeed to the title and she would be ousted. There was a natural animosity between Charles and his stepmother that had only grown with time, and with Raine's increasingly proprietorial behaviour.

In her determination to refurbish Althorp according to her own idiosyncratic ideas, Charles later estimated that Raine sold off one-fifth of the historic house's treasures. His resentment was deep and enduring, for he was himself acquiring a passion for his heritage. Johnnie's friend of many years, Lord Wardington, was called in at one stage to try to 'make peace between him [Charles] and Raine.' It was an almost impossible task, not least because Johnnie was obviously quite content to delegate his fatherly duty. Lord Wardington saw the full extent of Charles's anger. 'I got the subject on to Raine. Charles, who was still at Eton, told me he hated her. We had a long conversation during which I said, "She isn't your mother. Don't treat her as such, treat her as someone who is living here. Then you will get on better with her." I didn't do any good.' In the midst of adolescence, highly intelligent and with a strong love of history, Charles Spencer could only watch impotently as, with his father's acquiescence, his heritage flooded out of his own front door, his bitterness only held in check by the knowledge that one day he would have his revenge. Any emotional vulnerability and insecurity he might have felt was made much worse because it was clear that Lord Spencer had chosen Raine above his once longed-for son and heir. The message to Charles from his father was clear: 'My happiness is more important than yours.'

Johnnie Spencer behaved with cruel ineptitude, as well as staggering selfishness, at a time when his teenage son most needed him. It was no wonder, therefore, that Charles, his loyalties divided, turned to a man whom he had grown to love, trust and respect – Peter Shand Kydd. Their association reached back to when Charles had been a small boy, when Peter had treated him, as he had all Frances's children, with gentle humour and a kindly understanding. Since then, he had continued to prove his steadfastness and loyalty. He became an invaluable friend, and many years later, as a mark of his love, Charles asked Peter to be godfather to his son, Louis.

Away from Althorp and all its tensions, Diana continued to build her glittering social life. Invited to Balmoral in August 1979, just a few weeks after she had turned eighteen, as a guest of Prince Andrew, she again chatted easily with the Queen, perfectly at home in royal company. As usual, she charmed everyone, always on her best behaviour, aware that this was the best way to win the affection of Prince Charles, even though he was not at Balmoral at the time. The month that had begun so lightly, however, ended in tragedy. On 27 August, Lord Mountbatten, while on holiday in Ireland with members of his family, was killed instantly when an IRA bomb exploded on his boat, during a fishing trip near his home in the Irish Republic; others on the boat were also killed or seriously wounded. The nation was stunned that terrorists could murder so prominent a figure with such apparent ease, while Prince Charles was shattered at the loss of a man who was in many ways his surrogate father. Amid intense security, he flew back to Britain from a holiday in Iceland to prepare for the ceremonial funeral. Diana watched it on television, and saw the visible pain on Charles's face. He was clearly desolate. She empathized with his suffering, and longed to comfort him.

Mountbatten's death made the Prince question his own mortality, as he ended the flirtation with his mentor's granddaughter, Amanda Knatchbull. It was, perhaps, no wonder that a love match that had been urged on by Mountbatten himself should fade in the face of such terrible calamity, for without his guiding hand their relationship, always more like that of brother and sister in any case, became redundant. Charles was now free once more to set about the business of finding a wife.

Then something happened that was to change Diana's life. In July 1980, she accepted an invitation to spend a weekend in Petworth in Sussex, at the home of Commander Robert de Pass, a friend of Prince Philip, and his wife Philippa, a lady-in-waiting to the Queen. Diana arrived with the purpose of providing amusement for the Prince of Wales, and left knowing that she was within reach of her goal.

She spent the day watching the Prince play polo before going to a barbecue in the grounds of the house. She sat next to him on a hay bale and they talked for a while. After a certain amount of idle chit-chat Diana took a risk and turned the conversation to her feelings on watching him at Lord Mountbatten's funeral.

Prince Charles, an awkward man at the best of times, had always struggled with his own feelings. Not only was he in mourning for his great-uncle, but he also had to come to terms with his brutal murder. This young girl, barely nineteen, had reached out to him by daring to broach a subject that few others would even mention. She treated him as a person rather than simply as a prince. More than that, however, she possessed all the right qualities to make her acceptable as a wife at the highest level of society. Diana, it seemed, was the answer to a prayer: high-born, chaste, young, malleable, light-hearted, yet also sensitive and responsible.

Charles stayed talking to her late into the night, scarcely daring to believe that he had finally found what he was looking for – a woman whom the Queen would accept as her successor. Next day, saying that he had to drive back to London on urgent business, he asked Diana to go with him. She, however, despite a strong urge to leave with him, was mindful, as always, of others' feelings, and declined. This was not altogether altruistic, for she also believed that it was best to keep the man who has everything still wanting more.

By now, the press had picked up the story and, like the Prince, they too wanted more. Whom Prince Charles would marry was virtually a national obsession, and any hint of a lead as to who that might be always sold thousands more newspapers. Diana soon became the prime, if not the only, candidate, and, significantly in the press's eyes, she was keeping suspiciously quiet. This served only to inflame the media's interest. Photographers noticed that she kept her head down, eyes cast to the floor. Journalists nicknamed her 'Shy Di' and clamoured for her to speak, each hoping to have the first quote from a potential queen.

Five hundred miles away on Seil, Frances was acutely aware that if the relationship was to have any future, then it would lie in Diana's ability to maintain a judicious silence. Sarah had sunk her own chances after her candid outburst on the slopes (although, to be fair, she had no intention of marrying Prince Charles). Diana, however, remained the epitome of discretion; even the Robertsons, her American employers, had no indication of what she was up to. Mary Robertson could hardly believe her young nanny's story when she finally told it:

> She [Diana] told me that when I left for work I would see photographers and reporters at the end of the mews. I couldn't imagine what they were doing there and she admitted they were following her.
>
> I did a double take and said 'Goodness Diana, what have you done?' And she said, 'Well, I spent last week up at Balmoral Castle.' She was blushing and looking down at the floor and very modest, very demure; you know, very Diana, very understated. She said, 'Actually I've been with Prince Charles.' And I just couldn't believe it. I said, 'Oh, that's terribly exciting, do you think anything is gonna develop?' And she blushed again and said, 'No, I don't really think so. After all, he's thirty-one and I'm only nineteen.'

Diana's face began to appear everywhere on television and in newspapers and magazines. When driving her new red Mini Metro she was pursued by journalists, and she was accosted while walking in the street. One lunchtime, she was snapped running to get a sandwich for the teachers at the Young England Kindergarten. Suddenly, through her association with the Prince of Wales, she found herself in an international goldfish bowl. Everyone wanted a little part of her. As interest intensified, photographers tracked her down to the nursery. In her naivety, she agreed to be photographed, hugely embarrassed, with the children in her care, hoping that this would satisfy the media's obsession with her.

It did nothing of the sort, however, partly through an accident of the light. The ensuing furore caused by the publication of a chance, hazy, sunlit shot of her, with her enviably long legs silhouetted through a light summer dress, created a frenzy both in Fleet Street and Buckingham Palace. How could this juggernaut of publicity be contained? Of course, it could not; it was far too late for that.

By now Frances was desperately worried about her daughter and her relationship with the Prince. Moreover, she felt duty bound to protect her, especially when journalists traced the Royal Train to a secluded siding in Wiltshire late one night, and discovered that it was being used as a secret rendezvous for Prince Charles and a mystery blonde woman (later identified as Camilla Parker Bowles). The implications of such a late-night tryst were highly damaging to a young girl trying to protect her reputation. In an attempt to defend her daughter's honour (and, perhaps, Prince Charles's intentions) Frances wrote to *The Times*, which published her letter on 2 December 1980. In it she wrote:

> ... My daughter has spoken to the press about her work, and her affection for children. She has also denied, with justifiable indignation, her reported presence on the Royal Train. At no other time, and on no other subject, has she given her views to the press.
>
> May I ask the editors of Fleet Street whether, in the execution of their jobs, they consider it necessary or fair to harass my daughter daily from dawn until well after dusk? Is it fair to ask any human being, regardless of circumstances, to be treated in this way? ...

The tactic, well intentioned and well timed, brought Diana a temporary respite. In Parliament, sixty MPs supported Frances by drafting a motion 'deploring the manner in which Lady Diana is being treated by the media'. The Press Council spoke with editors, urging them to exercise some restraint. Nevertheless, it was not to be long before the flame of media interest exploded into an inferno of press intrusion.

For Prince Charles, the time to make a decision had finally arrived. By early February 1981 he still did not know which way to turn, and under pressure from his father, his friends, and Palace advisers who had the unenviable task of dealing with the media – as well as, albeit in a different way, his own inability to commit – he chose a desperate course of action. Cornered, required either to marry or to dump Diana fast, and out of a misplaced sense of duty rather than love, he decided to propose marriage to her. Somewhat ironically, he asked this young kindergarten teacher to agree to become the future Queen of Great Britain in the nursery at Windsor Castle. It was hardly a romantic setting, but Diana did not care. She had got what she had wanted for so long: the prince she loved.

She agreed at once with a characteristic giggle, and he, assured of her consent, left immediately to telephone the Queen with the news. It was the highest point in Diana's life. Like her fiancé, she too could not wait to tell her mother, although in her case it was not from any sense of correct protocol.

CHAPTER EIGHT

Duty Calls

A T 11 A.M. ON 24 FEBRUARY 1981 the long-awaited announcement was broadcast to the nation: His Royal Highness the Prince of Wales was engaged to be married to Lady Diana Spencer. Flags flew, crowds cheered and almost audible sighs of relief were heard from senior members of the royal family and their advisers. Later the same day, Frances switched on the television to watch the official photocall and subsequent interview at Buckingham Palace. Nothing she heard or saw surprised her – except the words, 'Whatever "in love" means,' followed by 'You can put your own interpretation . . .', which Charles mumbled to cover his embarrassment when questioned as to whether he was in love.

Three weeks earlier, immediately after she had telephoned Frances to tell her the news and warn her of the impending formal announcement, Diana returned home to Coleherne Court and, amid screams of delight and much hugging and laughter, told her friends what was about to happen. She then sneaked out of the flat to avoid any lurking press. All, including Frances, were sworn to secrecy until the Palace issued the news formally.

When Diana accepted Charles's proposal, she did so with the unswerving confidence of youth. She had pursued and won her man; that was all that mattered. 'It wasn't a difficult decision in the end. It was what I wanted,' she told Gordon Honeycombe. Even so, the days before the engagement was made public proved to be a time when Diana needed her mother more than ever before. Once the news was out, and she found herself in the spotlight of the world's media, the pressure upon her would be immense. Nor was Frances's task easy. She had to keep Diana in firm contact with reality so that she could be certain that she was doing the right thing. In these heady circumstances even the strongest and most mature woman might be swept away. Diana, a teenage dreamer, and immature even by her own reckoning, was in love with the idea of being a princess, as much as she was with her fiancé.

Drawing on her own experience, Frances sought to prepare her daughter for the almost unattainable – a successful marriage in the full glare of press scrutiny. Yet, at nineteen, and having almost no experience of relationships with men, Diana was unconcerned with the weight of the responsibility that was about to fall on her – not just in terms of being married to royalty, but in terms of marriage in general. Frances realized that supporting her sometimes wilful daughter without appearing to override her would need careful management.

Given the weight of attention and pressure from 'The Firm' – that is, the royal family – it became an onerous task to keep the media at arm's length. Journalists and photographers continued to dog Diana, even though they were still ignorant of her engagement to Prince Charles. Frances therefore worked out a plan that would give her daughter breathing space, as well as prepare her for life as Princess of Wales. This was put into operation speedily and secretly, for she told only the handful of people who needed to know, and whom she trusted to keep a confidence, that they were leaving the country. As though on the run, she, Peter and Diana packed a few belongings and boarded an aircraft for the twenty-eight-hour flight halfway across the world to the safety and seclusion of the sheep farm in Yass, New South Wales. 'I was determined to have what my daughter and I knew to be our last holiday together,' Frances said later.

It was very hot in Yass, the sun beating down on their somewhat basic homestead, with its tin roof, noisy swirling fans and the plainest of wooden verandas. It was a very far cry from the splendour of royal palaces. The 2,000-acre farm was so remote that they all realized that it was the perfect place to hide. The sky was beautifully clear so that at night they could gaze at the stars of the southern hemisphere in all their splendour. Somehow it helped to put life into perspective.

There, Frances and Diana, shielded by Peter, relived time and time again the events leading up to the Prince's proposal, and the moment itself. As any mother would, Frances asked, 'What did he say?' to which Diana replied, 'Would I be prepared to take him on?'

'And then what did you say?'

'I said, "Of course," and told him I loved him so much.'

'And his reply to that?'

'He said, "Whatever 'in love' means" . . .' Diana admitted that she had first heard that strange expression when Charles proposed, though she had dismissed any reservations it might have engendered in her in the exhilaration of the moment.

Frances immediately felt deep concern at so insensitive and joyless a response to her daughter's declaration of love. She knew better than to question Diana's feelings, however. Instead, she diplomatically suggested that her daughter 'think hard' about the changes such a decision would make to her life. More than fifteen years later when talking about Diana's engagement, Frances would say, 'I think at the end of the day, everyone marries because they've made up their mind to marry. I was only in the position of accepting the situation.' She recognized Diana's infatuation with the Prince of Wales, and knew that any words of caution she might offer would fall on deaf ears. At nineteen, Diana knew her own mind, just as a headstrong Frances had done many years before when she married Johnnie Spencer, twelve years her senior.

Diana having fled the country, rumours started to circulate that she was now off the scene and that Prince Charles had lost interest in her. It was not true, of course, but the flit from England served to put the press out of the picture – for a time, at least.

They were very nearly discovered at one point, however. A couple of days into the break, the distinctive sound of an approaching helicopter was heard in the distance, rapidly drawing closer. Peter dashed out, to discover a contingent of pressmen preparing to land. Thinking quickly, he waved wildly then, cupping his mouth with his hands, yelled up at them, 'You've got the wrong continent . . .' Luckily they took him at his word and their aircraft flew off into the blue sky. Barely able to believe that they had got away with it – for now – the small group of conspirators prepared to move on before they were found out. Contacting a close friend, they arranged to stay at a beach house some miles away. It had the advantage of being both anonymous and discreetly tucked away. Ironically, the Shand Kydd property in Yass was right beside that owned by the media baron Rupert Murdoch. How irritated he must have felt when he learned that the future Princess of Wales had been staying on a farm next to his own. He – or rather, his papers – had just missed a world-class scoop.

Thanks to Frances and Peter not even the most intrepid journalist or photographer managed to track Diana down. Indeed, no one found her, including Prince Charles who, despite having been given the telephone number, never once called to ask how his fiancée was, or to reassure her about the times that lay ahead. Not unnaturally, Diana pined for him, second-guessing what the silence meant and how he might feel about her. In these moods, there was little Frances could do to reassure her daughter, except listen. Looking back, it can be seen that the Prince's behaviour was a sign of things to come.

Sea and sand provided the perfect distraction, and the beach house proved to be the ideal place to recharge. Diana tried to rest while Frances stuck to practicalities, outlining to her daughter what a royal life might hold. They got well ahead with plans for the wedding, discussing dresses and going-away outfits as well as the range of clothes that would be needed for the honeymoon. There were moments of immense pride, certainly, but also sometimes vague feelings of unease, or even panic. Frances, Peter and Diana took long walks along the shore and talked things over as they went. Later, after the engagement had been announced, Frances was to affirm publicly Diana's intense love for Prince Charles, knowing perfectly well that his courtiers would be scouring the press for stories about his fiancée. She wanted him to be in no doubt about her daughter's feelings. 'We were just swimming and surfing,' she told one paper. 'It was like a real family holiday. Of course we talked about Diana's future life – I would be a very abnormal mother if we hadn't. I enormously approve of my daughters marrying the men they love so much.'

Peter and Frances snatched sidelong glances at each other as Diana swam through the surf. They had watched her grow up, and both hoped that she would be treated with the love and respect she deserved. Small twinges of doubt or concern were already creeping in, however. The reports that had circulated about the identity of a blonde woman seen to board the Royal Train in the early hours of a morning had been disconcerting. Frances knew Prince Charles's mysterious visitor had not been her daughter, but Diana's trust was being tested to the limit, and with alarming regularity the name of Camilla Parker Bowles would crop up. As one of the Prince's old flames, and even though married herself, it was clear that she had never truly been extinguished. Diana, young and in love for the very first time, was in danger of marrying a man who neither loved her nor felt it necessary to tell the truth. Frances knew only too well how destructive a lack of trust can be. Having conducted an illicit affair while still married to Johnnie Spencer, she also knew the dangers of secret assignations, and this story had left her feeling very uneasy. As she says, '. . . trust is . . . the biggest gem there is and very fragile. If you can keep trust it's there for ever, if you break it once, it's gone for ever.'

Having returned to London, Frances and Diana shopped at Harrods on the day before the engagement was announced and emerged with a selection of clothes, including the deep-blue suit and white blouse she would wear for the official engagement photographs. 'I literally had one long dress, one silk shirt, one smart pair of shoes and that was it,' said Diana. 'Suddenly, my mother and I had to go and buy six of everything. We bought as much as we thought we needed but we still didn't have enough.'

During the next day's television interview with the couple inside Buckingham Palace, the camera closed in on their faces and Frances heard Charles repeat the words he had spoken to Diana when he proposed to her: 'Whatever "in love" means'. Known to be awkward with the media, he was initially forgiven his bumbling reticence. It is rarely noted, however, that over the interviewer's voice he then adds by way of explanation, 'You can put your own interpretation . . .' Somewhat embarrassed by this, the interviewer fills in, adding, '*Well*, it obviously means two happy people.' Charles, however, unable to maintain the lie, looks down at the floor and mumbles, 'Yes, absolutely.' Diana's mouth visibly tightens and her face flushes, while Charles's face contorts. In every important respect, Diana is publicly humiliated before their life together has begun. Her fiancé's own 'interpretation' was clearly well established; he knew exactly what he meant by 'in love', and it had nothing to do with Diana. Nor was either of these two people 'obviously happy.' Penny Junor, Prince Charles's friend and biographer, says of his behaviour, 'I would have been devastated . . . I think it was a terrifically insensitive thing to have done.'

Diana's engagement had an effect quite the opposite of what Frances had envisaged. She had thought that the Spencer family would be left alone and under the protection of the royal family and the Palace, but instead media speculation about her private life and those of all her children intensified. Privacy, it seemed, was the price they all had to pay for Diana's decision. Frances acknowledges their innocence: 'Looking back, as a family we were very naive. We thought that a few months after Diana got married we'd be left alone but we're bit pieces in the soap opera, aren't we?' One of the royal press officers, Ronald Allison, remarked of that time:

> Once the engagement was announced, the focus of the press was even sharper on Lady Diana Spencer than it had been before. They were no longer speculating about who the Prince of Wales was going to marry, they were absolutely concentrating wholeheartedly, one hundred per cent, on the person he was going to marry.

Diana left her flatmates, and her own home, with just two suitcases for life in a royal palace. She was to reside at Clarence House until the wedding as a guest of the Queen Mother. This was supposedly to help protect her, and also so she could be schooled from 'commoner' to 'queen-in-waiting'. Her grandmother, Ruth Fermoy, was a regular visitor, and Diana would sit listening as the two older women discussed matters of protocol. It was a world very distant from the one she was used to. Three weeks earlier she had been teaching small children and having pillow fights with her flatmates, and now she was sitting, with legs crossed in the approved fashion, while courtiers presented her with dusty books about heritage, etiquette, precedence, and other arcane subjects. She left them rebelliously unread.

One courtier looked on sympathetically as Diana struggled:

> She was trying terribly hard to get it right. She cut herself off from her Sloaney friends, which was part of her attempt to try and get it right. That was the

streetwise Diana. She would have realized all her old chums and kindergarten friends would have stuck out like sore thumbs in the Palace. Once she was in there, what does she do? Who does she talk to?

It has been claimed – partly by Diana herself – that neither the Queen Mother nor Ruth Fermoy did anything to ease her way into the royal household and royal ways of doing things. This is hard to believe, however, and would have been self-defeating, considering that neither wanted to be associated with an unsuccessful union. There was neither benefit nor glory to be had from a failed marriage between a future king and queen.

Ruth Fermoy did in fact believe, however, that Diana's character was altogether too similar to her mother's, as though the 'flighty' Fermoy gene was destined never to accept authority or do as it was told. More than ten years later, Ruth conveniently admitted to Jonathan Dimbleby that she had had grave misgivings about Diana's suitability from the first. Instead of voicing her opinions, however, as she had done powerfully in the past with such devastating results, she apparently saw fit to mention her disquiet this time only in an aside to her granddaughter. She whispered to Diana, 'Darling, you must understand that their sense of humour and their lifestyles are different, and I don't think it will suit you.'

Diana had no wish to hear such views; besides, and by Lady Fermoy's own admission, she was unlikely to take her grandmother seriously. She also quickly discovered that her mother, the one source of trust, warmth and sanity in the chaos and confusion surrounding the engagement, remained a target for ridicule in royal circles. The Queen Mother loathed Frances because of her divorce many years previously, and that view pervaded the family into which Diana was supposedly being welcomed. It placed her in an impossible position, as she recalled years later: 'Whenever I mention my mother's name within the royal family, which I barely do, they come on me like a ton of bricks. So I can never do anything in that department. They're convinced she's the baddie and that poor Johnnie had a very rough time.'

Frances tried to live as normal a life as possible, rather than isolating herself in an ivory tower. Just prior to the wedding she bought A. and M. Menzies, a gift shop in Oban high street, which stocked souvenirs, postcards and other small items of interest for both visitors and locals. She enjoyed the contact with people that running the shop brought her. Some visitors came in especially to watch her at work, hardly believing that the mother of the future Queen would occupy herself with such a routine existence. Frances carried on working. She was treading carefully, however, aware that criticism was now being directed at Johnnie for commercially exploiting his relationship with Diana.

Although it was strenuously denied, the shop on the Althorp estate now stocked cheap imitation engagement rings, similar to Diana's; foreign visitors were offered tours of England which included – for a price, of course – an evening at Althorp in the company of Johnnie and Raine; and huge sums were being asked for early photographs of the soon-to-be new princess. The publicity was both unwelcome and highly embarrassing for Johnnie.

One company that organized parties confirmed that Althorp was heavily promoted as a venue for corporate and private events. After an agreed fee had been paid Johnnie and Raine undertook to 'meet and greet' the guests before pointing the way to the dining room. This would normally require about half an hour of their time, after which they would disappear, leaving the paying guests to their dinner. A member of the company who dealt with the Spencers said:

> We paid them £5,000, for a party of thirty guests. Johnnie didn't seem to know what was going on, bless him, and looked rather dishevelled and disorientated. It was obvious Raine was completely in charge and the servants, who we were instructed to sit with downstairs, all seemed frightened of her. Although she wanted to appear aristocratic, she didn't have the lightness of touch, or the charm you normally associate with that set. She tried too hard. I can't think why she allowed it all to go on. It's not as if she needed the money – she could easily have sold another painting for far more.

Frances tried to avoid any potential criticism of her own actions by sending early photographs of Diana to Buckingham Palace, to allow them to choose which to release for publication. Fearing that she would be tarred with the same brush as Johnnie and Raine she issued a pointed statement via the media:

> I'd never think of making a penny out of my daughter's wedding. I think it's terrible. I feel very strongly that it's not a time for any members of our family to consider making money out of the wedding. I have been asked to sell pictures of Lady Diana. But the answer is a very firm 'No'. Large sums have been mentioned, but the whole thing is totally alien to me.

Knowing her daughter was under such intense pressure, it was both a disappointment and a shock to Frances that Diana – a mere nineteen years old – was being treated so tactlessly and the press not brought under control. She herself continued to handle the media better than did the Palace, remaining supportive of Diana, while never undermining her. As Frances told journalists that February, 'It's an unknown world for her, but I'm sure she can cope and learn very quickly.'

By now, Frances was aware that her youngest child, Charles, was also undergoing intense press scrutiny. Aged seventeen and still at Eton, his world was also turned upside-down. A schoolfriend recalls:

> He was in the sixth form when Prince Charles announced his engagement to Lady Diana Spencer. I think that produced some problems for him. I remember one occasion when a press photographer walked into Charlie's room and took his picture, and then later on, when some reporters were nosing around. There are twenty-five houses at Eton with fifty boys in each house; everyone had his own room but none of the doors had locks on them so anyone could wander in . . . Diana would visit her brother occasionally, driving herself down.

Within days of the engagement announcement, Diana began to fall into the grip of bulimia nervosa, a serious eating disorder in which sufferers gorge on food and then deliberately make themselves sick in an act of self-hatred and purging. From February to July, her weight plummeted by more than 2 stone (28 pounds), and her waist contracted by 6 inches. It was an alarming change that many people noticed, but in particular her mother.

When her eldest daughter, Sarah, was diagnosed with anorexia, Frances had read widely on the subject, and on eating disorders in general, and had taken much professional advice. She knew that she had to tread a fine line between becoming over-solicitous, and not taking enough notice of the illness. She worked hard to keep her nerve when Diana displayed the classic symptoms of someone suffering from an eating disorder.

Behind her resolve, however, lay grave concern. Frances had been aware of Diana's problem almost from the start, but she now grew fearful of the speed at which it progressed.

> I saw it immediately because I'd had previous experience with my eldest daughter, Sarah. It's a very stressful illness and I knew quite a lot about it. There were plenty of photographs around at the time but you can tell things on the end of a telephone. When Sarah had it I sought a lot of medical help so I recognized all the symptoms very quickly with Diana . . . There are an enormous number of reasons for anorexia and bulimia taking hold and you have to know those reasons to be able to help. One of the main reasons is unhappiness.
>
> Because of having known anorexia with Sarah, I did as I was medically advised with Diana. It's a very difficult area because you are told you mustn't pander – that you can accentuate the problem – but if you don't take enough notice that can be damaging too.
>
> . . . Every mother has an affinity with her children which makes her more aware and sensitive to their well-being and contentment. Therefore whether it is a sadness or joy in one's children you perceive it. I listened to, and supported her in every way I could.

Frances openly acknowledges that in times of trouble, eating also becomes problematical for her. Unlike Sarah and Diana, however, she has always retained greater control over herself. 'I have a problem with eating, when I get fussed . . . However, I have tackled this very strongly and the time comes when I know I must eat. I have friends who ring up and say, "Have you eaten?"'

Choosing the wedding dress was a useful diversion, for it allowed Diana to assert herself and at the same time prevent the Palace from having total influence. Amid great excitement Frances joined her daughter when she visited the designers, David and Elizabeth Emmanuel, whom Diana had met previously during a photo session at Lord Snowdon's studio. They were determined to better all expectations, creating a dress the likes of which had never been seen before. The Emmanuels also did their homework, finding out the length of the longest train for any royal wedding dress, and then adding on a couple of extra yards. It was twenty-five feet long and featured 10,000 mother-of-pearl sequins and pearls, while material for the ivory silk taffeta dress was spun at the only silk farm in Britain, at Lullingstone in Kent. Mother and daughter delighted in this game of mild one-upmanship against an Establishment ignorant of their rather girlie motives. Yet no one had anticipated the extra fittings Diana would have to attend to accommodate her plummeting weight, which was discreetly dealt with. So too were the disastrous attempts by make-up artists to try out new looks. Frances says that after the first session she ended up looking like Coco the Clown but then, after some major tonal adjustments, scared herself with a face reminiscent of a resident of a mortuary. In the end, she elected to apply her own make-up.

At 10.10 a.m. on 29 July 1981, Frances, dressed in azure blue, and Peter Shand Kydd left Clarence House for St Paul's Cathedral with Charles Spencer, who, like his stepfather, was in morning dress. The next time Frances saw her daughter she would be about to take the vows that would make her a princess. Years later, using a phrase reminiscent of George VI on his reluctant accession to the throne, Diana said that she felt like 'a lamb to the slaughter'. In Britain alone, 39 million people – out of an audience of 750 million worldwide – watched as she walked up the steps of St Paul's on the arm of her father. Johnnie, weakened after his almost fatal stroke, but resolute, hesitated only once on a lower step before regaining his balance and taking Diana's arm.

Almost equally nervous, Frances sat between her husband and her son, Charles, his characteristic mop of rebellious sandy hair somehow brushed into order. Beside him was Frances's mother and sometime betrayer, Ruth, Lady Fermoy. The two women had scarcely spoken since the divorce hearing until shortly before this wedding day. Charles leaned closer to talk to his grandmother, but Frances sat rigid, barely able even to look at her. Although their faces revealed nothing, the body language was clear. What lay between them went too deep ever to heal. To the informed observer, here was a hidden cloud on what was supposed to be a perfect day.

Frances peered out from beneath her wide-brimmed hat as her daughter spoke her vows. She was delighted to see that Diana had worn the diamond drop earrings she had lent her as the 'something borrowed' of tradition. She smiled in sympathy when the nervous bride fluffed the order of Charles's forenames, saying, 'I, Diana Frances, take thee, Philip Charles Arthur George', instead of 'Charles Philip Arthur George'. She understood what it was like to be married with so many eyes upon you at such a young age. In his address, the Archbishop of Canterbury, Robert Runcie, grandly pronounced that the marriage was 'the stuff of which fairy tales are made'. It now transpires, however, that even he had doubts about the match, and was aware at the time that Charles's real love was for Camilla Parker Bowles. Far from being a fairytale affair, Dr Runcie later privately acknowledged that it was an 'arranged marriage'.

With the ceremony completed, members of both families, royal and aristocratic, moved off together, while the congregation waited, fidgeting, for the reappearance of the bride and groom. The Queen, Prince Philip, Princess Anne, Prince Andrew and Prince Edward accompanied Earl Spencer, the Hon. Mrs Peter Shand Kydd, and Ruth, Lady Fermoy to sign the registers, one state, and one royal.

It was done. Frances's beloved youngest daughter was now Princess of Wales.

Frances left St Paul's Cathedral seated beside Prince Philip in an open-topped landau for the short journey to Buckingham Palace and the wedding breakfast in the Ball Supper Room. Ahead, behind the carriage carrying Charles and Diana, Johnnie, obviously enjoying the moment, travelled beside the Queen, waving enthusiastically at the throng.

Frances waved her daughter off from Buckingham Palace with a mixture of joy and trepidation. Diana, unwell and fragile, desperately needed a break from the unprecedented pressure under which she had lived for so long. Frances trusted the Prince to care for her daughter, to treat her with love and kindness. Yet at the back of her mind was the cold ruthlessness of which, she knew, royalty, and those close to them, were capable, an attitude epitomized by Ruth Fermoy, her own mother. It was a world where duty took precedence over all other matters, and where people were dispensable. She prayed that this attitude would never be adopted with Diana. Yet, had she known it, the signs were already there. When Prince Charles later described his wedding day, it was with a direct reference to his country, rather than his future queen: 'I remember standing at my window trying to realize what it was like, so that I might tell my own children . . . It was something quite extraordinary . . . I was quite extraordinarily proud to be British.'

After the first three nights together, Charles and Diana boarded the Royal Yacht *Britannia* at Gibraltar for a Mediterranean cruise. Intimacy was impossible, given the yacht's crew of close on three hundred. Sir Joshua Hassan, Gibraltar's Chief Minister, observed Diana, 'peering out of the porthole and tears welled in her eyes. She was overwhelmed by it all.'

The differences between the newly married couple were immediately apparent, as one onlooker noted: 'He did a lot of reading and painting. She got bored and wandered down to the mess decks. She was eating ice cream, surrounded by lots of sailors. She was doing something innocent but there was gossip and disapproval.' One crew member recalls an incident which, while typical of the behaviour of many twenty-year-olds on holiday, nevertheless spoke volumes about the relationship between the Prince and his bride:

> They'd gone on an excursion and landed on a deserted beach. Next thing I know the Princess is careering across the beach, pissed out of her mind – she'd discovered Pimm's. She had seaweed all over her. The poor old Prince is standing around, talking about the navy. She was hustled back to base. He was very gloomy. As they climb up the steps, she tips a bucket of water over him. He gets very angry, and looks like a hurt spaniel. You can see why – he's heir to the throne.

The last sentence is a telling one: in effect, Prince Charles would tolerate nothing that offended the person or the dignity of the heir to the throne. His wife and his marriage came a long way second to that august position.

Diana's mood darkened further when Charles callously decided to wear a pair of cufflinks engraved with the intertwined initials 'CC', for 'Charles and Camilla', a gift from his former lover. Diana was astounded as well as hurt, and from then on began to nurse an obsession with all things Camilla. Lonely, trapped aboard a floating palace in the middle of the Mediterranean, constrained by rules and royalty, she longed to go home to Britain.

In time she got her wish and, once back at Balmoral, to which she and Charles returned from *Britannia*, immersed herself in her family. At the end of August Frances and Peter joined Diana and their new son-in-law, and Sarah also came to stay, as did her brother Charles Spencer. Diana even invited her former flatmates to Balmoral, knowing that they would provide some much needed fun. In this relaxed atmosphere, once more among family and friends, she worked hard to get closer to the Prince of Wales.

Despite the difficulties that had attended the early days of the marriage, Diana quickly became pregnant, just as her mother had on her honeymoon. When the news was announced, the country seemed to go into a frenzy at the prospect of a royal heir. Frances watched with incredulity as the nation all but begged for a boy to complete the fairy tale. She herself wanted a healthy grandchild, and nothing more. Pregnant, Diana was grateful to have such a wonderful diversion, while Frances hoped that the birth of a child would bring her daughter the sense of security she needed.

Diana's initial excitement soon waned, however. She suffered terribly from morning sickness, while continuing to battle bulimia. She felt wretched as her weight fluctuated. Charles, entirely ignorant as to how to handle his pregnant wife, was also too proud or too arrogant to ask Frances, or anyone else, for that matter, for advice. To have done so would have been an admission of weakness; it would also have been an admission that his wife's well-being should take precedence over his own. The Queen considered Diana's welfare to be none of her business – rather, that was something for Frances to deal with. By April, too, Britain was at war, for the Argentinians had invaded South Georgia and the Falkland Islands and her younger son, Prince Andrew, was on active service with the Task Force as a helicopter pilot, a dangerous role. Compared with the conflict in the South Atlantic, Diana's temperamental behaviour became an irritant. In an attempt both to please and to distract her, Prince Charles handed her the task of choosing the interior design at Highgrove, their Georgian country home in Gloucestershire. Diana engaged Dudley Poplak, who had decorated Frances's London flat. Mother and daughter enjoyed choosing the designs, and for a time the project helped take Diana out of herself, while allowing Frances to offer reassuring motherly advice about the impending birth. All too soon, however, Diana's concentration was once more submerged beneath her anxieties, while her work on the house proved to be a hollow gesture. Charles did not like the results, and Diana took this as yet another indication that she had failed. For her part, Frances remained convinced that Charles would soften over time and that the birth of Diana's baby, especially if it should be a boy, would give him everything he desired.

Prince William was born on 21 June 1982 in the private Lindo Wing of St Mary's Hospital, Paddington. Like her mother before her, Diana's first labour was long and arduous. After sixteen hours and an epidural – an injection in the spine to provide pain relief – she finally pushed the baby boy into the world. For a brief moment the Waleses forgot the past and focused on their beautiful son. He was blond and had the Roche saucer eyes; better still, Diana had achieved the ultimate goal and borne a boy at the first attempt, unlike her siblings and her mother. Relieved and overjoyed, she felt at last that the royal family would consider she had done something right.

Frances, delighted with the news, was the first to see her newborn grandson, ahead of the Queen, a gesture intended to soothe Diana. Waiting for the birth had proved an anxious time for Frances who, like any mother, worried about how her daughter would cope with labour, and about the well-being of mother and child afterwards. For a woman who had lost a child at full term, however, the period of waiting was doubly hard. Immediately after the birth she told the press:

> One is always anxious until the birth is over and one knows that mother and baby are well. The hours spent waiting for a grandchild are the longest in any mother's life.
>
> When Baby Wales finally arrived safely the hours that followed were the happiest I've ever spent. He is a beautiful child and Diana is very, very radiant and very, very well.
>
> I love children. I always have. I had five of them in nine years. But I don't know if Diana plans to follow my example and have a large family.

Diplomatically, she also mentioned her first grandchild by her younger daughter, Jane. 'I have been so lucky. My other daughter, Lady Jane Fellowes, has a beautiful little girl aged two, and now I have a grandson.'

After William's birth, Frances made plain that her role was one of support, but not interference. 'I am a firm believer in maternal redundancy,' she said, 'When daughters marry they set up a new home. They should be free to make their own decisions and make their own mistakes. Whatever you taught them at a certain age . . . that is finished.'

From the moment Diana gave birth, she discovered that she needed her own mother more than ever. Far from her husband providing stability in her life, she sought and found it in Frances. The mother who had not been able to share fully her daughter's life while she was growing up, was now at the very centre of it.

CHAPTER NINE

Crumbling Marriages, Shattered Dreams

For Frances, the births of her grandchildren and the spectacle of Diana becoming a princess, to rapturous approval from around the world, were some of the most precious moments of her life. As a mother and a grandmother, they brought feelings of immense satisfaction and contentment.

As a wife and a sister, however, she found herself on the brink of a long period of emotional turmoil. On 19 August 1984 came news that was both unexpected and devastating: her beloved younger brother, Edmund, highly strung by nature and plagued by depression and self-doubt, had killed himself. He was just forty-five. The tormented fifth Lord Fermoy had woken early, taken his shotgun, walked into one of the stables on his 700-acre estate, Eddington House near Hungerford, Berkshire, and there turned the gun on himself. The violence and despair of the act were truly shocking.

Educated at Eton and then Sandhurst, Edmund was commissioned into the Household Cavalry before eventually becoming a farmer, although his skills as a rider had seen him triumph as a successful steeplechase jockey and polo player. He had succeeded to his father's title in 1955, aged just sixteen, and in 1964 had married Lavinia Pitman, who bore him two sons and a daughter. By the 1980s he had been suffering from depression for some time, made worse when he was subsequently exposed in the press as one of the clients at a massage parlour also frequented by Major Ronald Ferguson, the Prince of Wales's polo manager and an old flame of Frances's. For Edmund, a proud, sensitive and private man, the shame of exposure in the press must been shattering – and perhaps pushed him over the brink.

To Frances, losing Edmund was almost unbelievable, and certainly unthinkable. From the day he was born, she had loved and protected him, and they had always been extremely close. He had once asked her how she managed to remain calm and optimistic in the face of adversity, whereas he was troubled by his relatively straightforward life. She answered thoughtfully, and with characteristic simplicity, 'It's how you come out of the egg, Edmund.' When his first child, a girl, was born in 1965, he named her after Frances. The shock of his death reverberated around the entire family, and Diana was especially saddened. Taking his death to heart, and less than a month away from giving birth to a second child, she cancelled a planned trip to Balmoral in order to help Frances with the funeral arrangements and to comfort her three cousins, Edmund's now fatherless children.

One of Diana's abiding memories of her uncle was of an incident during a hot summer's day two years after her parents' divorce. Edmund flew into the Sandringham Estate in his helicopter and landed on the lawns of Park House, while Diana was leaping in and out of the swimming pool.

He stepped from his aircraft like a secret agent on a mission and strode over the lawn towards the pool. Mary Clarke, the nanny at that time, dressed in a bikini top and shorts, jumped up to introduce herself, 'before my rather vivid imagination took too strong a hold. The reality was that I was not an Ian Fleming heroine and Lord Fermoy was certainly not James Bond! I introduced myself and explained who I was and that Lord Althorp was away for the afternoon.'

Edmund's jaw dropped – nannies in his day came dressed head to toe in uniform, and would never have allowed themselves to be seen so casually attired. Diana, along with Sarah and Charles, came running over to see who the glamorous figure was, and greeted him enthusiastically before dashing off to get cool drinks. When they returned, Edmund took a few sips and said, much to the amusement of Diana, 'Tell Lord Althorp I dropped in.' He then stepped back into his helicopter and flew off as swiftly as he came.

Only six weeks after Edmund's death, the family received yet more horrifying news – Frances's former brother-in-law, the Conservative MP Sir Anthony Berry, had been killed in the bombing by the IRA of the Grand Hotel at Brighton, where many senior members of the party were staying during their annual conference. The Prime Minister, Margaret Thatcher, only narrowly escaped with her life. Frances immediately rang her sister, Mary, who had married the then Anthony Berry in 1954, although they had quietly divorced in 1966, after she had borne him four children. Now she had lost a brother and an ex-husband, the father of her children, in a matter of weeks. In the midst of such sorrow, Frances resolved to find strength in desolation. As she says, 'Death is not new to me. My brother took his life and six weeks later my brother-in-law was murdered. So in six weeks, all seven of my nephews and nieces had no father.'

Frances dealt with her sorrow by taking long walks along her favourite beach in Seil. It gave her time to think, to remember and to grieve. She worked hard to avoid becoming cynical in the face of such tragedy, and found that looking at the 'big picture' helped to bring the arbitrariness of life into perspective.

Yet the seclusion that Frances and Peter craved, and never more so than after the trauma of the deaths of people they were close to, was fading. Peter was becoming increasingly restless, and made frequent journeys away. Frances, having been preoccupied with Diana and the panoply of her engagement, wedding and royal life, was still having to fend off relentless press interest in her family's every move; not least hers, for she was now not only a mother to royalty, but a grandmother to a future king.

It was all a far cry from the early days, when her children had come to Scotland as carefree young teenagers, and she and Peter had worked to make their visits idyllic. Frances then had been kept busy with the mundanities of running the house and helping with the farm, and even of ensuring that the ponies she bred were well treated after they had been sold. Sadly, One mysteriously found its way on to the menus of French restaurateurs, having being passed to an abattoir by a local farmer. Frances was aghast when she discovered the truth, having been promised that the pony was on its way to a good home, and vowed never to let such a thing happen again. As a result, she subsequently found it hard to delegate tasks to others, on the principle that only if you did something yourself would you know that it had been done properly.

Having become one of the most sought-after mothers in the land, Frances stoically coped with the pressure. She had no press officer to field the numerous telephone calls and interview requests, since she was determined to keep her life as normal as possible. She continued to run her shop in the town and the farm on the island. Yet despite her huge reserves of energy, she was silently suffering. Something had to give.

By now, the intensive physical work of farming was starting to affect Peter's health. A large and powerful man, he had always thrown himself energetically into any job that required extra muscle power, despite Ardencaple's team of labourers and farmhands employed to keep the farm operating smoothly. As a result, he became frustrated when he damaged his back and found that he was no longer able to do as much of the physical work he so enjoyed.

The broadcaster Gordon Honeycombe describes Peter as a gentle giant. 'He was very broad, not bulky but a large man, very imposing with a wide strong face, a very engaging smile and twinkling eyes. His tanned face had very strong lines – he looked characterful.'

Peter's back problem was only aggravated by the long-haul flights to and from Australia, squeezed into small aircraft seats for hours at a stretch. The

12,000-mile journey became such an ordeal that he became less and less inclined to make the trip. Frances tried to be positive in this time of misfortune, joking that she was in some ways relieved the journey to Australia had become infrequent as it saved her 'talking to sheep' all summer. Nevertheless, she lamented to Gordon Honeycombe, 'We will have to give up Yass at some point because Peter can't manage the trip any more. He can't sit for that length of time and the flight is too long.'

The problems with his back came as a considerable blow to Peter and the chronic pain affected his mood, frustrating to someone always regarded as charming and convivial. Yet underneath his very extrovert exterior lurked an extremely private and discreet man. As a former submariner and farmer, he tended to like his own company as much as he enjoyed others'.

The years when he had worked in the family wallpaper business were probably the hardest for him, confined by office walls and the red tape of conventional business. From his early years in the navy to the outback farm in Australia and then Seil, it is clear that he was never a man to seek limelight. The peace and quiet of wide-open spaces were what he craved, whether he was sailing or farming, while his wealth meant that he could do most of the things he wanted without any real restrictions. Such a lifestyle had also suited Frances. During the Diana years, however, Peter began to find the incessant media attention both irritating and stifling; it led, too, to an agreement between the couple never to speak about their relationship, an agreement they kept even after they had gone their separate ways.

For, sadly, what gave in the end proved to be their relationship. Placed under a strain Frances had not anticipated, she and Peter were now doing less together and more apart. Their interests diversified, Frances organizing and answering the incessant mail and calls and faxes, while Peter occupied himself in sailing and farming. He became moody and withdrawn, and avoided talking about the state of the marriage. Certainly, things had changed. They were no longer simply Mr and the Hon. Mrs Peter Shand Kydd, they were the stepfather and mother of the future queen, step-grandfather and grandmother to a future king. It was clear that Peter hated the spotlight and, having been used to Frances's undivided attention, minded the changes in their life together.

The split, when it came, seems to have been due as much to the very pressures Peter always sought to avoid, as to any specific problem in the relationship. He detested publicity, and once Diana's life was put on public show he began to feel pursued. Eventually the pressure became too great and he could no longer live with the intrusion.

Even so, Frances always made time for Diana and her two children (Prince Harry had been born in September 1984), often inviting them to Seil where they could relax away from the intrusive media. Ken Wharfe, the Princess's police protection officer from the late 1980s to the early 1990s, came to know Frances well, and to admire her:

> There was only one 'Supergran' – Diana's mother . . . To Diana she was simply 'Mummy', the one person in the world to whom she could always turn . . . Diana and 'Granny Frances' (the boys' pet name for her) enjoyed a close and loving relationship. When Diana was at her most troubled and really needed the most private of counsel, it was to her mother that she would always turn.
>
>   Whenever Frances came to Highgrove, or when we went to her home near Oban in the west of Scotland, William and Harry were ecstatic. Journalists tended to assume that because the Princess and her mother lived so far apart geographically, contact between them must be limited. In reality, they kept very much in touch, and whenever Diana wanted to escape with her sons we would decamp en masse for Scotland to her mother's remote hideaway for a healthy dose of normality. The young princes loved these visits and they were always a tonic to Diana . . .

Frances became adept at mixing diplomacy with her well-known habit of straight talking. Knowing that relations between Diana and Prince Charles were deteriorating rapidly, she used her quick wit and incisive manner to deflect the tension between the two of them; in short, she would go where others feared to tread. As Ken Wharfe again recalls, 'Diana's mother was an excellent mediator, and at Highgrove was one of the few people capable of breaking the bitingly cold silence that reigned between Charles and Diana.'

Yet such efforts were at a high personal cost. Frances's attempts to ensure the success of her daughter's marriage were leading to her sacrificing her own. The closeness that had so typified the early love between Frances and Peter was dying in the wake of her devotion to her daughter. Desperate to cling on, to repair the damage, Frances believed that it would only take a little time together to rekindle what they had once had. By now, however, it was too late. She says philosophically, 'When Peter and I drifted apart, I thought if I hung in long enough and tried hard enough we'd find calmer waters. Well, we didn't.'

The break-up of Frances's first marriage and her subsequent vilification in the press made her very wary of revealing details about her relationship with Peter. Indeed, her desire to keep this chapter of her life private is a determined attempt to draw a line and protect her children and herself from unnecessary intrusion. She has always refused to allow the substance of her second marriage to become public property. And to this day she still refuses to speak badly of Peter – or of Johnnie, for that matter. 'Pass – personal opinions I won't do,' she says adamantly.

Diana identified with her mother's way of dealing with her own problems, and recognized that it often masked considerable suffering. She was grateful she had inherited or acquired this trait, for it helped her enormously in carrying out her public duties. 'I've got what my mother's got,' she declared. 'However bloody you're feeling you can put on the most amazing show of happiness. My mother is an expert at that.'

The Shand Kydds' marriage staggered on, but there was soon a new interest in Peter's life – a Frenchwoman, Marie-Pierre Becret Palmer, whom he had met as a result of his love of fine wine, for she ran a champagne-importing business in London. She was younger than Frances, voluptuous, chic, enticing, and she gave Peter the attention he was missing. Frances did not recognize what was happening until it was too late.

By the summer of 1988 matters had come to a head, and on 20 June a terse statement was issued, through Frances's solicitors, to the press: 'I would like it known that my husband and I have separated. This is a great sadness for us both. No one else is involved and neither Peter nor I will be making any further comment.'

Even if the statement had not kept to the strict letter of the truth – for there was someone else involved – Frances was true to her word. Callers at Ardencaple, where she remained alone after Peter left, were intercepted by a lodgekeeper and turned away as newspapers, starved of hard information, began to speculate that Peter was returning to his first wife, Janet, now an antiques dealer in Chelsea. Others, however, blamed the split on his fondness for alcohol. 'He liked a tipple,' a neighbour was quoted as saying. 'Every time I met him, he would have a drink in his hand. I never saw him staggering or falling over, but he could knock it back.' An Oban resident added, 'We've been wondering for some time if everything was well with the marriage. Mr Shand Kydd has hardly ever been seen in Oban. And you could count on the fingers of one hand the number of times they have been out as a couple.'

The separation and subsequent divorce were a harrowing time for Frances. Left by the man she trusted and adored for a younger woman, she was inconsolable. Still desperately loving Peter, it took her more than four years to recover, yet she refuses to apportion blame or descend into bitterness.

> We aren't around to judge, we are around to love. Marriage is harder nowadays than for my parents because they lived in a big house, someone cooked their meals, looked after their individual needs, there were buffers. To be in a small flat cooking the scrambled eggs, when you're both home, never getting away from each other, is difficult. If things are going wrong what you really want is peace, not pressure, to see what you can do.

Three years later, after Peter and Frances had divorced, he and Marie-Pierre were married. They divided their time between their homes in Chelsea, where Marie-Pierre's champagne business was based, in the medieval hilltop village of Goult in Provence, and in the French ski resort of Savoie. Their relationship lasted until April 1995, when Peter returned to Aldeburgh in Suffolk, to live close to his first wife Janet. Marie-Pierre, an independent countrywoman known for wearing jodhpurs and tan boots, said of Peter at the time of their separation, 'Provence is just not his scene.' Then she added, 'I know about Frances, but I have nothing in common with her. Peter likes to spend time with his first wife Janet. She is, after all, the mother of his children and she lives in Suffolk too. I am not a headmistress supervising all he sees.'

Digging deep within herself, Frances found reserves of resilience. Her determination to see positive aspects in often terrible times is remarkable. Speaking of her life, she says, 'I knew enormous happiness in both marriages and I think it's one of the worst things you can do in life to talk about a break-up when you've been happy. I believe the currency of loving and happiness, whether it was brief or long, is silence.'

By misfortune, both mother and daughter were under enormous emotional strain at the same time. As Frances's second marriage ended, so Diana had almost completely withdrawn from Prince Charles. Shortly after Prince Harry's birth on 15 September 1984, the Prince and Princess were living separate lives, holding the semblance of a relationship together with cold politeness and protocol. Nothing, it seemed, could deflect Prince Charles from his views as to how things should be. At Harry's christening, he tactlessly told Frances of his disappointment that he had another son, and not the daughter he had hoped for. Diana recalled that, for once, Frances lost her temper: 'Mummy snapped his head off, saying "You should be thankful that you had a child that was normal."'

It was an ill-chosen remark of the Prince's, especially to a woman whose first son had died within hours of his birth; it was also indicative of his lack of sensitivity. Frances's characteristically direct response was automatic. She chastised the future King without a moment's thought, saying precisely what she felt. By leaping to the defence of her daughter and grandson she made her position plain; she neither feared the Prince nor, when he made such remarks, did she respect him. Inevitably, a frostiness descended upon her relationship with her son-in-law. He took the reprimand as a deep personal insult, seeing no fault in stating his views in any way he saw fit. As Diana noted, 'Ever since that day the shutters have come down and that's what he does when he gets somebody answering back at him.'

Undeterred, Frances continued to provide solace to her desperately unhappy and disillusioned daughter, offering the peace and normality of Seil whenever Diana became desperate to escape the glare of publicity, the prying lenses, and a disaffected husband who apparently had no interest in repairing their marriage.

In fact, that marriage was dying, but from bitter experience Frances knew the damage that in-fighting between husband and wife could cause, especially to their children. She was also acutely aware that Diana could not just uproot her children and leave her husband, as she herself had tried to do almost twenty years before. The royal family would never let the princes go. Ken Wharfe saw at close quarters the effort Frances made. 'She did everything she could to support her daughter, but also to save Diana's marriage, if only for the sake of William and Harry. Her wisdom, her experience, her kindness were always at Diana's disposal and the Princess knew it and was glad of it.'

By now, however, Diana was becoming increasingly paranoid, and especially nervous of Palace insiders. In July 1987 her trusted police protection officer (and Ken Wharfe's predecessor), Barry Mannakee, was killed in an accident while riding as a passenger on a motorbike. Mannakee's employers, Scotland Yard's Royalty Protection Department, believing that he and the Princess had become too close, had summarily removed him from his post with her a year earlier. Learning of his death, a deeply upset Diana believed that the accident had been a set-up; that he had in fact been murdered by the Establishment because of his closeness to her.

A persecution complex was one thing, but Diana's judgement was also in question during her heady love affair with a Guards officer, James Hewitt, whom she had met in the previous year at a drinks party at Buckingham Palace. Although always in danger of being exposed, she conducted the secret liaison in an extremely cavalier manner, sending him hundreds of personal and explicit letters, and showering him with often expensive presents and even, on one occasion, a large sum in cash. It is said that Prince Charles was well aware of the liaison and welcomed it, perhaps even encouraged it, since it allowed him the freedom to pursue his own rekindled affair with Camilla Parker Bowles.

Frances knew all about the frustration and heartache that went with being in love with someone other than your husband. For her to have judged Diana over her extramarital relationships would have been hypocritical, and therefore, to her, unthinkable. Indeed, such episodes helped the two women work through unfinished business. Diana as a child had found it hard to come to terms with her parents' divorce. Now, as an adult caught in a loveless marriage, and prone to offering her love if not wisely, then too generously, she gained a different perspective. Frances, whose own experience gave her the benefit of hindsight, adopted a calmly non-judgemental view of her daughter's future:

> I really believe you have to accept people the way they are and if they have
> something which, after a long time, they feel must be done or should be said,

well, who are we to criticize even though we have deep feelings that they are hurting rather than healing themselves?

You must respect everyone's opinion. The big issues in life aren't done hastily, they are done in time and with thought.

Frances, having herself suffered greatly at the hands of the Establishment, in the form of the law and of closed-ranks upper-class society, was mindful of the backlash her daughter's problems would provoke, were they to become widely known. Knowledge of a pending separation, or even of strain within the marriage, might well place merciless pressure upon an already delicate Diana.

Constitutionally, the breakdown of the Prince and Princess of Wales's marriage raised many complex issues, issues that Diana had no wish to consider. She was both the wife and the mother of a future monarch, and also a public figure with the weight of history, tradition, duty and precedent pressing heavily on her shoulders. Whether she would ever be crowned queen now seemed increasingly doubtful. Her two boys were her first priority, and however unwillingly, she had to accept that they would be raised in the royal way of life. To the Palace, the issue of paramount importance was how the wife of a prince of the blood royal could extricate herself from her marriage with minimum damage to the monarchy.

Diana and Charles no longer slept, or even lived, together, the boys were away at boarding school for much of the time, and Diana had carved a role for herself through her dedication to an array of charitable causes. She had lovers, and a close circle of trusted friends. Frances, however, preached caution. Keep up the illusion and live your life as best you can, she urged her daughter. Don't rock the boat; there are ways of steering a course into calmer waters. It was not what Diana wanted to hear, of course, but none the less reflected her mother's wiser philosophy:

> You must give your children roots and wings, above all wings. As they fledge you still watch with a great mix of pride and anxiety. There comes a time when the ground rules for living draw to a close and there's nothing more boring than parents who interfere along the way. I said to all my children, 'OK, you have independence and with that goes responsibility. Don't whack someone if you've done something that wasn't a good idea.'

Diana, however, tried beyond endurance, could no longer stand the hypocrisy of a Palace working actively against her, the lies in press accounts circulating about her state of mind, and the maliciousness of stories saying that her charity work and public appearances were no more than an attempt to pander to an already adoring public. Frightened and hurt, she wanted desperately to put her side of the story, an idea that, at the time, seemed impossible, for the consequences, in terms of the vengeance that would be wreaked on her by an infuriated Establishment, were unthinkable.

In the midst of these dilemmas, Diana insisted that Frances join her on a secret three-day trip to Italy, where they were to be guests of Frances's friend the Contessa Maria Cristina Guerrieri-Rizzardi. There Diana relaxed at last, telling her detective, Ken Wharfe, 'I am sure the air is different here, Ken. It tastes cleaner – crisper.'

One night, after attending the open-air opera in the Roman arena at Verona, to hear Pavarotti sing in Verdi's *Requiem*, the Princess suggested on a whim that they should see Venice by moonlight, even though the heavens had opened and brought the performance to an early close.

'Let's live a little,' she urged.

The party jumped into cars and, escorted by Italian police, drove the seventy-odd miles to Venice at breakneck speed. When they arrived, Diana flung herself out of the car and went splashing through the puddle-filled streets like an excited child. Watching her, an Italian policeman mused, 'I thought it was only we Italians who are crazy.' After a midnight boat trip along the Grand Canal, the party sauntered through a deserted Saint Mark's Square and ate hot croissants and freshly cooked bread in the shadow of Saint Mark's Cathedral. Drinking straight from a bottle of wine, Diana whispered, 'If only I could have this freedom once a month it would make the job worth it all the more.'

Back in Britain, reinvigorated by the success of her secret trip, she saw a piece sympathetic to her by a former royal correspondent, Andrew Morton, who had written several books on her early life at the palace and other royal subjects. His name came up again as she seriously considered how best to tell her side of the marriage and free herself from the oppressive burden of living a lie, as well as take her revenge upon the royal family and the Palace hierarchy that supported it.

Using an old and trusted friend, James Colthurst, a physician and surgeon turned alternative therapist, as a go-between, with whom she secretly recorded extensive and detailed tapes, Diana poured out her heart. Colthurst smuggled the tapes out of Kensington Palace and handed them over to Morton in a covert operation worthy of Watergate.

Diana's sole condition was that the author, and anyone else involved with the book, must never admit that she had been connected in any way with it, something which, despite intense pressure, was indeed kept secret until after her death. With *Diana: Her True Story*, the Princess found a way to exorcize her sadness and tell the entire truth, while also taking a daring swipe at Prince Charles and the Palace. That this appealed to her sense of the dramatic and her urge for vengeance is unquestioned; in the end, it also bought her freedom. She told her brother of her plans and he agreed to help. Through her family, she provided previously unpublished photographs from the Spencer family albums and even 'organized' a press shot with her friend Carolyn Bartholomew, who was quoted as one of the sources for the book, standing next to her to authenticate the publication.

When, in the summer of 1992, the first serialized extract of the book was published, with its tales of bulimia and attempted suicides, infidelity and a stultifying life inside the royal family, the public reaction was overwhelmingly in Diana's favour, although the Establishment, largely in the form of the Palace and the supporters of Prince Charles, tried desperately to discredit the book and its author. Diana knew, as did Frances, that she had successfully arranged her ticket to a separation and a future on the periphery of royal life. The Palace, hell-bent on finding the 'traitor' who had talked to Morton, suspected Diana, but even in an interview with her brother-in-law, Sir Robert Fellowes, now the Queen's Private Secretary, she successfully denied any involvement, although the suspicion followed her. The other royal courts lashed out, each making a frenzied attempt to discredit its opposite number. St James's Palace, for Prince Charles, questioned Diana's mental state, while Kensington Palace, for Diana, questioned.Charles's fitness to rule.

Nervous of the implications of Diana going public about the state of her marriage, Frances always kept her fears, and her daughter's secrets, to herself. 'Since my children grew up I've never told one what another has told me, it's up to them to transmit their news. I'm a great one at keeping confidences, an absolutely zipped-up oyster!'

Andrew Morton's book became an immediate and massive international bestseller, and changed the course of Diana's life. There was fury within the royal family, and Prince Charles was said to have been overcome with rage. Such tale-telling went against everything the monarchy stood for; worse, the public image of peace, harmony and deference had been shattered, possibly for ever. Diana had chosen her own rough road, rather than the one that had been mapped out for her by the royal family. While she had now bravely thrown off the chains of her supposed masters, her action had also exposed not only her, but her family. Frances waited anxiously for what would happen next. She knew that the aftermath of Diana's exposé might rebound on to her other children, remarking, not without an implied criticism of her younger daughter's behaviour and love of the limelight:

Some people thrive on publicity, but as Diana's mother I was very concerned not only for her but the effect her marriage had on my other children. I'm enormously grateful for those who knew me as the mother of all my children and who recognized I did indeed have other children. Sometimes Diana would be having a particularly poor time and the other children had the spin-off from what she was feeling.

Post-Morton, the public were made even more aware, thanks mainly to the tabloid press, of the precarious nature of the royal marriage. On New Year's Eve 1989, in what was arguably an orchestrated attempt either by the Palace or by Prince Charles's supporters to discredit Diana, an intimate telephone conversation between Diana and a man identified as an old and close friend, James Gilbey, was illegally recorded, possibly by one of the government security agencies. It was broadcast continually over the airwaves, with the result that at least two radio hacks managed to record the conversation. One of them sold his tapes to the *Sun* newspaper which, at first fearful of publishing such explosive material, kept them locked up for more than two years before finally releasing them in August 1992. In the tapes Diana, who was calling from her bedroom at Sandringham, is at her most candid, complaining about being 'sad and empty'. 'I'm going to do something dramatic because I can't stand the confines of this [i.e. the royal] family,' she says, going on to describe her life as 'torture.'

The publication of the transcripts of the 'Squidgygate' tapes (so called because Gilbey addressed Diana as 'Squidgy' or 'Squidge' several times during the conversation) left the Princess even more exposed and vulnerable. It was a feeling that Frances knew only too well. She was, too, scathing in her criticism of telephone buggings: 'I was horrified as anyone with a streak of decency would be. To me it was shocking . . . I don't know how anyone can ever feel comfortable with that sort of pressure.'

If Diana was a source of deep concern to Frances, so too was her son. Charles Spencer had had no doubts about supporting his sister, not least because he was becoming increasingly uneasy at being the Prince of Wales's brother-in-law. He and Diana had always been close. When he left Oxford with an upper-Second degree in Modern History, therefore, it was not altogether surprising that he should buy a house in Notting Hill, not far from his sister Diana's home at Kensington Palace. Good-looking, clever and charming, he began a career as a journalist with the American TV station NBC, beginning with light features before being sent to report from the world's trouble spots. The job suited his impetuous, daring and assertive nature, and Frances was delighted by the success he made of it: 'With Charles, I was very keen on him having a career or doing what he wanted in spite of his title, not bucking the reality of it but expressing himself. I don't think any parent is in a position to say "you must, you should" or "this'll be good for you".'

Being a handsome, rich and titled foreign correspondent was not lost on the women he met, and Charles enjoyed a lively social life. He tended to wear his heart on his sleeve, however, admitting, 'I am very impetuous when it comes to matters of the heart. I'm a romantic and can fall head over heels in love very easily.' True to his word and following in the footsteps of his sister, Sarah (who had admitted that she was a 'whirlwind kind of lady' after her five-week romance with the man she married), Charles proposed to Victoria Lockwood, a model, within ten days of having met her.

Frances was in a kind of double quandary. Her youngest child was about to marry a woman whom he hardly knew, and her youngest daughter's marriage was collapsing. Knowing what to say, and when – or when to keep silent – became one of her chief concerns. Furthermore, although she liked her son's fiancée, Victoria, and found her to be kind as well as pretty, she was concerned about her health. Having gained considerable experience of anorexia and bulimia from Sarah and Diana, she could tell that Victoria was suffering from a similar problem. As a result, Frances trod very carefully around the couple, so young and so obviously infatuated with each other, anxious not to disturb their frail happiness. She saw, not for the first time, shades of herself in her starry-eyed son:

> Your own faults are very clearly mirrored in your children. I sometimes think, 'What a pity I've handed that on.' I'm still unsure whether you're a better mother to the children you are naturally in tune with, those who have some of your genes so you know what they mean. Or whether you're a better mother to a child who has a mixture of genes, who thinks differently, so you make a conscious effort to understand them.

Charles and Victoria's wedding, which took place at Great Brington church on 16 September 1989, also brought more than its fair share of difficulties. Raine, as was her practice, snubbed Frances during the rehearsal the day before, refusing to exchange pleasantries, even though they were seated next to each other. Diana, spotting this slight, moved in for the kill, but Raine was ready and spat, 'You have no idea how much pain your mother put your father through.' The effect was as though she had lit a fuse. Diana exploded at her stepmother, leaving Frances astounded to hear her daughter defend her so publicly.

The wedding itself had a theme that echoed Frances and Johnnie's union so many years before. The pages (Prince Harry and Alexander Fellowes, aged six, Jane's son) were dressed similarly to the third Earl Spencer in a portrait by Reynolds painted in 1779. The bridesmaids (Emily McCorquodale, aged six, Sarah's daughter, and Eleanor Fellowes, aged four) wore dresses like that of Lady Georgiana Spencer in a portrait by Gainsborough dating from 1763.

History aside, Victoria's dress cost £16,000 ($24,000) and was a distinctive shade of champagne achieved by using domestic bleach; she also wore the Spencer tiara. One fashion critic found the outfit too bizarre, however, saying that she looked 'like Anne Boleyn going to her execution'. The weather was foul, and Jane skidded on a corner and sent her car into a ditch after leaving the reception with her three children. Fortunately no one was hurt.

The newlyweds moved into The Falconry, Charles's house on the Althorp estate – for Johnnie and Raine occupied the main house, and Charles had not the least intention of living with his stepmother – and Victoria set about adding her personal touch to the bachelor dwelling. 'All I want to do is look after Charles,' she was quoted as saying, somewhat passively. Despite earlier declarations that they would not have children immediately, on 30 December 1990 the Hon. Kitty Eleanor Spencer was born at St Mary's Hospital, Paddington.

Charles was twenty-six, and his relationship with Victoria was already under stress when he confessed to an affair in the period between his wedding and Kitty's birth. Contrite, he admitted that he had caused his wife, 'more grief than I would wish her to have in a lifetime with me. I accept full responsibility for the folly of my actions.' Questioned by the press, Johnnie put the fault firmly at Charles's door. 'He is married to a splendid girl in Victoria but I think he's a little immature. He'll get over it all, just you wait and see. I love my children but they have gone a bit haywire.' Charles had not expected sympathy from his father, but a public dressing-down was more than he had bargained for. Rather than confront his ailing father, however, and after patching up his troubled marriage, he focused his resentment on Raine and her wrongdoings. Then quite suddenly, his life was turned upside-down.

In March 1992, Johnnie was taken ill with pneumonia and was admitted to the Humana Hospital in St John's Wood, London. Diana came at once to see him there, but his condition was not considered critical and she left for a skiing trip with the boys and – most rarely – Prince Charles on 28 March, reassured by the doctors that Johnnie would soon be back at Althorp.

A day later, on 29 March, while Diana was in Lech, a ski resort in the Austrian Alps, her father died from a massive heart attack. Grief stricken, she flew back immediately, and the family gathered at Althorp for the funeral. Raine was not there, for Charles Spencer had already had his revenge, telling her to leave Althorp the moment he inherited the title. He now contemplated life as Lord Spencer, with the title and the estate he had been born to embrace. It was, he thought, a mixed blessing:

> From the outside it must look like an incredible life and lifestyle. But, nowadays, living somewhere like this is an enormous effort really. I suppose I'd

always thought that I'd come here in my late thirties, early forties. But my father's early death has obviously brought all that forward . . . Ideally I would have liked to have waited a few years but, now it's here, it's a great challenge. It gives a purpose to your life looking after something like this.

His wife did not share his enthusiasm. Soon pregnant again, this time with twins – both girls – Victoria felt ill, fat and terribly insecure. Beyond that, however, she had still not produced an heir in a family obsessed with lineage. Charles Spencer himself had expressed the perennial obsession that so perturbed the male side of the Spencer family when he told a journalist: 'There aren't many men alive in my family at all. My father has one male first cousin who's now over sixty years old, unmarried with no children. Then there's me. I don't know of any other male Spencers anywhere who are directly connected to the title. So if I die and my cousin dies without an heir, then that's the end of the earldom.'

History, it seemed, was repeating itself. The Spencers' all too public problems would once again rock the Establishment; worse still, they were about to shatter the Windsors' credibility. Divorce, aristocratic and even royal, was in the air. While Diana sank deeper into the morass, Frances knew that it was time to embrace a new way of living. Things had to change, for she sensed that otherwise they would break.

CHAPTER TEN

Soul Searching

B Y THE TIME she had reached the age of fifty-two, Frances had already joined what she calls the 'Home Alone' Club. The phrase, the title of a film which stars McCauley Culkin as a young boy accidentally deserted by his family and forced to fend for himself against housebreakers, aptly described the circumstances in which she found herself in 1988.

The breakdown of her relationship with Peter after nineteen years of marriage shook her to the core. In a rare show of vulnerability, she admitted that 'It left me lacking in all confidence.' In the last two decades she had lost her children, her home at Park House, her Sandringham friends and her reputation. Now she was on the brink of another divorce. It was undoubtedly a low point in her life, and her usual optimism quickly evaporated as she struggled to come to terms with the end of her second marriage. 'There were certainly occasions when I wondered "Is this the way it's going to be all the rest of my days?" There was a huge void. I was very bad about getting my act together. It took a long time.'

Where many others would have cracked under the strain, Frances buckled but did not break. Her wealth and comparatively high profile only complicated her recovery as she faced having to rebuild life alone, isolated, yet constantly under the gaze of a prying press and an intrigued public. The shock of being in a large property by herself was compounded by the responsibility of running the farm. Everything became more difficult without the steadying hand of Peter. The rambling old farmhouse was creaky at the best of times, but now seemed even more so. Sleeping became difficult. Frances did not relish the prospect of being on her own for the first time in her life. She was used to the cut-and-thrust of company and the vitality that another presence brought. Suddenly to find herself in what amounted to solitary confinement called on all her reserves of nerve and strength: 'I'd actually never lived alone, having married from home when I was eighteen. It [fifty-two] wasn't a brilliant age to start going it alone for

ABOVE: Lord and Lady Fermoy, with their second daughter, the Hon. Frances Burke Roche in her nanny's arms, after her christening in 1936.

BELOW: Frances (*right*) and her elder sister, Mary, a photograph sent by Lord Fermoy in 1936 to his American friend and former lover, Edith Travis, with whom he corresponded for some forty years until his death in 1955. He annotated the picture with the children's names and the date.

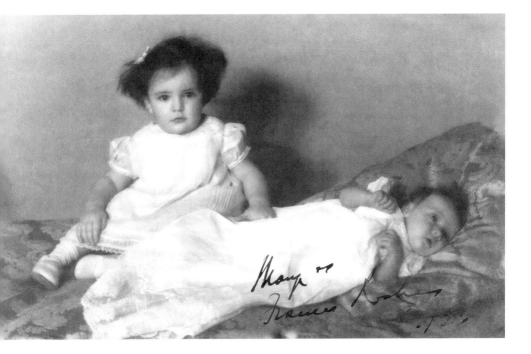

Lord and Lady Fermoy with Mary and Frances (*at right*), at the coming-out dance Ruth Fermoy gave for both girls in May 1953. Maurice Fermoy started the proceedings by dancing with his wife's close friend, Queen Elizabeth, the Queen Mother.

'The Children of Lord and Lady Fermoy' – a typical photograph from one of the 'society' magazines of the day, taken not long after Edmund Roche's birth in 1939, when Frances was three. The original, rather gushing caption states that the Fermoys 'are near neighbours of the King and Queen at Sandringham'.

A bystander fixes the buttonhole of Lord Fermoy at the wedding of his daughter Frances to Viscount Althorp, 1 June 1954. The photograph does much to confirm Maurice Fermoy's unsnobbish charm and graciousness towards others.

The society wedding of the year – Viscount and Viscountess Althorp leave the West Door of
Westminster Abbey, followed by the many pages and bridesmaids, and beneath an arch of swords
provided by the guard of honour from Johnnie Spencer's regiment, the Royal Scots Greys. Among
the guests were the Queen, Prince Philip, the Queen Mother, and Princess Margaret, all of whom
signed the register.

ABOVE: Frances and Johnnie at Park House on the day before their marriage in 1954, in another typically posed 'society' photograph.

IN LOVING MEMORY OF
JOHN SPENCER
SON OF VISCOUNT AND
VISCOUNTESS ALTHORP
BORN AND DIED
JANUARY 12TH 1960

LEFT: The grave in Sandringham churchyard of Frances's third child and first son, John, who died some ten hours after his birth. Frances was never allowed to see or hold him, and the fact that he was born malformed was kept from her.

RIGHT: The longed for son and heir: Frances holding her son Charles before his christening in London in July 1964. By now, as well as the death of her firstborn son, she had suffered a miscarriage which, as a result of the pressure upon her to produce an heir, she kept secret.

BELOW: Ruth Fermoy had trained as a concert pianist, latterly in Paris, before her marriage, when she gave up her professional career. She remained an extremely good pianist; here she accompanies the conductor and cellist Sir John Barbirolli at the 1962 King's Lynn Music Festival, a festival which she had helped to found.

ABOVE: Frances's brother Edmund, by now Lord Fermoy following Maurice's death in 1955, with his wife Lavinia at the christening of their daughter Frances in June 1965. Edmund was later to take his own life.

LEFT: Diana and Charles, aged six and three, playing in the grounds of Park House, which Johnnie leased from the Sandringham Estate, before he and Frances divorced, and she lost two court actions for custody of the children. Diana and Charles were often together, because the two older girls, Sarah and Jane, were away at boarding school for much of the time.

ABOVE: Charles Spencer, Viscount Althorp, escorts visitors around his ancestral home in Northamptonshire in 1977. By now his father had married Raine, the former Countess of Dartmouth.

BELOW: Lady Sarah Spencer, as she was styled after her father succeeded to the earldom, with the Prince of Wales at a polo match at Windsor in July 1977. She had outspokenly told a journalist that she had no wish to marry the Prince as she was not in love with him.

ABOVE: 29 July 1981 – Frances rides in an open landau with Prince Philip from St Paul's Cathedral after the wedding of her daughter, Diana, to Prince Charles. When, later, Prince Andrew became engaged to Sarah Ferguson, Frances wrote to Sarah's mother, an old and close friend: 'So glad there's another rotten apple with me at the bottom of the barrel'.

BELOW: The Earl and Countess Spencer in their hotel suite during a visit to Munich in 1981, the year that Diana married. By now, Raine had been instrumental in selling off an estimated one fifth of the treasures at Althorp, to the fury of her stepchildren, and especially Charles Spencer.

ABOVE: Raine and Johnnie Spencer, Charles Spencer, Frances Shand Kydd, and her mother, Ruth, Lady Fermoy, at a ceremony granting the Freedom of the City of London to Diana in July 1987. There is an air of tension to the photograph, unsurprising given the years of resentment and ill will between the protagonists.

RIGHT: Diana, holding Prince Harry's hand, walks beside her mother at Great Brington church, close to Althorp, a few days before Charles Spencer's wedding there in September 1989. Prince William walks ahead with his cousin, Alexander Fellowes, son of Diana's older sister, Jane.

LEFT: Frances and Diana in the entrance to Great Brington church as they arrive for Charles Spencer's wedding to Victoria Lockwood. The marriage ended in divorce, and Frances was to be unfairly censured by the press for her apparent insensitivity to her daughter-in-law's anorexia.

ABOVE: The Princess of Wales with her grandmother, Ruth, Lady Fermoy, at a concert at Hampton Court Palace in 1991; with them is Diana's aunt, Mary, Frances's older sister. Like her mother, Diana was to suffer bitterly from the social and moral strictures that her grandmother applied.

ABOVE: The Hon. Mrs Frances Shand Kydd, flanked by her daughters Lady Jane Fellowes (*left*) and Lady Sarah McCorquodale, arrives at Westminster Abbey for the funeral of Diana, Princess of Wales, 6 September 1997.

BELOW, LEFT: A rare shot of Peter Shand Kydd, taken in 1995, some years after his divorce from Frances, although they remain friends to this day. The photograph well illustrates his absolute refusal to have any truck with the media.

BELOW, RIGHT: Frances Shand Kydd arrives at Oban Sheriff Court for her trial, in which she denied charges of driving while under the influence of alcohol. November 1996.

RIGHT: Frances will never be free from her famous daughter's legacy, whether for good or ill. Here she arrives at court on 24 October 2002 to give evidence in the trial of Diana's former butler, Paul Burrell, for allegedly stealing property belonging to the late Princess. The trial collapsed spectacularly, and Burrell was released without further charge.

ABOVE: The bungalow on Seil, the Scottish island where she has lived since 1973, which Frances bought in 1992, after her divorce from Peter and their sale of Ardencaple, their farm on the island

BELOW: Frances Shand Kydd on Seil. Now sixty-seven, she faces declining health with the same courage, resolution and fortitude that she has always displayed throughout her extraordinary life.

the first time. At that stage in life you don't have the resilience that you do in younger years.'

A month after the separation, Frances was virtually housebound on Seil as the press, anxious to report on the break-up of her marriage, resorted to round-the-clock surveillance. 'They were camped outside my house for four days, twenty-eight of them,' Frances said. With typical panache, she enlisted the help of employees and friends in order to sneak out unseen: 'I used to leave the house in sheep trailers to avoid being detected.' She could hardly resist a smile as, hidden in the trailer, she rumbled past the line of press waiting with cameras and notebooks.

What remains remarkable is the absolute loyalty she has engendered not just among her friends and family, but also among the people on Seil, whether she knows them or not. They stick rigidly to the unspoken law that details of Frances's life are for her to reveal. They have all, without prompting, adhered to this vow of silence, with the result that very little about her life on the island has leaked out for public consumption. A former housekeeper at Ardencaple stuck resolutely to this code, and refused to give the slightest hint of what life was like with Frances and Peter. 'Not now. Not ever,' she declared. She was not alone, for this is a common response from islanders, who remain protective of their most famous resident.

At first, Frances, desperate to mend the marriage, worked hard to persuade Peter to come back to Scotland. He, however, had had enough. His unexpected role, and the responsibility that went with it, as stepfather to the most famous woman in the world was something that he could no longer live with. Furthermore, he distrusted Frances's renewed interest in their marriage after she had been so long preoccupied with her daughter's life. In the end, she reluctantly had to admit that the relationship was over.

> I realized very early on that any chance we might have had was just killed by the press. They just followed, followed and followed our every move. When you first separate there's always a question mark: is this the right thing to do? You can't find out by continuing to live together under the same roof, you need space. We were never given that opportunity.

With all hope of saving the marriage gone, Frances knuckled down to the practicalities of daily living. She soldiered on, continuing to farm at Ardencaple, dealing with her staff and ensuring that the animals – cattle and horses mainly, but also some sheep – were looked after. But daily trips into Oban became increasingly impractical, and in the end, reluctantly, she had to give up her gift shop. Quite apart from the behaviour of the media, the excessive attention from people who came to gawp at the spectacle of Diana's mother working behind a counter at her shop made life intolerable for

Frances and the rest of the staff. It was pointless pretending to be normal in such an abnormal situation.

Diana, who had always had a deep affection for Peter, was extremely upset when she learned of the separation. More than that, however, she felt a sense of responsibility for having placed her family in such a highly conspicuous position simply by her choice of husband. The Princess, who was by now leading a life separate from Prince Charles, sympathized with her mother's situation, and they spoke regularly on the telephone. Yet Frances declined Diana's frequent invitations to stay at Kensington Palace, believing that it was more important to search for solutions to her problems rather than run away from them. It is a philosophy she maintains to this day. 'When in doubt, standing still is the hardest thing to do,' she says, adding that there are many benefits to be had from letting matters develop gradually without forcing them, since this allows one's life to evolve, rather than simply exist within a tight structure.

Diana respected her mother's wish to remain on Seil and to get her life in order, although she knew from experience what a personal toll that takes. Even Frances realized that she needed to get away – from Ardencaple, from the press, from the gawping public, from her own lonely existence. At the end of 1988, therefore, she organized and paid for Diana and her two sisters to go with her to the Caribbean for a 'girls only' holiday. Having booked in under the name Barry, they flew to the exclusive Mosquito Island. In April 1989 Diana returned the compliment and asked Frances to accompany her, once more with her two sisters and this time with all seven grandchildren, to Necker, Richard Branson's private island in the Caribbean, which he had generously put at the Princess's disposal free of cost. The week they spent there gave Frances time to relax among her family and Diana valuable breathing space, away from the cameras and the now almost constant speculation about the state of the Waleses' marriage.

As greatly as they enjoyed themselves, even private family holidays could become a trial for Diana, especially when sunbathing by the warm waters of the Virgin Isles. The ever present 'rat pack' of photographers and journalists were never far behind, each hunting for a front-page headline or a valuable photographic scoop. Worse, the media had got wind of the fact that while Diana was on Necker, Prince Charles was on his own holiday in Scotland. To appease the press who had followed Diana to Necker, Ken Wharfe arranged photocalls in a deal whereby they would get these shots, and then agree to leave the Princess in peace. This worked well, but back in England, the knives were being sharpened. With no indication from the Palace to explain the increasingly noticeable differences between Charles and Diana, the separate holidays created a furore in the press. The Prince was slated for being an absent father, preferring to spend his time alone in the Scottish Highlands, rather than with his wife and young sons.

The Caribbean hideaway left such a lasting impression on everyone that a year later, in March 1990, Diana returned to Necker with her mother, her sisters and her recently married brother, Charles, and his wife, Victoria. Diana had planned the holiday as a surprise second honeymoon for the newlyweds, but this time it was even harder to keep the press at bay, to her irritation. Eventually she was persuaded to appear for a photocall, a one-off trade designed to guarantee the group some much-needed privacy in exchange for a few pictures. Diana had become well versed in manipulating the press to her own advantage.

It was during these holidays on Necker that it became transparently clear to Frances that Diana was in the throes of an affair with the handsome Captain James Hewitt. There was a sexual chemistry between them never before experienced by Diana. Hewitt's interest and affection brought her the emotional security she was looking for and an escape from the rigours of royal life. Their relationship won, too, the tacit approval of Prince Charles, as was clear when he invited Hewitt to his fortieth birthday party in 1988. If it remained discreet, Hewitt's affair with Diana kept the heat off Charles, for Diana, when happy, was far less likely to make trouble for him, and assuaged his guilt over his own continuing relationship with Camilla Parker Bowles.

Diana sometimes fantasized about living with her lover in a cottage in Devon, a carefree ordinary life. Hewitt recalls that she wanted 'To find some small, cottagey-type longhouse in Devon – nothing big, grand or majestic but somewhere that's cosy and comfortable. A bit of a sort of dream cottage.'

Ultimately, however, what Diana wanted most was what her mother had found (and now lost) with Peter – love, friendship and fun. Trying to live her fantasy of becoming an ordinary wife, she became close to Hewitt's mother, Shirley, and his sisters, often spending weekends with them at Shirley's home in Devon. According to Ken Wharfe, however, these visits were not always easy: 'Shirley Hewitt was a little bit difficult. I think she would have preferred the relationship not to be there because it put a lot of pressure on her – with her son bonking the future King's wife in her own cottage.'

Although Frances knew of Diana's secret love, Ken Wharfe confirms that Hewitt 'never went to Seil; I don't think she'd [Frances] ever allow that.' Yet her daughter's illicit liaison did prompt Frances to examine her own philosophy of life and, from that, her religious beliefs. She sought a new kind of peace after Peter, and was grateful to be able to focus on her own personal life, without troubling others. She admits, 'I actually don't like asking people to help me. I like to fight my own battles.'

In the end, however, it was the appalling human suffering caused by the Lockerbie air disaster that provoked Frances back into action. Although only months after her divorce, she forced aside her own feelings when the scale of the tragedy became known. Four days before Christmas 1988, a Pan-Am Boeing 747 jumbo jet, en route, via London, from Frankfurt to New York, was destroyed by a terrorist bomb high above the small Scottish town, killing 270 people: all 243 passengers and 16 crew, as well as 11 Lockerbie residents on the ground. The fall of the shattered aircraft caused extensive damage in the town, and debris was scattered over some 845 square miles between Lockerbie and the North Sea, while the attempt to find those responsible for the outrage and bring them to justice resulted in the largest criminal investigation ever undertaken in the United Kingdom.

The disaster brought out the best in Frances. In particular, she was touched by the plight of Steven Flannigan, whose family had been killed when the wreckage struck their home. The young boy only survived because, moments before the explosion, he had left the house to mend his sister's bike. To help him recover from the loss of his parents and sister, Frances took him to Australia, on a holiday to the sheep farm she and Peter still owned in Yass. One Lockerbie resident said of her support, 'A lot of people know what she has done for Steven but everyone is very protective of him. Everyone knows what a marvellous woman she is. She has done so much behind the scenes to help the children of Lockerbie.'

Modest herself by nature, but swift to credit others, Frances wrote to the newspapers, praising the attitude of the townspeople:

> Deep and resolute caring is given to the families of the victims who come to Lockerbie from all corners of the world. During their time in the town, the bereaved are cherished in a remarkable, practical and supportive way. Many remark on leaving Lockerbie that they wished the world knew of the kindness and comfort, given so freely to them by the people of Lockerbie.
>
> . . . I feel strongly that such heroic courage and Christian example should not go unsung.

By a somewhat sad irony, a few months later Frances won a pair of 'His-and-Hers' towels in a raffle in aid of the Lockerbie victims' families. Reflecting on her recent divorce, she smiled wryly at the embroidered wording, opting to hand the towels back for someone else to win. 'I'd have trouble finding a use for these,' she said, trying to make light of the end of her marriage.

Her divorce, Diana's marital problems and now her affair with Hewitt, and the terrible events at Lockerbie that had shown her ordinary people at their bravest and most compassionate, all set Frances on a path of deeper reflection. Her thoughts were gradually being drawn closer to the Church, and to a spiritual life within it. Having been brought up as a member of the Church of England, on moving to Scotland she had swapped easily between denominations, trying to discover a creed with which she felt comfortable. Gradually, one began to take prominence above the others, for she found the services at the Roman Catholic cathedral in Oban, St Columba's, remarkably calming, and the people welcoming. The plain, almost austere building was designed by Sir Giles Gilbert Scott, the same architect who created the famous Anglican Cathedral in Liverpool. The large granite and oak church, erected on the same site as the older cathedral, built in 1886, looks out over the sea towards Iona, the sacred Isle of St Columba, who brought the Christian faith to Scotland in the sixth century. For Frances it seemed to offer sanctuary, a place without fear.

There was more to this than her liking for the cathedral, however. The Catholic Church's emphasis on forgiveness, repentance and the necessity to live in the Christian faith at all times was hugely attractive to her. She was searching for something that required her complete commitment, something all-consuming, a belief that would never desert her, ideals that she could trust and live by, for ever. It is little wonder, therefore, that she described her growing interest in Catholicism as being like finding her 'spiritual kennel'. It was not perhaps the most felicitous of phrases, but it did convey a sense that she had, in terms of her faith, finally come home. As she said on another occasion, 'I . . . decided, quite literally, to go on a spiritual tour and find out what most suited my needs. I attended services of all the main branches of Christianity in Oban – Episcopalian, Church of Scotland and the Catholic Church – and I simply felt at home in the Catholic Church.'

Frances's devotion to the Catholic cause became known nationally when she helped to found a campaign that was close to home, as well as to her heart. Needing £100,000 ($150,000) to build the first Catholic house of prayer for four hundred years on the Scottish island of Iona, she became appeals secretary and treasurer to the Colmcille Trust. She then used her media profile to offer interviews in exchange for donations to the trust. In twelve months she wrote 10,000 letters, and sold bricks for the new building to sponsors at £5 ($7.50) each to raise yet more money.

While turning to Catholicism may have been Frances's salvation, the Establishment took a different view, deeming her participation provocative because no British monarch is permitted either to be a Catholic, or to marry a Catholic (the Sovereign being the head of the Church of England, and thus Defender of the Faith). As the grandmother of a future monarch, Frances's religion was seen as a potentially unwelcome influence on an impressionable young man; indeed, being close to Prince William, she was perceived by some as an ecclesiastical threat. Freedom of religion may have been all very well for the average person, but it became extremely complicated where an heir to the throne was concerned. Critics even raged that Frances's new faith was a deliberate, two-fingered baiting of the monarchy, a way of getting back at the Establishment that had shunned and scorned her.

Frances found all this risible. Nothing could have been further from the truth, for she would never consciously do anything that might hurt her children or grandchildren. She had turned to Catholicism because it gave her spiritual roots, and for no other reason. Nevertheless, in an effort to avoid further controversy, it was only after six years that she finally converted to Catholicism. It was something of a cloak-and-dagger exercise, for she asked none of her family to be present to avoid unwanted media attention.

> I had wanted to be received during a public service without a journalist there but that ruled out St Columba's Cathedral in Oban as the church was being watched. I had actually become rather twitchy about the press because I'd been followed for ten days by two tabloid reporters so it was decided I should go to Morar, near Mallaig, a couple of hours' drive north. In order to shake the press off my trail I went to mass in Oban at 10 a.m. dressed very scruffily. I then left by a back entrance and took off, changing when I got to the other end. My dearest wish was then realized – it was a public daily mass amongst my fisherman friends.

Some of her local friends thought that they might see changes in Frances as a result of her conversion, not necessarily for the good. She laughed out loud at the suggestion. 'Various of my friends cast a rather wry look at me when I said I was joining the Catholic Church. Their main concern was that I was going to become holy or pious. Some hope! They now acknowledge how happy it's made me. Without it I would quite simply have been crushed by the rocks of daily living.'

Even so, the scepticism of others bewildered Frances who, from the first moment she encountered it, never doubted that the Roman Catholic Church was the right choice for her. She found its precepts a wonderfully fruitful way of living, both in the faith's acceptance and its constancy, two things her life has lacked. Being attracted to the humanity of the Catholic faith along with its compassionate priests and warmly spiritual services brought her tremendous contentment – something that no one could take from her. Within the clergy she discovered both trust and understanding, and has made lasting friendships among Catholic priests. Her commitment is neither negligible nor temporary; instead, it does indeed seem to be her home. As she says:

Like the tradition of Catholicism, when everything around you is at sixes and sevens, it remains constant. I never understand why people are so dubious and nervous of the Catholic Church, it's wonderfully warm and friendly. Catholicism, for me, is trying, rather late in life, to live my faith seven days a week. It's the kernel of my living and I love it.

Undoubtedly her past played an enormous part in Frances's conversion. In particular, it is clear that the death of her first son, John, is still something that she finds difficult to accept, quite apart from the many traumatic moments of her married life at Park House. The effects of being denied the chance to see and hold her dead child, for however brief a time, can still bring her to tears. She feels entitled to her quiet grief, in the knowledge that, through her faith, they will meet again in another life. 'I still think a lot about John, the baby I lost. Perhaps one of the reasons I love the Catholic Church is its root in dual living in a place we call Heaven. The church recognizes John and I'm no longer denied him. I believe I'll see all my children again after death.'

Her decision to convert came at a time when her mother, Ruth Fermoy, was nearing the end of her life. Aware that time was running out, Frances visited her mother in London as often as she could, and strained attempts were made at reconciliation; 'I spent a lot of time with her in her last few years, when she suffered heart problems.' The sadness and sense of loss she had experienced through her mother's behaviour during the custody case could never be completely healed. 'You can imagine how much it hurt,' she has said, choosing her words with the extreme care of someone who will never forget the pain of rejection.

Ruth, Lady Fermoy died on 6 July, 1993 aged eighty-five. A lifelong friend and ally of the Queen Mother (who, although older, outlived her by nine years), these two grand dames of the Establishment had colluded for over sixty years, privately making clear their views whenever the duty and traditions they embodied were threatened. For her devotion to royalty Ruth was rewarded with position and titles. After becoming a Woman of the Bedchamber to Queen Elizabeth the Queen Mother, and having been appointed to the OBE for her part in founding the King's Lynn Festival, she was subsequently appointed CVO in 1966 and DCVO* in 1979. Towards the latter part of her life she dramatically fell out with the organizers of the King's Lynn Festival and furiously demanded that her name should never be used in publicizing the event again – although, as was her style, she refused to give her reasons.

---

* Respectively, Companion of the Royal Victorian Order and Dame Commander of the Royal Victorian Order, honours which are in the monarch's personal gift.

Her funeral was a suitably grand affair, marked by a lack of colour and of flowers. Instead, her coffin alone was covered in white lilies, 'one for each year of her life, so it was rather smothered because there were eighty-five,' said Frances.

Some days after Ruth died, Frances was sorting through her mother's effects when she noticed a tall pile of 'society' magazines, dating back many years, at one side of the room. That in itself was no great surprise, for Ruth had been an avid reader and kept every magazine she felt was of interest. Upon closer inspection, however, Frances found, interleaved between the yellowing pages, personal notes, letters and memos, hidden away in the most obvious of places. It says something strangely apt about Ruth's true nature that her almost obsessive desire for privacy was delineated in personal notes captured between the gossipy pages of popular magazines.

If Ruth Fermoy's relationship with Frances remained politely strained until the day of her death, that with her granddaughter, Diana, was almost equally fraught. Although the latter's rank, as Princess of Wales, was far above her own, she did not hesitate to call the younger woman to account if she felt that Diana had, in any way, let the royal family down. Furthermore, although Ruth never publicly commented on the perilous state of her granddaughter's marriage (and by the time of her death, the Waleses had officially separated), one source close to her revealed that 'Ruth has been appalled by what she sees as Diana's refusal to put duty before her own wishes. She feels that Diana ought to have accepted the Queen's suggestion that she and Charles appear in public and lead separate private lives . . .' On one occasion, before her separation, Diana visited Buckingham Palace for what proved to be a slightly sticky interview with the Queen about the 'suitability', in Her Majesty's eyes, of some of her charity work. As Diana was leaving the Palace, somewhat upset by what the Queen had said, she met her grandmother, who berated her soundly for having the temerity to wear trousers to an interview with the Sovereign, implying that she was, as a result, little better than a 'strumpet'. That the trousers were part of an extremely well-cut and expensive outfit was not something likely to sway Ruth Fermoy from her purpose.

Cut loose from the psychological grip of such a controlling and disapproving parent, Frances found herself in a time of deep grief and tremendous liberty as she pondered what to do with the rest of her life.

After becoming a member of the Catholic Church, she befriended the priests at Oban, Sean Macauley and Roderick Wright. Having been, in effect, deserted by Peter, she needed to rebuild her trust in men, and these unconventional relationships brought Frances a companionship not unlike first love – fresh, innocent, and wholly unexpected. The two priests became her companions and escorts on trips abroad. On one occasion they were seen on an aircraft together, attentive and absorbed in each other's company. Whatever the world – or the press – might have thought, there was in truth nothing very strange about a friendship between a twice-divorced Catholic convert and two men of the cloth. As Ken Wharfe says, 'Frances has some very good male friends in the purest sense of the word because she is a very engaging woman. Great woman to be with, lots of fun, very quick, very attractive, very bright.'

None the less, Frances did not want media speculation to hurt her new friendships, as it had done her marriage to Peter. In order to protect herself, and others, after her divorce, she stopped going to dinner with male friends anywhere in public. She also vowed never to marry again, having come to see that a relationship with any man was likely to be too fraught with difficulties because of who she is – a target for the media on whom there is open season.

She also found that being single often brought the wrong kind of attention. 'There is something about me that attracts obsessives who seem to feel they know me and are in love with me,' as she once said. In August 1988, a wealthy businessman, Thomas Rountree, thought he saw something special in Frances as they brushed past each other during an agricultural show. Unfortunately for him, Frances was not of a like mind. Rountree, a bespectacled, balding, slightly rotund fifty-seven-year-old, had simply mistaken eye contact for an expression of mutual attraction. His infatuation grew and he began to inundate Frances with chocolates, cards, flowers and love letters in which he addressed her as 'horse'.

Frances never responded to any of his gifts or notes, preferring instead to call in the Royalty Protection Department, whose task it is to guard the royal family and those close to them, as well as senior diplomats and visiting dignitaries. They tried, vainly, as it turned out, to discourage her importunate admirer. Instead of taking the hint, Rountree called at Ardencaple after booking tickets for a ballet in Birmingham that Diana was due to attend. His stalker-like behaviour finally spooked Frances, who called the police; he was arrested and successfully prosecuted for causing a breach of the peace. In a sad twist of fate, Rountree was killed in a car accident some years later.

Perhaps there is nothing very surprising in this; after all, 'celebrity stalking' is virtually a fact of modern life. Frances receives numerous crank letters each year, most of which she has learned to deal with, and treats with a pinch of salt. One man, a Norwegian, is regularly in contact claiming he is Diana's father. Another offers to be her part-time chauffeur and slave. Luckily, most of these correspondents live far enough away not to cause concern, but sometimes these missives can be much more threatening. 'A letter was put through my letterbox saying: "I am here. I am coming here." He wants a long discussion with me,' she noted with concern. Letters like this go straight to the police, who deal with them with despatch, since Frances's position as Prince William's grandmother inevitably makes her a potential target.

Frances finally accepted that, as beautiful as Ardencaple was, she no longer felt safe there. The large old house with its 1,000 acres was 'unmanageable on my own' and running it and the farm was becoming a chore. She started looking around for a more suitable property – 'it was time to give up' – and Ardencaple was put on the market for £700,000 ($1,050,000). Yet Frances could never leave Seil. She wanted somewhere smaller, although finding the right place on a tiny island would be tricky.

At a dinner party many years earlier, she had asked the singer Kenneth McKellar to grant her first refusal if he ever sold a simple whitewashed bungalow on the island which he used as a holiday retreat. He retired to Australia to be with his children after his wife died, and shortly afterwards suffered a stroke, although he and Frances stayed in touch. Then one day he called her at Ardencaple. 'The phone rang and he said, "Here's your first refusal."' She could not believe her luck.

The timing could not have been better and Frances wasted no time in having the papers drawn up. Buying the bungalow proved to be a major turning point, for the simplicity of her new home mirrored a clearing-out of the emotional clutter left behind after her marriage to Peter. Having bought the property, the first home she had ever owned alone, for £100,000 ($150,000), she set about making it a place that would be both comfortable and comforting. The property, which was called 'Callanish' (after the place on the Isle of Lewis in the Outer Hebrides where there are mystical standing stones dating from around 3000 BC), was furnished functionally when she bought it, and retained the air of a holiday bungalow rather than a home, with its coarse sea-grass carpets, austere paint scheme and windows from which the paint was peeling. There were two bedrooms, a dark windowless bathroom, and a reasonable-sized kitchen well enough equipped to allow her to cook for friends. A separate dining room doubled as an office, and afforded a good view of the front of the house, which would allow Frances time to spot and ward off any approaching press or uninvited visitors. The house stands alone and is reached by an unmarked steeply winding road, which means that anyone approaching it can be seen long before they reach the front door. As an extra security measure, she also had several CCTV cameras installed to provide round-the-clock security. The back garden offered privacy, but Frances preferred to sit on a bench at the front of the bungalow, overlooking the island, watching the sailing boats in Seil Sound below. From the sitting-room window she had a panoramic view of the sound, and she placed her large chesterfield sofa to face it.

The Isle of Seil has been fundamental to Frances. Not only has it provided a haven from prying eyes and the stultifying, often slavishly conservative or snobbish ways of the Establishment, but it also allows her space. After divorce for the second time, she was facing a period of reassessment, a time to question her own motives and beliefs, even her own identity. Where the latter is concerned, she has always found it hard to accept that she is most widely known as the Princess of Wales's mother, rather than as a woman in her own right. Only children, she says, see through that label to the person beneath.

> The marvellous thing about children is that whatever they've heard they are totally accepting. They might say extraordinary things like, 'I don't believe my Mum. She says you're Princess Diana's mother – where's your crown?' But on the whole they accept you as being yourself – and boy, it's hard for me to be myself, just Frances. Children are so wonderfully resilient and direct. They may surprise you but they are honest, straightforward and far better able to cope with what happens in life.

Living on Seil has helped to alter that uncertainty about herself and made Frances feel individual once more, giving her an anchor when she was most adrift. Slowly, she began to adjust to her new life, encouraged by her friends to get on with things. 'I value their friendship and loyalty enormously. It's great to have really good friends who give you a verbal thumping when you're out of order and follow it up with a hug.'

Selling Ardencaple also gave her the confidence to simplify another part of her life – her ownership of the sprawling 2,000-acre ranch at Yass in New South Wales. It had become uneconomical to maintain a farm halfway across the world which Frances would only visit for six weeks in any year. Yet it was a place that Peter loved, with the result that it was a long time before Frances felt comfortable about selling it.

In 1995, however, she finally relented and the farm was put up for auction. At £800,000 (($1,200,000) it sold for well over the reserve price, to their nearest neighbour, the media tycoon Rupert Murdoch. Frances said, with typical understatement, 'I'm very pleased indeed,' adding, 'I feel enormously lucky to have owned a wee piece of this wonderful country for the past 26 years.'

In 1995, Peter and Frances flew out to Sydney for the final time together. When the Yass property was finally auctioned off, it marked the end of an era for both of them. They took the opportunity to sort out their possessions and arrange the transfer of the ranch to its new owner, while at the same time acknowledging each other's new life. Despite being separated for over seven years, the long journey proved that the friendship between them had survived the turbulence of divorce. They had metaphorically moved on, yet had managed to remain on good terms – a rare feat.

Ironically, as Frances began to rediscover a purpose in her life, her son's was becoming increasingly miserable. Charles Spencer had inherited Althorp and the earldom sooner than expected, and though he now had three daughters, as yet he had no son and heir. His marriage to Victoria, as she struggled against anorexia and alcoholism, was rapidly deteriorating into a complicated mess, not least because she also had to contend with her husband's admitted infidelity with a journalist, Sally Ann Lasson, in a Paris hotel, which had been discovered and widely publicized by the press. Try as she might, Victoria could not re-establish the lost trust, or rebuild her self-esteem.

Charles was working hard to put right the inappropriate changes introduced by Raine, but was also under considerable pressure from the financial constraints of the estate. Althorp was costing half a million pounds ($750,000) a year alone to maintain, and he therefore increased the entrance charges for visitors and explored the corporate-entertainment market to help meet these costs. The sheer expense, coupled with the responsibility of inheriting the title and estate so young, weighed heavily on his mind, as he told a journalist:

> My wife and I live a modest lifestyle with all the resources earmarked for the perpetuation of the house. I would hate it if, a hundred years from now, my great-grandson was sitting in a council flat cursing me. It is, therefore, very important for me that I leave Althorp in such a way that it is worth keeping and not a millstone around my successor's neck.

On 14 March 1994 Charles Spencer at last got his wish with the birth of his long-awaited son and heir, Louis Frederick John Spencer, Viscount Althorp. Charles had not known that the baby was going to be a boy, but Victoria had. She had kept the knowledge from him, holding secret the one thing that he wished for above anything because, she said, she did not want to 'to take away from his joy on the day'. When he heard the baby was a boy, he was 'dumbstruck', and later described how he 'sat there in the corner with my head in my hands reeling from shock'. Yet the truth was that Althorp and the title broke Victoria. One of the servants noted, rather sniffily, that, 'The new Countess Spencer was a scared rabbit of a young woman. She never seemed happy there, or in her husband's presence.'

The christening became a double celebration, for a date was selected to coincide with Charles's thirtieth birthday. Peter Shand Kydd, chosen as one of the godfathers, was one of the guests. It was a further sign that Frances had managed to overcome any resentment she may have felt towards Peter, and the day marked the start of a deep friendship between them, even after divorce. She later described their renewed relationship: 'We enjoy a robust, trusting friendship. I see him regularly . . . There's nothing any more between Peter and me except tremendous friendship. We're simply friends.'

Relations between Charles and Victoria had reached their lowest point, however. Carried away with the knowledge that Althorp was now safe for another generation, Charles released his hold on his marriage. In what was, at best, a crass and ill-advised attempt at humour, he publicly humiliated his wife at the party. Getting up to speak, he recalled a conversation he had had with his father about what he should look for in a wife: 'The ideal bride, in his opinion, was one who would stick with me through thick and thin. Well, those who know Victoria know she's thick – and she's also thin.'

For Victoria, it was the final straw. Stripped bare of confidence and with her self-esteem crumbling, married to an unfaithful husband and wrestling with demons of her own, she knew their relationship had gone beyond the point of no return. With the christening over, she agreed to undergo treatment at an addiction clinic in Surrey, and demanded a trial separation.

Frances found her loyalties divided, for while she felt it important to show her support for Charles, over the years she had become fond of her daughter-in-law, and had a close bond with her grandchildren. Later she was to rally round both her younger children, citing her own experience to show that she did not feel that she had any right to judge them: 'Neither my son, Charles, nor Diana expected their marriages would break up. That also applied to me.'

In January 1996, Lord and Lady Spencer announced formally that they would not be getting back together. With the children, they deserted Althorp for Cape Town in South Africa, where they bought separate properties and, at last relatively free of the intrusive media that had reported their marital problems with avidity, licked the wounds of a broken marriage. By April of that year Charles had settled into an impressive house in the fashionable part of Cape Town, relishing his new life – and new romances. Victoria and the children were a short drive away, and all of them felt happy in South Africa. It had been a good move.

The family balance seemed at last to have been restored, and Frances heaved a sigh of relief. It was all working out. The darkest days – in her own marriage, and in those of her two youngest children (for Diana had formally separated from Prince Charles at the end of 1992) – appeared to be behind them.

CHAPTER ELEVEN

Power and Protocol

FRANCES HAD SUFFERED TERRIBLY during her battle with Johnnie over custody of the children. Besides losing her beloved daughters and son, she learned what it felt like to be condemned as unfit and uncaring. Vilified by the Establishment, she was rejected by her own class, by the judiciary, and almost unbelievably, by her own flesh and blood.

The whispering campaign to blacken her character worked to such great effect that she was forced to abandon the society she was born into. Her mother's treacherous behaviour made her acutely aware of the value of loyalty. It is a quality she treasures, and nothing in the world would ever make her turn on any of her children with the viciousness she experienced, however much she might disapprove of their actions.

Even so, in the early 1990s, when Diana stood her ground against the House of Windsor, unable to accept any more their arcane and archaic way of life, Frances feared for her. She knew the power and influence of the enemy Diana was facing.

An ancient aristocratic family, the Spencers have always been closely aligned to the monarchy, although never so closely as to suffer the responsibility that rests upon a head of a state. Their wealth, which grew enormously over the centuries, brought each successive generation power and a grand, privileged lifestyle. By the time Sarah, Jane, Diana and Charles were growing up, they wanted for little materially, something that allowed them, almost in reaction, to indulge their emotional desires. And in most cases, these ran riot.

Sarah's disruptive behaviour as a teenager preceded her anorexia, which was in turn followed by a whirlwind romance, a precipitous dash to be married. Diana's search for love and security began at an early age, and led to her becoming obsessed with the fantasy of marrying a prince. Charles, once he had overcome an initial shyness, discovered a love of the dramatic as a foreign correspondent and an almost insatiable desire to date beautiful women, which continued even after he had married; like his oldest sister, he too fell in love and proposed within days. Only Jane, studious, quiet, and largely content to be one of life's onlookers, escaped the often tortured psyche of her generation of Spencers. (She had, however, married a senior courtier, and so always walked a very fine line with her younger sister.) Whether disruptive or romantic, the free-spirited, independent nature of the Spencer children was a trait that Frances had passed to them. It was both a benefit and a burden, often setting them apart from others, and sometimes landing them in trouble.

Nor did these shared characteristics preclude the family from arguing furiously among themselves; indeed, it was often these inherited similarities that caused clashes. Moreover, their inherent passion seemed to precipitate rifts of almighty proportion. One such row, between Diana and Charles, serves as a good example. In early 1993 Diana was hoping to move from Kensington Palace, 'It's like returning to prison,' she moaned of what had become her main residence, since she would no longer go to Highgrove after separating from Prince Charles. Yet she was wary, were she to move somewhere else, of the added cost of all the extra security that would be needed, and felt that her popularity might well take a dive if she opted to decamp to some discreet but salubrious location abroad. In any case, she wanted to be near her boys, and knew that they would always have to remain in Britain and close to the seat of royal power. This situation appeared to find a happy resolution when her brother Charles made a protective gesture. Brother and sister had always been close, and now that he was lord of the Althorp estate, he could afford to come to the rescue of his older, if better-connected, sister.

In April, he offered her the four bedroom Garden House, near the main house, for what was, even then, a tiny rent of £1,000 ($1,500) a month. Diana was delighted: 'at long last I can make a cosy nest of my own,' she said happily. She went to Althorp, and while her two sons were shown round she discussed blue and yellow colour schemes with the interior designer she planned to engage, Dudley Poplak, a friend of Frances's and the man who had worked on the interior of Highgrove, to Prince Charles's displeasure. Her detectives, Ken Wharfe and Peter Brown, were then shown to a small house next door where they could stay, thereby assuring the Princess of her privacy without compromising her security. It seemed the perfect solution.

Initially, the idea of his sister's and nephews' presence on the estate pleased Charles Spencer, who now radiated genuine pleasure when talking about Althorp. The austere, foreboding home of his youth, especially during the years when Raine was chatelaine, had swiftly faded from his memory as he and his own wife and family took over the rooms.

Whatever his visions of life at Althorp with Diana and the two young princes *in situ*, however, within weeks the plan had gone horribly wrong. When he realized the additional police presence that would be necessary to protect his sister and her sons, Charles performed a complete volte-face.

The Royalty Protection Department advised that police officers armed with machine guns and sniffer dogs should be on twenty-four hour duty at the estate to give the highest level of security to the Princess and her sons. As Diana's senior police protection officer, Ken Wharfe advised against the move, and Charles, after consideration, decided that this level of intrusion could not be lived with. He feared that the armed officers would frighten his children, while their presence would threaten his own privacy. Having worked hard to establish a good life at Althorp, he was not about to sacrifice it, even for his marooned sister. He therefore telephoned Diana and promptly withdrew his offer.

Diana was distraught at his decision, and their conversation soon escalated into a blazing row. The rift deepened as the weeks passed. Letters were returned unopened, a Spencer habit. Proud and impulsive, neither would back down, and the quarrel between them became a complete impasse. Diana felt deeply let down, while Charles felt misunderstood. Caught in the middle, Frances, like many mothers, tried to see things from both sides. She felt, however, that Diana and Charles were adults and had to fight their own battles; it was not for her to take sides. She tried to dampen the argument, suggesting that the difference of opinion would soon be smoothed over – 'There are spits and spats in any family,' she says sensibly. It would blow over eventually. It always did.

Unhappily, the same could not be said when it came to Prince Charles and the Windsors. With the publication of Andrew Morton's book Diana had crossed a personal Rubicon. Although her part in *Diana: Her True Story* was only suspected and not yet confirmed, none the less she made, through Morton, a compelling case. Highly critical and consciously and deliberately biased, Diana exposed her in-laws as cold, calculating and prepared to go to any lengths to protect their position and their legacy. Fundamental differences were highlighted between the Spencer and Windsor dynasties, differences that could no longer be papered over. One day, Prince William would be king, his very existence a merging of the Windsor and Spencer blood lines and a manifestation of these two houses' polarized philosophies of life, and of duty, honour, privilege, tradition and service. Without modernization and a loosening of its tight formalities, Diana believed, the monarchy would shrivel up and lose all relevance in contemporary society. As the most popular member of the royal family, revered for her common touch, as well as her beauty and sense of style, she undoubtedly had a point.

Prince Charles's fury at the book and at his wife's betrayal (for, like most of the royal family and the Palace hierarchy, he was certain that she had been closely involved in its writing) was slowly replaced by a calculated strategy for fighting back. Among other measures he discussed with his advisers, he earmarked over £300,000 ($450,000) a year to be paid directly from the Duke of Cornwall's Estates to nine different strategists.* He and his supporters were certainly becoming well versed in the art of spin, and their discussions culminated in the idea of an official biography of his own. His Private Secretary, Richard Aylard, put forward the name of the respected journalist Jonathan Dimbleby, who, after some resistance, agreed to work with the Prince and write the book.

Dimbleby's 620-page biography, published in 1994, was only given the green light by the Prince of Wales after he had meticulously checked through every word. It attempted to counter many of the statements and impressions offered by Andrew Morton (and therefore by Diana) in *Diana: Her True Story*. Yet it showed a prince ill at ease. Critical of his own upbringing, Charles blamed his remote mother and bullying father for many of his problems in what was little more than a self-pitying appeal for sympathy.

Even before Dimbleby's biography was published, Prince Charles had gone out on to another limb. Against the advice of his mother, his father, and Camilla Parker Bowles, he agreed to allow a film crew to follow him for a number of weeks. The result was a two-and-a-half-hour television documentary, *Charles: The Private Man, The Public Role*, which was aired in June 1994. Little is remembered of the film, however, except Charles's admission of adultery. When, during the programme, he was asked by Dimbleby, 'Did you try to be faithful and honourable to your wife?' he squirmed while replying 'Yes . . .' before adding, 'until it [his marriage] became irretrievably broken down.' Here was the future King and head of the Church of England blatantly compromising himself before the world.

Diana, obsessed with her own public image and determined that any press focus on her husband should be limited to insignificant and dismissive articles rather than front-page stories, got wind of the programme. Infuriated by what she suspected would be yet another whitewash of her husband's character and behaviour, and jealous of the media attention he was about to receive, she struck back in characteristically dramatic fashion.

On the night that the Dimbleby documentary was screened, Diana made a grand entrance at a charity benefit at the Serpentine Gallery in Hyde Park wearing perhaps her most sensational outfit to date – a low-cut black cocktail

---

* As Prince of Wales, Prince Charles is also Duke of Cornwall. The duchy's estates provide him with a substantial revenue.

dress by the Greek-Armenian designer Christina Stambolian. Her appearance caused, as she had known it would, a feeding frenzy among the paparazzi. Her attempt to upstage Charles at what should have been his finest moment proved wholly successful – the following day's papers were full of her alluring new look and her relaxed and confident manner, while questioning how Charles could even consider straying.

It is hardly surprising that, in admitting that he had broken his marriage vows, almost every other aspect of the documentary was ignored – he was, after all, the country's future king and head of its church, and therefore of considerable public interest, if not concern. The tabloids, in particular, had a field day, the *Daily Mail* headlining its story, 'Charles: When I Was Unfaithful,' while the *Sun*, with a characteristic, if feeble, pun, declared, 'Di Told You So'. The broadsheets, among other commentators, though more restrained, questioned whether this adulterous prince was fit to be king. The Prince of Wales had effectively shot himself in the foot.

Once again the Prince was furious, this time that two years of planning could so easily be eradicated. In the fight between the warring Waleses, the gloves were now well and truly off.

It was now that Martin Bashir, a journalist with BBC TV's flagship current-affairs programme, *Panorama*, entered the ring. He had information suggesting that the security service MI5, and the secret service, MI6, had colluded and authorized spying on Diana and the Spencers. After discreet discussions with her brother, Bashir was granted an audience with Diana, whose suspicions were already high after the release of the Squidgygate tapes. Having met the journalist and reflected upon her position, she decided that the airtime allocated to Bashir for a *Panorama* programme about the state of the monarchy could be put to better use. If she granted him a private audience, she said, he could expect nothing less than full disclosure. This was a sensational offer, and Bashir and *Panorama* seized their chance, shelving the planned documentary and preparing to interview the Princess, under conditions of the greatest secrecy, at Kensington Palace.

Seeking advice from no one, and not even revealing anything to her equerry (later her Private Secretary), Patrick Jephson, Diana followed her instincts, meticulously planning the interview that would finally seal the fate of her marriage.

Twenty-three million viewers in the UK watched the *Panorama* programme of Bashir's interview with the Princess when it was aired in November 1995. Frances watched with the nation as her daughter explained what it was like to be married to Prince Charles.

Time and again, Diana's darts found their mark. Of her formal separation from Prince Charles, she said that it had not been her idea, because she had 'come from a divorced background, and I didn't want to go into that one again'. Bashir then turned to her affair with James Hewitt. 'Yes, I adored him,' she admitted. 'Yes, I was in love with him. But I was very let down.' Now both husband and wife had publicly confessed to adultery, although it was the Prince who was to suffer for it.

The programme caused a furore. Here was a classic example of David and Goliath, the lone Princess squaring up to the giant in the shape of the royal family and the Palace. As an exercise in putting across her own position, the interview succeeded triumphantly. Frances – and indeed most of the nation – rallied to Diana's pleading, agreeing that she had been victimized and ignored, and finally betrayed. Wearily, Prince Charles's advisers and supporters went back into action to try to undo the damage, largely by attempting to discredit his wife. In this, too, they were doomed to failure.

One of the things Diana had made clear in the *Panorama* programme was that she wanted a way of life for her sons different from the stultifying world in which her husband had been raised. His parents had remained aloof as he was trained for the role to which he had been born. Expressing emotion does not come naturally to the royal family and he admitted that he often found socializing difficult; 'I have always preferred my own company or just a one-to-one.' This feeling was entirely alien to Diana, who had grown up in a house full of noisy children and who later, as a mother, had done all she could to love, support and protect her boys until they could find their own way. As Frances aptly put it, she wanted to 'give them wings'.

Prince Charles and the Queen communicate by notes; they shake hands after weeks apart, and defer to royal etiquette in private as well as in public – throughout his marriage, Charles always poured the Queen's drink ahead of his wife's. To him, Her Majesty was his sovereign before she was his mother, and he would therefore never dare to defy her.

In contrast, Diana and Frances had always talked, laughed, hugged, and sometimes rowed and then made up again, but always engaged with each other. Diana had unwittingly married into an institution rather than a family, an institution constrained by hundreds of years of duty, protocol, tradition, precedence – and repression. Yet it still had immense influence; neither living within it, nor disengaging from it, was ever going to be easy.

In the long period between Diana's separation in December 1992 and her divorce in August 1996, Frances saw her role as that of 'the supportive mother'. Divorce is hard, she said, and anyone experiencing such times, 'and that includes Diana, needs compassion to come to terms with a very sad situation'. Retreating behind a well-worn theme, she went on to blame her family's ills on the media's incessant appetite for the Spencers: 'There is no doubt in my mind that the constant media speculation has been a contributing factor in the breakdown of three marriages – my own, my son's and my daughter's.'

Diana took a different view of the press, however – or at least did so when it suited her, as it did now. Afraid that she might, like Frances, lose her children, she was playing the Prince at a public-relations game. More streetwise than her mother, she created her own camp not only among her supporters, but among sympathetic journalists, in order to fend off attack. Young, beautiful and gifted with the common touch, Diana became hugely popular not just through her charm and her natural sympathy, but through the efforts she made on behalf of often unfashionable causes. Comforting a man with AIDS, holding the hands of a leper, hugging a child disabled by landmines, brought huge benefits to those whom she sought to help. Beyond that, however, it created a public profile that she could use to her advantage. As the people's champion – 'a queen in people's hearts' – she could keep control of her own destiny. Meanwhile, the Prince of Wales's efforts and causes suffered from the comparison with his wife's charitable work.

By her own account, Diana never wanted to divorce. Like many an unhappy wife before her, she implored her mother-in-law to intervene, hoping that his mother could persuade Charles to try to make their marriage work. The Queen, however, refused. Despite the looming constitutional crisis and the personal unhappiness caused by the continuing animosity between the Waleses, Her Majesty felt unable to offer advice – other than that Diana should allow the marriage time to heal. The monarchy was reeling as scandal after scandal was reported, to the horror of loyal subjects (and her own). The Queen was at a loss to understand the messy marriages of her children, much less their behaviour and that of their spouses. Like her mother, she believed uncompromisingly in the sanctity of the wedding vows. The taking of mistresses or lovers, while long accepted tacitly as part and parcel of royal and aristocratic life, she would never openly condone. Prince Charles was therefore in a quandary: his mother disliked the thought of his separation from Diana, and regarded the idea of a divorce with horror; equally, she disapproved strongly of his by now quite open relationship with Camilla Parker Bowles.

In the midst of such turmoil, it might have seemed natural for the Queen to speak to Frances, so that they might together try to understand and find a way through the unhappiness afflicting her son and daughter-in-law. Yet she chose to remain silent. For how could a woman confront emotion within her family, when by all accounts she denied it in herself?

Diana repeatedly described the destructive attitude within the royal family as swift to criticize when someone had done something wrong, but unable to praise when things had been done well. Living outside 'the loop', Frances, to whom such an attitude was abhorrent, was unable to bring any of her own experience to bear on the royal family. She was limited to trying to lift the mood, although she well understood the need to be able to laugh at oneself in order to keep a balanced outlook.

> It's . . . terribly important to give praise not just to children but to everyone. If they do well, say so, if you look well, say so, if you've done badly you might comfort that distress or remain silent. Maintain a sense of humour and laugh at yourself, that's vital. With my children some of our best times are laughing at things that have gone utterly wrong.

The year of Diana and Charles's separation ended with the devastating fire at Windsor Castle, leading a usually stoical Queen to describe 1992 as her '*annus horribilis*'. The public's perception of the royal family, especially its younger members, as a group of parasites living the high life funded by the general populace might not have been far from the truth. The Royal Train, the Royal Yacht, the aircraft of the Queen's Flight, all added to the image of polo-playing, grouse-shooting playboys with little better to do than argue with their beautiful, bored wives.

Bowing to opinion, albeit somewhat belatedly, the Queen agreed to pay tax on her private income for the first time. She also agreed to scale down the Civil List – the sum, fixed by Parliament and reviewed periodically, accorded to the Sovereign for the payment of the expenses of the royal household – to include only the Queen Mother and the Duke of Edinburgh. The monarchy, forced to modernize, was, without acknowledging it, taking a leaf out of Diana's book. Yet the Princess of Wales, by now the royal family's most famous and best-loved icon, had become its most estranged member.

The Queen, no longer able to tolerate the constant and very public power play between the Waleses, eventually decided that the time had come to force Diana's hand. The media's reporting of the now almost constant war between the Prince and Princess had gained a powerful momentum, leaving Diana playing a role in royal life that was damaging and dangerous. If a stop was not made to the continuous leaking of barbed comments, the Queen felt, rightly, then her own position would be undermined. As Christmas 1995 approached, she wrote to both Prince Charles and Diana. She had had more than enough of the public bickering, for the couple were endangering the institution she held so dear. Start divorce proceedings, she told them . . . and start them now.

Diana was shocked at the suggestion of divorce, for it was what she most dreaded. Patrick Jephson recalled: 'I could not forget the catch in her voice when she read the Queen's letter to me over the phone shortly before Christmas. "Do you know, Patrick, that's the first letter she's written to me."

She tried to laugh, and for once she failed.' Unable to face the reality of a decision, she chose to stall, refusing to answer the Queen's letter. Such a course was unheard of, and under increasing pressure from courtiers, in February 1996 she grudgingly arranged a private meeting with Prince Charles to thrash out divorce terms.

Having boldly detailed her demands, and without waiting for an official response from the Palace, she returned to Kensington Palace and impetuously had her staff release a statement to the effect that she had agreed to Prince Charles's request for a divorce. The press statement ended with the words: 'The Princess of Wales will retain the title and will be known as Diana, Princess of Wales.'

The Queen took Diana at her word. The Princess had not mentioned, either at the meeting or in her statement, her other title – the courtesy title 'Her Royal Highness'. To Her Majesty's way of thinking, Diana, as the soon-to-be former wife of the future King, had no need of it. In an echo of King George VI, her father, denying the Duchess of Windsor the same honorific, the Queen slapped Diana down, as sovereigns have done for centuries, by the removal of an honour. It was a public humiliation enacted, through the media, on an international stage. It was the revenge of one mother of a future king against another, and it wounded Diana deeply.

By early 1996, having gone some way to achieving what she wanted as a roving ambassadress, Diana crumpled. Paranoid and cornered, and behaving increasingly strangely, she became convinced that her rooms at Kensington Palace were bugged and that her own people were working against her. Her temper flared as she took out her frustrations on her staff. Patrick Jephson, who had been central to establishing the international ambassadorial image of the Princess, as well as a key figure in negotiations over the separation, resigned, believing that he was soon to be sacked.

In May, Diana flew to Majorca to stay at Richard Branson's luxury hotel La Residencia. According to guests who were staying at the same time, she appeared to be in fine spirits. One onlooker commented 'It was as if in her mind she had moved on and this was a girlie weekend.' Other subtle changes could be seen in her behaviour. Another guest remarked, 'I met her several years before and there was an innocent and undeniable inner beauty about her, which made her very special. But now she seemed altogether harder and more calculating. She was constantly on her mobile phone. It seemed the stuffing had been knocked out of her.'

With the agreement to divorce and the loss of her courtesy title, Diana seemed also to lose perspective. Like many people, she would often take out her frustration on those she cared for most. A close friend, Vivienne Parry, explains: 'Divorce was the very last thing that Diana wanted and she was devastated by it. I remember she was sobbing her heart out. She was utterly desperate about it, because she felt that she had failed.'

At her most vulnerable, she would lash out at those closest to her – 'There wasn't one friend she hadn't fallen out with at one time or another,' Vivienne Parry remarked sadly. If not treated with kid gloves she was liable to explode with rage. No one, she believed, could truly understand her situation, and it frustrated her. For, paradoxically, the most famous woman in the world was almost pathologically insecure, and tended as a result to take any criticism, no matter how well-meaning, to be a slur on her character. 'What she didn't understand was that sometimes people criticize you because they love you, not because they don't,' Vivienne Parry added.

On one occasion, Rosa Monckton, another close friend, found herself cast into the wilderness for four months after suggesting some changes that Diana might make in her life. 'Then as usually happens, she just picked up the telephone one day, said "Rosa, how are you?" and off we went again.' Such behaviour was, it seemed, part of the turbulent relationship that friends and family had come to expect from a woman both untrusting and increasingly distanced from normal life. In August 1996 her divorce from Prince Charles became final, which served only to deepen her unhappiness.

The following year, even her own mother was ostracized. Rationally, Frances's wholehearted support for her daughter throughout her marriage, separation and divorce, should never have been in question. Yet that month, after the publication in May 1997 of the first instalment of a two-part interview Frances had given to *Hello!* magazine, Diana backed away.

Inevitably, the question of Diana's recent divorce was raised during the interview as well as the loss of the 'HRH' tag. Frances, typically, put a positive gloss on Diana's new status. Asked what she thought about the courtesy title being taken from her daughter, she replied, 'I thought it was absolutely wonderful. At last she was able to be herself, use her own name and find her own identity. It's a very personal thing and I don't understand why it became so important to so many people.'

She went on to admit that she had concerns about the future, especially for Diana: 'I hope and pray she will find contentment. Contentment I think is more important than happiness, it is a general feeling of well-being, mental and physical. Of course there's always sadness when a marriage fails and its even harder when it's one of your own children.'

When Diana learned that Frances considered the loss of the royal title to be 'wonderful,' she was furious. She interpreted the well-intentioned words as a slight, rather than the indication of Frances's pleasure that Diana would now be freed from the constraints of the Palace. Instead of recognizing that her mother had her best interests at heart, she responded petulantly and quite disproportionately, immediately cutting off all contact with Frances.

Sally Cartwright, the publishing director of *Hello!*, tried to ease the tricky situation. 'Diana knew her mother had given a long interview to *Hello!* to be published in two parts . . . most of the newspaper coverage suggested that the Princess was extremely unhappy with what her mother had said.' The magazine diplomatically offered Diana sight of the copy for the second instalment of the interview. It arrived at Kensington Palace on the day before the Princess was due to leave for Pakistan. Sally Cartwright reme mbers that:

> In the event she claimed she didn't have time to look at it, which was curious since it takes ten hours to fly to Pakistan, ample opportunity to read what her mother had said. Her excuse suggested one of two things: either, that she genuinely wasn't troubled by what her mother might have said or, that she didn't want the responsibility of having looked at it and then possibly having to tackle her mother on certain points contained within it.

Frances attempted to resolve the impasse by writing a letter to explain her actions. It was returned unopened, the childish slight that Diana had learned from her brother Charles. Frances, dismayed but determined, tried to call her daughter, but was unable to get through. Temporarily left out in the cold, she reacted as she always had in these circumstances. She waited, knowing that one day the telephone would ring and it would be Diana, laughing as if nothing had happened, and they would pick up the strands of their relationship where they had left off, without a mention of what had gone before.

In fact, Diana's trip to Pakistan may also provide a clue to her ambivalence towards her mother at that time. She had fallen deeply in love with a London-based heart surgeon, Hasnat Khan. He was a Muslim whose family were in Pakistan and she was subtly trying to ingratiate herself with that family in the hope that they would accept her as a suitable bride for him. In the first flush of love and its mind-altering state – 'I want to marry him and have his babies,' she reportedly said – all Diana could think about was Khan. Almost everything else was an irritation. This was a man she loved and wanted, but their different religions stood between them, not on her part, but on his family's. Her mother was the last thing on her mind. Besides Frances, as Diana knew, would probably have counselled her against becoming too involved with another man, especially before her divorce had been made absolute.

In truth, whenever Frances expressed her views publicly, her daughter never took well to it. Any statement considered to be critical, however truthful or supportive, might and often would be misconstrued by the Princess. In the *Hello!* interview Frances accurately predicted that her daughter would suffer 'long-term difficulties' because of her own openness. At the time Diana was angered by that comment, while privately acknowledging that it was indeed true. This was later confirmed by Hasnat Khan who revealed, 'She was upset . . . that she had talked about too many personal things. She wished that she had not because, in her heart, she felt later that these were not the sort of things to be discussed in public.'

The summer came and Diana planned her first holiday as a free woman. She wanted to make it special for Princes William and Harry. She had made no impression upon Hasnat Khan's family, and was growing impatient. So when Mohammed Fayed (a friend of Johnnie and Raine's) suggested that she and the princes spend time at his home in the South of France and cruising the Mediterranean aboard his yacht, Diana agreed. It sounded like the perfect way to spend the boys' vacation and her own. As Patrick Jephson wrote, 'The trappings of royalty suddenly reappeared: the jets, the yachts, the bodyguards, and the happy disregard for the cost of anything.'

Frances watched her daughter's holiday play out in the press and on television, for journalists and photographers followed Diana at every turn. She saw the pictures of Dodi Fayed and Diana kissing. She smiled, pleased that her daughter was having a wonderful time, apparently enjoying life once more. She knew that it would not be long before Diana called her. Then they would have so much to talk about: it was after all exactly a year to the day since Diana's divorce had become final.

How could Frances have known that she was never to speak to her daughter again?

CHAPTER TWELVE

Death of a Daughter

THE LAST WEEKEND OF SUMMER, before August tumbled into September, was perfect. That Saturday, daylight stayed until late and only faded to half darkness as the day ended. On Seil, so far to the north, days are long and darkness hardly falls at that time of year. In her bungalow on the island, Frances lay asleep in her bedroom. Then her telephone started to ring. It kept ringing, the sound piercing the natural quiet. She jolted awake and reached for her clock – it was nearly two o'clock on the morning of Sunday, 31 August. Through a haze of sleep, she found herself hoping it would be the one person who always made calls at an unearthly hour – Diana. 'Stay with me,' she would say as she answered, 'the more I wake up the better I get.' This was the call for which Frances had waited all summer long, the chance for her to tell her daughter how much she missed her, for the silence between them to be over, for their great friendship to resume. Reaching for the receiver, she expected to hear her daughter's warm and bubbly greeting.

But it was not Diana. Instead, she heard the worried voice of a friend from the town. Frances recalls that night vividly:

> I was rung shortly before 2 a.m. by Janey Milne in Oban, who said, 'I had to wake you because there's a news flash on Sky News. Diana's been hurt in a car accident in Paris.'

Janey, shaking as she dialled Frances's number, had not wanted to make the call, but had felt that she had no choice. Urged on by her husband, she offered to drive to Seil straight away to support her friend. In the confusion, initial reports claimed, conflictingly, that Diana appeared to be either walking around uninjured, or that she had suffered a broken arm. The details of the crash in Paris were changing so rapidly that it was hard to work out the truth. Another bulletin stated that Dodi Fayed was dead, and news of Diana's condition suddenly seemed ominous.

Frances reached out to switch on her bedside light. Needing time to gather her thoughts, she firmly instructed Janey to stay at home in Oban for now, assuring her, 'I'll ring you if I want you.' Getting out of bed, she pulled on her dressing gown and walked the short distance into her sitting room. Turning on a lamp, she flicked the television to Sky News and watched as sombre journalists in Paris and London tried to piece together the night's terrible events. Almost at once, the telephone rang again. This time it was a newspaper editor, asking for a comment. She declined, ended the call and walked into her office, where she switched on her answering machine, which would allow her to screen calls and keep the press at bay. 'They think of me as someone they can pull into line,' she says disparagingly of the media in general, a view reinforced by their behaviour that night.

Back in the sitting room, its cream chintz curtains tightly drawn, Frances sat down on the large brown-leather chesterfield sofa and stared at the television. She remained bolt upright, watching images of her daughter flash repeatedly across the screen. Reaching towards a side table, she pulled a cigarette from a packet there and flicked her lighter. Chain smoking one Silk Cut after another, she inhaled deeply, a long curve of ash hanging from the cigarette held unsteadily between her trembling fingers until she nervously ground the butt into an ashtray. She glanced repeatedly at the photographs of Diana cuddled up with William and Harry that stood on a chest of drawers. Unable to concentrate, she pushed aside a cushion embroidered with the words 'If you can't fish in Heaven, I'm not going' and stood up.

Walking into the bright, white kitchen, her bare feet recoiling from the cold of the tiled floor, she used the remote control to turn the volume on the television higher. At the sink she filled a kettle with water and set it to boil, then opened the fridge, filled a jug with milk and set it down on a tray, ready to make a cup of tea. The solitude of those early moments, the droning news reports so at odds with the still, eerily silent night beyond the window, and punctuated by the shrill ringing of the telephone, will live with her for ever. She waited, listening to the start of each message, becoming ever more anxious to hear a family voice. Her line was almost constantly engaged, however, as increasingly desperate journalists tried to contact her. 'The telephone rang all night, which it made it impossible for my family to ring me because they couldn't get through on the fax or telephone line. One paper was calling on both lines. That was pretty harsh.'

Sipping hot tea in between puffs on yet another cigarette, Frances walked back into her bedroom, opened the wardrobe, pulled out a suitcase and dropped it on to her bed. Hastily grabbing a selection of what she hoped were suitably dignified clothes, she folded them into the case, feeling an overriding desire to be with her daughter. 'I didn't know how long I'd be there, which hospital I was going to or what was up. But it seemed quite natural to go to my wounded child.' At the time, she still believed, as well as hoped, that Diana would survive whatever injuries she might have suffered.

Desperate to obtain accurate information, she waited for a lull in the telephone's ringing and dialled her eldest daughter, Sarah, at her farm in Lincolnshire, and then Jane, who was on holiday in Norfolk with her husband, Sir Robert Fellowes, the Queen's Private Secretary. Both lines were engaged. She then got through to her son Charles at his home in Cape Town – there is almost no time difference between Britain and South Africa – and despite the chaos of the night they managed to exchange the few details each had managed to gather. Still there was no word from Diana. Frances felt sure that if she had been able to, she would have called the family to say that she was all right. The silence was unbearable, hope and fear crowding her mind equally. As she said later, 'During that night, I went over all the possibilities and options in my mind.'

At Balmoral, a hundred miles away to the north-east, on the other side of Scotland, Prince Charles had been awoken by telephone calls from Sir Robin Janvrin, the Queen's Deputy Private Secretary. At 1 a.m. Janvrin had been informed by Michael Jay, the British Ambassador in Paris, that the Princess of Wales and Dodi Fayed had been involved in a car crash. The Queen and her eldest son met well away from the sleeping princes, William and Harry, and were swiftly joined by Janvrin, Nick Archer, the Prince's Assistant Private Secretary, and their protection officers and equerries. The news sounded grave.

Far away in London, the press worked frantically, journalists calling any royal contact they knew. Palace officials were soon being bombarded with calls. Mark Bolland, Prince Charles's Deputy Private Secretary, received a message from Stuart Higgins, the editor of the *Sun* newspaper, asking him to confirm that Dodi Fayed was dead and that Diana had been injured. The Prince's Press Secretary, Sandy Henney, heard the same rumour – for nothing had been confirmed as yet – from a journalist. Both Bolland and Henney called Balmoral immediately, seeking confirmation.

The Prince issued instructions for the television and radios to be removed from William and Harry's suite so that neither would inadvertently hear about the crash before they could be properly and sympathetically told. All through the early hours of that Sunday Charles and his mother, although under the same roof, did not speak directly. The 'grey men in suits', as Diana called courtiers, whisked from room to room, making one telephone call after another to ensure their employers' views prevailed. It was like a game of chess, though it was one that no one could win.

*

In Seil, the telephone rang yet again. Frances looked at it, hesitating momentarily before lifting the receiver. It was her daughter Jane, who had heard that Diana was alive but severely brain damaged and that Dodi had been killed.

Minutes later came the news that would, in the end, shock even the most hardened and cynical of people. This time, nothing could prepare Frances for the blow. 'She's dead,' she heard. Motionless, shocked into silence, she replaced the receiver. Frances was now expected to endure the longest wait of her life, for she was instructed to speak to no one until the news was formally announced.

> I knew of her death an hour before the news was given out. Protocol was such that heads of state had to be informed before it was made public. So I was left in an amazing, stunning situation of having an hour to wait knowing she was dead and unable to transmit this news or ask for help of a friend. I was literally in front of my television shouting, 'Come on, come on, tell the world!'

Utterly overwhelmed, she walked slowly back into her bedroom. She knew that protocol had taken over and that it must be followed. Her daughter's unique position meant that formalities were now in place to ensure that this terrible situation was dealt with in an appropriate manner; in other words, according to royal precedent. The death of someone so close to the Crown required a special contingency plan. After sixteen years on the fringes of the royal family, Frances understood that until she received word from the Palace, she must remain in Seil. Except that different factions within the Palace, for all its high sense of tradition and its comforting formality, could not agree on how to handle this unprecedented problem. The in-fighting had already begun.

In deep shock, Frances picked up her suitcase from where it lay in the corner, placed it on the bed and opened it. Carefully and methodically, she removed every item of clothing she had recently packed. Closing the case, she put it back in the wardrobe and returned to the sitting room. Then, at last, the news was made public as a sombre-voiced newsreader read a formal statement announcing that Diana, Princess of Wales had been killed as the result of a car accident in Paris earlier that morning.

Frances walked to the telephone, picked up the receiver and slowly dialled Janey Milne's number. 'I said, very calmly, "Can you come down? Diana's dead."'

Diana was officially pronounced dead at 4 a.m. Earlier, at 12.24 a.m., the Mercedes in which she was travelling had slammed at high speed into the thirteenth pillar of the Place de l'Alma underpass, ricocheted off the unyielding concrete and overturned three times. The roof was smashed down, the wheels and bodywork twisted and the entire front horrifically mangled. Although she was given emergency first aid almost immediately by a doctor who arrived on the scene, Frédéric Mailliez, the Princess's condition was critical. Dodi Fayed and the driver, Henri Paul, had both been killed on impact; in the front passenger seat the bodyguard, Trevor Rees-Jones, was also in a critical condition with terrible injuries.

Paramedics arrived within fifteen minutes, and while rescuers worked to cut her free, she suffered the first of two massive heart attacks. Among other injuries, her pulmonary vein – the major vein connecting the heart and lungs – had been torn. By the time an ambulance delivered her to the Hôpital de la Pitié Salpetrière, she was almost certainly clinically dead. For the next two hours, however, the cardiac team staunched the bleeding and worked frantically to save her, massaging her heart internally and externally. There was no response. Eventually they recognized that their efforts were in vain, and that Diana, Princess of Wales was dead.

A news conference was hastily arranged, and delayed by an hour to allow time for the news to be transmitted confidentially to the royal family. Dr Alain Pavie, head of the hospital's cardiology department, was given the unenviable job of announcing to the world that the Princess was dead. The British Ambassador, Michael Jay, steeled himself for the media onslaught that would follow, having earlier broken down on being told the news by the hospital, which he had immediately relayed to the royal household. 'The death of the Princess of Wales fills us all with shock and deep grief,' he said, when questioned by journalists.

Within hours, Charles Spencer was being filmed for television at the gates of his home in Cape Town, speaking from a prepared statement. With barely controlled anger, he lambasted the press for the death of his sister; every editor and proprietor who had paid for intrusive and exploitative photographs, he said, had 'blood on their hands.' Having someone to blame made the reason for Diana's death seem clearer; indeed, initial reports did in fact point the finger of guilt squarely at the media, and particularly those mercenary soldiers of the industry, the paparazzi. Poignantly, when Lord Spencer told his young children that Aunt Diana had died in a car crash, they smilingly assumed he was joking – 'No Daddy, not in real life,' said Eliza, one of his twin daughters.

On Seil, Frances opened the door to Janey and her husband. The three of them embraced in the hallway before he went straight into the kitchen to put the kettle on while the two women sat together on the chesterfield, watching the television. Frances drew up a list of people who needed to be told about

Diana, but quickly realized that she was too distraught to make the calls. She looked towards her trusted friend and made a decision. 'I asked Janey to ring [the names on the list],' said Frances. It was one less thing to worry about, and a huge burden lifted. Immersed in her loss, unable to focus, she could not contemplate speaking to others. 'Obviously your first thought is hugely personal. What you feel is for yourself and your children; you aren't desperately concerned about the rest of the world.'

As day began to dawn, Frances and the Milnes waited in the bungalow, hoping against hope for a call from the Palace. At one point, the fax machine clattered into life again and Frances rushed to the office hoping that here at last were instructions from Balmoral or Buckingham Palace. In fact, it was a message 'from a tabloid editor in longhand saying, "I'm sure I know more than you do about your daughter and our readers would love to know what you think. I am at my desk."'

She angrily dismissed as ridiculous any suggestion that she should meet this request, trying to remain focused, her mind occupied with a single thought: whatever had happened between Diana and Prince Charles, surely, in death, Frances would receive a call from the Prince or one of his staff? She knew that both her surviving daughters had been asked to accompany Prince Charles to Paris to bring Diana's body back to England. She wanted to go to her dead daughter. She wanted to bring Diana home. Beyond that, however, she felt that the family should be together at this time. It was bad enough that Charles Spencer was in South Africa, prevented by distance from reaching Europe in time to escort his sister home. Frances, almost beside herself with anxiety, thought of the Prince of Wales. 'Why hasn't he rung?' she asked aloud. 'What is going on?'

In Balmoral, however, discussions were still under way about protocol, an important factor as the Prince and Princess of Wales were divorced. Diana was no longer royal, and theoretically should be treated like any other private person, without special privileges. She was the responsibility of the Spencers, and the return of her body would therefore be a private matter for her family. The Prince, however, emphasized that his former wife was the mother of a future king. Himself shocked and deeply saddened by her death, he insisted that Diana should be treated accordingly. Nevertheless, this was easier said than done. Royal protocol and precedent are extremely complex matters, and there are rules and provisions for almost every conceivable situation, as well as detailed contingency plans for sudden events or emergencies. Diana's death, however, was so unexpected, and of such worldwide, as well as royal, significance, that there were no contingency plans in place to cope with it. The result was that the Queen and the Prince of Wales, together with their respective staffs, were faced with the necessity of holding long discussions in order to decide how best to meet this unprecedented situation. Her Majesty is known for her devotion to duty and protocol; indeed, she may be one of the few remaining people who knows exactly how things should be done, and in this she was supported fully by her Private Secretary, Sir Robert Fellowes, the Princess's own brother-in law. Protocol dictated that the Queen should not endorse the use of an aircraft from the Queen's Flight to bring home the Princess's body. Yet compassion dictated that a chartered flight would be wholly inappropriate, with the result that Her Majesty agreed to send an aircraft. It seemed that even after her death Diana was challenging the monarchy and its centuries-old certainties.

Princes William and Harry took the news of their mother's death with tremendous resolve. Feeling obliged to defer to their elders, in which, in any case, they had little choice, they attended the regular Sunday morning service at Crathie Church with their royal grandparents. As usual the family and its entourage arrived in a fleet of Daimlers, Charles, flanked by the two boys, all wearing black ties. Yet not one word was spoken of Diana during the entire service. The family carried on, and the service was conducted as though nothing had happened, while throughout the rest of the country the Princess's death dominated every church service. It was an omission of epic proportions, bordering on the bizarre. Perhaps the Queen wanted to prevent the young princes from being exposed to emotional condolences for which they could not yet be prepared. The service ended with the national anthem, 'God Save the Queen'.

Undoubtedly the younger new guard of Prince Charles's entourage were less bound by protocol than the Queen's old-guard staff, and many discussions between the two must have taken place in the search for guidelines for appropriate action. By now taking advice from the recently elected Prime Minister, Tony Blair, Charles recognized that he needed to be responsive to public opinion. Dissatisfied murmurs were already winging their way up to Balmoral because the Union flag flying over Buckingham Palace had not been lowered to half-mast. Charles was advised that if the royal family continued, as people perceived it, to ignore Diana's death, it was tantamount to signing away any remaining popularity the monarchy still commanded. In death, Diana had forced her husband's hand. The two royal camps agreed that an aircraft of the RAF's Queen's Flight, carrying the Prince of Wales accompanied by Lady Sarah McCorquodale and Lady Jane Fellowes, would fly that day to Paris to bring back the body of Diana, Princess of Wales.

The BAe 146 of the Queen's Flight picked up Sarah and Jane at RAF Wittering, then headed north to Aberdeen to collect the Prince of Wales before taking off again for Paris. Even now, however, the arguments within the Palace continued. Prince Charles was dismayed to discover that plans were in place for Diana to be taken to a public mortuary in Fulham. He ordered these arrangements to be changed and her body to be transferred directly to the Chapel Royal at St James's Palace immediately they landed at RAF Northolt.

In Paris, Diana's butler, Paul Burrell, who had flown there ahead of the Prince's party, arrived at the hospital carrying a suitcase he had brought from Kensington Palace. In it he had packed one of the Princess's favourite black cocktail dresses by designer Catherine Walker. Left alone with her body, he carefully dressed her and arranged her hair and earrings in preparation for the arrival of her sisters and ex-husband. Despite Burrell's efforts, however, Diana's body, which had already been embalmed, bore the marks of the terrible accident that had killed her, and her sisters were deeply distressed when they arrived at the hospital to see her for the last time.

Diana, Princess of Wales, the former Lady Diana Spencer, returned to England a full member of the royal family. Escorted by her ex-husband and her two older sisters, her coffin was draped in the Royal Standard; the Prime Minister was among those waiting, heads bowed, at RAF Northolt as at 7 p.m. the aircraft landed from out of a cloudless sky.

As the calls offering condolences poured in, and scores of bouquets arrived, many from complete strangers, Frances was both astonished and humbled. The level of public sympathy was quite beyond anything she might have expected. Knowing that she could not go to Paris, her thoughts turned to her grandsons. Later that awful day she managed to speak to William and Harry at Balmoral, desperately trying to find words that might comfort them. Then, in company with the whole nation, she watched her daughter's homecoming on television, knowing in her heart that she should have been there. Unable to contain herself, she suddenly bubbled over with fury:

'They [the Palace] thought, "She lives on an inaccessible island in Scotland, how would she get to Paris?" Well, damned easy – if you're asked.'

Frances had miscarried one baby and suffered the death of another, as well as losing her brother, her father, her mother, and now one of her daughters. She was not inexperienced in what she calls 'the grief stakes.' But Diana's death was different. It was not only tragic and wasteful, it was horribly public. Almost at once, it set the Spencers against the Windsors as both families fought over how best to mark Diana's life and lay her finally to rest. Frances remained inside her home on Seil during those first few terrible days, surrounded by the press and guarded by the police. She was visited by her priest, Father Sean Macauley, by her nephew Hugh Roche, and by her many local friends, including, of course, the Milnes. They all helped her with the countless arrangements that had to be made, although, resolute as ever, she played her own part with a kind of numbed, yet undaunted, courage. As she was to say later, 'When something like this happens your best friend is deep shock. Looking back, it's amazing how lucid your thinking can be and definite your actions, as well as your ability to grasp hold of what needs doing now, not later but now, imminent.'

Early on the Wednesday morning, 3 September, Frances, dressed entirely in black and accompanied by a detective, left Seil in lashing rain for the hundred-mile drive to Glasgow airport. She slowly wound down the window to pass over a handwritten note to the crowd of journalists that had gathered near her bungalow. It read: 'My heartfelt thank you's [*sic*] to everyone for their prayers, flowers and endless thoughtful kindness, following the death of my daughter, Diana. I pray for her and the two men who died with her, and for their families. I am so proud of William and Harry . . . and Diana's sisters Sarah and Jane and her brother Charles. I thank God, for the gift of Diana and for all her loving and giving – I give her back to Him . . . with my love, pride and admiration . . . to rest . . . in peace.'

Within moments of learning that Diana was dead, Frances had decided she would 'be as dignified and as good as I could be in facing her death'. Her tears would be shed in private and not for the public to see. 'Not that it matters, but it is important to me,' she said. In this she was following not just the age-old precepts of her background, her upbringing and her class, but also those of the character she had formed in the course of facing so many disasters. She intended to cope by keeping her days full and her life busy: 'I would get out and do and give myself charitable commitments that would give me deadlines and lift me out of myself, however hard it was.' She called this determination to carry on her 'options for life without Diana'. Only she would know, or even be able to guess at, what that effort cost her.

Unfortunately, the Palace was not as decisive. They dithered in their official mourning, and in their show of respect for the Princess. The Queen ruled out a state funeral. (In Britain, only four commoners have been accorded state funerals: Admiral Lord Nelson, Field Marshal the Duke of Wellington, Sir William Gladstone and, most recently, Sir Winston Churchill in 1965.) Prince Charles, however, aware of the tidal wave of emotion that had swamped the nation, and perhaps suffering from a sense of personal guilt himself, felt that it was vital that the royal family should honour Diana. Once again, therefore, he ventured to disagree with his mother and his Sovereign. Once again the staffs of the Queen and Prince found themselves at odds, until a Buckingham Palace official resolved the impasse by announcing that a ceremonial funeral for the Princess would be 'a unique event for a unique person'. Charles Spencer, who by now had arrived back at Althorp, maintained that he had no wish for a state funeral but felt arrangements on a grand scale were 'right and proper'. Frances remained perplexed and upset at not being asked or consulted about the funeral arrangements 'by the Prince of Wales' office', especially as she was 'the sole surviving parent'.

By Wednesday, Kensington Palace Gardens had become a sea of flowers. People were crying in the streets, and queuing for hours to write messages in specially opened books of condolence. Beyond that, however, they were watching every move that the royal family, and especially the Queen and the Prince of Wales, made, and frustration was turning to anger at what appeared to be the Palace's complete indifference to the mood of the country.

Within a few short days the arrangements for the Princess's funeral, down to the smallest detail, had to be in place, and all arguments ended. The Palace recognized that the ceremony had to be right for the Spencer family, while at the same time meeting the requirements of royal protocol, but it also had to satisfy the people. Diana's death had, it seems, polarized the nation's view of the royal family without the Princess, and Tony Blair advised Prince Charles that a constitutional crisis might arise if the warning signals, which were being loudly trumpeted in the tabloid newspapers, were ignored. 'Your People Are Suffering – Speak To Us Ma'am' shrieked one headline. Another demanded of the Queen, 'Show Us You Care'.

The Queen had wanted Diana's funeral to be a private affair held in St George's Chapel, Windsor Castle, with a burial at Frogmore, the royal burial grounds in the gardens of Frogmore House, a short distance from the castle. In that, she would at least have been treated like every other member of the royal family apart from Sovereigns (with the exception of Edward VIII), but without ceremonial. Prince Charles had won his battle, however, and was orchestrating a grand public funeral for his ex-wife. When Frances finally learned the details, she drew a deep breath. 'It was one of my daughters who told me, I can't remember when, that it was to be Westminster Abbey. She gave me the date and time.'

This information came as something of a shock to Frances. For just over forty-three years earlier, as a young woman on what was, then, the happiest day of her life, she had walked down the aisle of the great abbey. Now she was to return there as a grandmother to bury her own child. Faced with the news, she found that thinking with any clarity became almost impossible. 'It may seem odd that I don't recall the date or time [set for Diana's funeral] but that is simply because I had a huge overwhelming hiccup about it being Westminster Abbey, since the last time I walked up that aisle was in 1954 to marry Diana's father. So that was something I had to grasp, digest and get on with.'

As plans for the funeral took shape that week, and work began on the myriad details that needed to be worked out, the Queen, Prince Philip, Prince Charles and the two boys remained at Balmoral. Hidden from view in the aftershock of Diana's death, they had no intention of returning to London until Friday, the day before the funeral. It was a dangerous strategy. The public, displaying a kind of collective mass mourning, perceived the royal family's determination to remain in Scotland as symbolic of the monarchy's physical and emotional remoteness, and, in particular, of the Queen's disdain for Diana.

The Spencers, in complete contrast, threw themselves into action in the days after the Princess's death, despite being scattered around the country. Having been denied proper involvement in the kind of funeral that Diana was to have, the Spencer family considered it vital to make the service both dignified and personal. They scouted through Diana's telephone book to ensure that her friends and supporters were invited to the service, not just official dignitaries. As Frances put it, 'Faxes from the family were going like frisbees round the countryside, as we tried to find everyone connected with Diana's life to be at her funeral and have a big input in the service, so I concentrated on that. Jane was in London, Sarah in Lincolnshire and Charles at Althorp.'

The royal family, on the other hand, had become preoccupied with how high to fly its flag. Although flags across much of the world were at half-mast as a mark of respect for the dead Princess, the Palace refused to comply, the Union flag over Buckingham Palace remaining resolutely at full mast. This was viewed by the public with suspicion and anger: could there be a greater indictment of the royal family's treatment of Diana?

Faced with this undercurrent the Queen was again advised to take action, and her Press Secretary, Geoffrey Crawford, was ordered to sort out the mess. He went on the offensive, claiming to the media that the royal family had been 'hurt by suggestions that they are indifferent to the country's sorrow'. It was not enough, however. The people, egged on by the press, and the tabloids in particular, wanted more; they wanted a public declaration of Diana's contribution to the royal family, and a public demonstration of its senior members' sorrow and contrition.

Under this pressure, by Thursday the Queen and her advisers had relented and for the first time in history the Union flag flew at half-mast over Buckingham Palace. Beyond that, however, the Palace announced that the Queen would read a statement live on television the following day, Friday 5 September. Protocol had been swept away for Diana.

When Frances arrived in London on Wednesday, her daughter had been dead for four days. Yet still the Queen had not personally contacted her to offer her condolences or to talk about the grandsons they shared. A flag, it seemed, possessed her thoughts more than a mother's grief. These two women had, as had their fathers, known each other all their lives; their mothers had been close; they had been neighbours at Sandringham; their children had married each other; and, through William and Harry, their families were now joined by ties of blood. It remains almost inexplicable that the Queen, whose powerful sense of duty has been so often and so widely remarked, did not even telephone Frances to express her sorrow that Diana had died so suddenly, aged just thirty-six.

In London, Frances felt compelled to visit the area outside the gates of Kensington Palace, now immersed in a vast carpet of flowers. It had become a focus of pilgrimage; here people lit candles, left cards bearing tender and often grief-stricken messages, and held vigils through the day and night in homage to their lost 'Queen of Hearts'. The Sovereign's continuing silence was outweighed, if not shamed, by the people's show of love and respect for the Princess. Restless, and knowing she would be unable to sleep, Frances wandered among the crowds outside her daughter's home late into the night, reading some of the thousands of tributes, breathing the air thick with the scent of flowers, occasionally stopping to listen to people who felt that they too had seen a spark in their lives extinguished.

A succession of Diana's family and close friends visited St George's Chapel in St James's Palace, where her body lay, to pay their last respects. Sarah, Duchess of York, herself largely ostracized by the royal family after her divorce from Prince Andrew, broke down in tears, leaving a bouquet on which was a card with the words, 'My most darling friend, my Duch, I love you. My soulmate and partner. God bless you – Fergie.' Frances, too, summoned her courage and went to the chapel, where she sat silently and peacefully beside her daughter's encased body. For her, however, unlike her other daughters, there was to be no last glimpse or kiss. 'I didn't get the chance to see or touch Diana at St James's Palace because she was in a coffin, nailed down.' All she could do was whisper her final farewells.

Later, Frances would reflect that one of the greatest tragedies of her life had now been repeated. She had been deprived of seeing her baby son John in death, and now her daughter was to be taken from her without a final embrace. Such lost moments, she knew, could never be recovered. 'I do ache about it,' she admits. In abiding by the wishes of Prince Charles's office – 'I didn't go to Paris to bring Diana home to London because I wasn't asked' – Frances now had to live in the knowledge that her last memories of Diana could and should have been so different. 'It really seems somewhat ironic to me that having buried two children, for entirely different reasons, I did not see or touch or hold them when they were dead,' she says, not without bitterness.

At 6 p.m. on Friday, 5 September, having arrived back at Buckingham Palace only four hours earlier, the Queen finally addressed her subjects, live on television, in order to placate the growing mood of anger. It was an occasion that demanded the highest calibre of prose, and the senior members of the royal family and their advisers knew it. As she sat in Buckingham Palace with her back to an open window through which could be seen thousands of mourners, their noise clearly audible, she began to speak.

Since last Sunday's dreadful news, we have seen, throughout Britain and around the world, an overwhelming expression of sadness at Diana's death. We have all been trying in our different ways to cope. It is not easy to express a sense of loss, since the initial shock is often succeeded by a mixture of other feelings: disbelief, incomprehension, anger – and concern for those who remain. We have all felt those emotions in these last few days. So what I say to you now, as your queen and as a grandmother, I say from my heart.

First, I want to pay tribute to Diana myself. She was an exceptional and gifted human being. In good times and bad, she never lost her capacity to smile and laugh, nor to inspire others with her warmth and kindness. I admired and respected her – for her energy and commitment to others, and especially for her devotion to her two boys.

This week at Balmoral, we have all been trying to help William and Harry come to terms with the devastating loss that they and the rest of us have suffered. No one who knew Diana will ever forget her. Millions of others who never met her, but felt they knew her, will remember her.

I for one believe that there are lessons to be drawn from her life and from the extraordinary and moving reaction to her death.

I share in your determination to cherish her memory. This is also an opportunity for me, on behalf of my family, and especially Prince Charles and William and Harry, to thank all of you who have brought flowers, sent messages, and paid your respects in so many ways to a remarkable person. These acts of kindness have been a huge source of help and comfort.

Our thoughts are also with Diana's family and the families of those who died with her. I know that they too have drawn strength from what has happened since last weekend, as they seek to heal their sorrow and then to face the future without a loved one. I hope that tomorrow we can all, wherever we are, join in expressing our grief at Diana's loss, and gratitude for her all-too-short life.

It is a chance to show the whole world the British nation united in grief and respect. May those who died rest in peace and may we, each and every one of us, thank God for someone who made many, many people happy.

With those words still hanging in the air, Diana's body was placed in a hearse and driven, under escort, the twenty-minute journey from St James's Palace to Kensington Palace. Thousands of flashbulbs lit the way through the streets as the four-car procession followed the route down the Mall and around Hyde Park Corner. Even though the fine weather had broken and it was raining heavily, some 50,000 people, many holding flowers or lit candles, lined the streets and bowed their heads in sorrow as they watched the car bearing the coffin, which was draped in the Royal Standard and surmounted by a simple arrangement of arum lilies, Diana's favourite flower, drive slowly past. The flowers' heavy scent filled the hearse as people pressed forward in the pouring rain for a glimpse of the Princess on her final journey home. Grief-stricken and exhausted, Frances needed her faith now more than ever. Later that evening she attended a requiem mass at Westminster Cathedral, where she sat shoulder to shoulder with the Duchess of Kent, a fellow Catholic. Cardinal Basil Hume, Archbishop of Westminster and head of the Roman Catholic Church in England, himself a friend of Diana's, paid tribute, 'Thank you for the joy you gave the many. Thank you for being like the rest of us, flawed, but lovable. The agonies of the heart and anguish of the mind were often your companions in life.'

Frances found tremendous comfort in these sentiments. They had a greater truth than those belatedly broadcast by a compromised Queen to assuage the royal family's guilty conscience, and perhaps even to avert a constitutional crisis. She knew, however, that she faced an even sterner test. Yet she could only speculate about what tomorrow would bring.

CHAPTER THIRTEEN

Trying To Be 'Just Frances'

T HE PALACE HAD WANTED A FUNERAL with a strong military flavour, but the Spencer family would have none of it. Nor, in particular, would they countenance the attempts to push Diana's friends to the fringes of the abbey. Charles Spencer, having consulted his mother and sisters, stood his ground, made his demands and won. Facing squarely up to his brother-in-law, Sir Robert Fellowes, he was determined that the part the Spencers had played in his sister's life would be remembered.

His conviction had been cemented when, standing before Diana's coffin in the chapel at St James's Palace, he had decided to practise reading his speech – drafted in a single sitting in the early hours after the announcement of her sudden death – from beginning to end. Lord Spencer has said that it felt right straight away, and he could sense, even then, that it would gain public approval. It was not something in which he was going to be denied.

Thousands of people, young and old, camped out in the streets in order to secure a spot from which to see the Princess's final journey, just as they had done on her wedding day sixteen years before. Saturday, 6 September 1997, would see the funeral of the world's most famous woman, with a worldwide viewing public estimated at over two and a half billion – the greatest since President John F. Kennedy's funeral in 1963. The day arrived bathed in bright sunshine after the heavy rain of Friday, and the stage was set.

Frances had yet another sleepless night. She woke early, and, finding it hard to settle to anything, smoked an early-morning cigarette. As the time ticked away, she dressed in a black knee-length dress complemented by a pearl choker, pearl earrings and a bejewelled cross on a heavy gold chain around her neck, and on her head a striking large-brimmed hat. The few belongings she needed for the day were tucked carefully into a small black patent-leather clutch bag, which she held tightly in black-gloved hands.

The funeral had at least been planned with military precision. At 9.08 a.m., Diana's coffin, resting on a gun carriage drawn by six black horses, emerged through the gates of Kensington Palace. At once a haunting sound, a kind of wail from the crowd, pierced the air. The coffin, once again draped in the Royal Standard and covered in lilies, also bore, in pride of place, a wreath of pink roses and a single posy of tightly budded cream roses on which was a handwritten card that said, simply and poignantly, 'Mummy'.

As was the Spencer way, Frances had asked whether the family wanted the flowers to be placed on the coffin as though from them all as a group, rather than as individuals. They unanimously agreed to this sign of solidarity. 'That was my idea, it was following a family tradition. And I just thought, let's as a family united – siblings, nephews, nieces and Mum – all go together. There were thirty-six flowers [the lilies], one for each year of her life. They were from her sisters, brother and me, and her nieces and nephews.'

As the cortège reached St James's Palace it was joined by Prince Charles, Prince Philip, Princes William and Harry and Lord Spencer, who took their places behind the gun carriage as it processed to the abbey. Dignified in their silence and grief, but utterly alone in their own private thoughts, the three men and two boys made their way towards Westminster Abbey. The boys' heads were lowered and their hand clasped as they moved past the hushed crowd watching their Princess on her final journey. With the traffic stopped there was a heavy silence, punctuated only by the sound of the horses' hooves and the gun carriage's wheels, the shuffle of the mourners' feet, and occasional sobs and the sound of thrown flowers landing on the roadway. Under the temporary shelter of the arch at Horse Guards, Charles laid a reassuring hand on Prince Harry's shoulder before the eyes of the world were upon them once again.

When the procession reached Westminster Abbey, Frances watched the invited mourners form a procession behind her son and grandsons. Yet again Charles Spencer had got his way, making sure that his sister Jane, in conjunction with her husband, Robert Fellowes, should be allowed to organize the seating plan in the abbey. Of the people who filed into the great church, many were Diana's friends, and many others the ordinary people whose lives she had touched – charity workers, disabled people, trusted servants, those Diana had lived to help. They all filed in along with heads of state, politicians, film stars and other celebrities. Some were dressed casually, others were in uniform, some in suits. Taken together, they represented the many faces of the Princess.

Frances, shocked but resolute, was flanked by her daughters, Sarah and Jane, accompanied by their husbands and children. The family gathered together knowing this day was about showing their love and respect for Diana, but also about being strong and brave.

Walking through the great West Door of Westminster Abbey at 135 a.m., Frances made the sign of the cross as she stared straight ahead. 'I saw the cross on the High Altar and thought, don't look left or right. I remember as we went by the tomb of the Unknown Warrior there is a left-hand bend. Sarah said, "You should remember that bend, Mummy."' Frances carried on tentatively up the aisle, achingly aware that the first time she had taken these steps, forty-three years ago, it had been to marry Johnnie Spencer. She set her face towards the altar, where in a few minutes she would be staring at her daughter's coffin. It had been agreed between the organizers and the television news teams that none of the family, especially the young princes, would be filmed during the funeral service. Those moments inside the abbey were just too personal.

Frances took her seat with the rest of the Spencer family in the area known as the North Lantern, facing the royal family. The tolling of the bell – a single peal every minute – signalled that Diana was approaching. At ten minutes before eleven the Queen, in company with the Queen Mother and Prince Edward, arrived in a large black Daimler and made their way to join the rest of the royal family in the South Lantern

On the stroke of eleven o'clock the cortège arrived at the West Door and the congregation stood to sing the National Anthem. Eight pallbearers from the 1st Battalion the Welsh Guards – especially chosen to be of equal height – expertly lifted the 700-pound coffin on to their shoulders and slow-marched the length of the aisle between the congregation, before lowering it solemnly on to the catafalque placed before the High Altar. The first hymn, 'I Vow To Thee, My Country', which had also been sung at Diana's wedding to Prince Charles in 1981, was followed by a poem read by Sarah, 'Turn Again To Life' by Mary Lee Hall. It sums up the essence of the Spencer optimism: 'If I should die and leave you here awhile, /Be not like others, sore undone, who keep /Long vigils by the silent dust and weep. /For my sake – turn again to life and smile . . .'

Jane, sounding all too eerily like her younger sister, recited a Spencer favourite, 'For Katrina's Sundial' by Henry van Dyke: 'Time is too slow for those who wait, /Too swift for those who fear, /Too long for those who grieve, /Too short for those who rejoice, /But for those who love, /Time is eternity.'

Elton John delivered his specially penned version of 'Candle In The Wind', with its newly written words, at which Prince Harry was visibly reduced to tears. His father bent to hold and comfort him. The song also set a contemporary tone for Charles Spencer's eulogy. As the young earl rose to his feet in front of his godmother, the Queen, Prince Charles must have wondered what the next few minutes would hold. Despite requests to do so, neither he nor his mother had seen a copy of Spencer's tribute to his sister. They would soon learn. For the next five minutes they were to receive a global dressing-down as the Spencers, descendants of the old English aristocracy, declared war on the Windsors. Charles Spencer's moment had come.

He began in conventional form: 'I stand before you today the representative of a family in grief, in a country in mourning before a world in shock', before going on to praise his sister's many qualities. The first shock came at the end of his second paragraph, electrifying the congregation, the thousands listening outside the abbey as his voice was relayed over loudspeakers, and the millions listening to or watching the live broadcasts on radio or television. Diana, he said, was 'Someone with a natural nobility who was classless and who proved in the last year that she needed no royal title to continue to generate her particular brand of magic.' It was a deliberate reproof to the Queen, whose decision to relieve Diana, on her divorce from Prince Charles, of the right to use the courtesy title 'Her Royal Highness' had been widely condemned as spiteful, if not vindictive.

In what was, by any yardstick, a bravura performance, Lord Spencer went on to commend his sister's work with important but often unfashionable causes, emphasizing his point by showing that, for all her glamour, beauty and power to inspire others, she remained deeply insecure at heart. Here too, perhaps, was another reproof aimed at the royal family, who by now were seen by a majority of the public as unemotional and unfeeling beings who had made no effort to understand, and certainly not to help, their troubled Princess. He reserved his greatest contempt for the media, for paparazzi photographers and newspapers that belittled her 'genuinely good intentions'. This, had baffled his sister, he said, before adding witheringly:

> My own, and only explanation is that genuine goodness is threatening to those at the opposite end of the moral spectrum.
>
> It is a point to remember that of all the ironies about Diana, perhaps the greatest was this; a girl given the name of the ancient goddess of hunting, was, in the end, the most hunted person of the modern age.

If the Queen and the Prince of Wales had felt some relief as Spencer's attack shifted to the media, it must only have been short-lived. As he moved to the end of his lecture – for it was hardly a eulogy in the ordinary sense of that word – he turned his attention to Diana's sons, openly suggesting that the Spencers would do all in their power to save the young princes from the sort of treatment their mother had received not only from the press, but from the royal family:

> She would want us today to pledge ourselves to protecting her beloved boys, William and Harry, from a similar fate and I do this here, Diana, on your behalf. We will not allow them to suffer the anguish that used to regularly drive you to tearful despair. And beyond that, on behalf of your mother and sisters, I pledge that we, your blood family, will do all we can to continue the

imaginative way in which you were steering these two exceptional young men so that their souls are not simply immersed by duty and tradition, but can sing openly as you planned. We fully respect the heritage into which they have both been born and will always respect and encourage them in their royal role, but we, like you, recognize the need for them to experience as many different aspects of life as possible to arm them spiritually and emotionally for the years ahead. I know you would have expected nothing less from us.

Struggling to keep his composure, Charles Spencer sat back down. For a moment there was a stunned silence, then the congregation heard the rippling sound of hands clapping outside the abbey, swiftly taken up and sweeping to a crescendo of wild applause both inside and out. He had seized the moment and read the mood of the people perfectly. For that instant, like his sister before him, Charles Spencer became the face of truth and justice. Yet it was a dangerous thing to do. He had made promises and statements that will for ever direct a spotlight on his own behaviour.

The service came to its dignified and moving conclusion, prayers and anthems followed by a final blessing. No one stirred as Diana's coffin was raised aloft and carried out into the bright light for the journey back to Althorp House in Northamptonshire, where, despite the Queen's wishes, the Princess was to be buried. Traditionally, as a Spencer, Diana should have been laid to rest alongside her father, Johnnie, and ancestors in the family vault in the thirteenth-century church at Great Brington, close to Althorp. Yet during the week since Diana's death, Frances had become adamant that her daughter should have peace, now more than ever. To inter her body within the church would have left her burial place vulnerable to mawkish curiosity and overrun with tourists. 'I was fussed about her being buried in the local church at Althorp. I couldn't bear the thought of people walking all over her grave and gawping.'

Despite the acrimony of her divorce from Johnnie, which coloured her view of Althorp, as well as her early dislike of the place after her son Charles had inherited the title, Frances had come to enjoy the large estate. It was private and had beautiful grounds, while a happy balance had been struck between the house and grounds being open to the public and its use as a family home. Charles had transformed the stuffy and rather formal old rooms into something altogether more welcoming and Frances had begun to feel easier on her visits. Not far from the house is a lake with a small wooded island in the middle, known as the 'Round Oval'. To Frances, this seemed a perfect place for Diana's grave, but she was reticent about saying so, anxious not to pressurize Charles into making a decision. Unwilling to force the issue, she kept her idea to herself. 'I actually thought the only place she could be buried was on the island, but I resisted saying it to Charles because then he's left with that for the rest of his life.'

As it turned out, she need not have worried. Charles Spencer, struggling with the same dilemma, revealed his own thinking in an early-morning telephone conversation with Frances. His views and hers coincided almost exactly, except that Charles had thought beyond the actual burial itself, deciding that a temporary bridge, erected to allow family and friends to pay their respects for some while after the funeral, would improve the plan. Frances could hardly contain her relief. 'The very next morning, after another sleepless night, he rang and . . . told me about his idea for the island. I said, "Do it. Great! Fantastic!"'

Outside Westminster Abbey, Diana's coffin was carefully placed inside the hearse for its final journey. All along the seventy-seven-mile route to Althorp, the crowds lined the roadway to throw bouquets or single flowers in the car's path. As the vehicle approached the motorway on the outskirts of London, it was so covered in flowers the driver was forced to stop to clear his windscreen. He carefully lifted the bouquets and placed them by the side of the road, before resuming the slow, dignified journey to Northamptonshire. People strained forward to catch a glimpse from behind barriers and ran across bridges as the hearse passed underneath.

The Spencers, with Prince Charles, travelled by Royal Train and then by car to Althorp, together with the two young princes. It was neither the time nor the place for small talk, especially after Charles Spencer's implied criticism of the way William and Harry were being raised.

On arrival, Frances, with her children and grandchildren, crossed the temporary wooden bridge, which had been specially built by the army, to the island for Diana's interment. It was a strictly private, family affair conducted by a close friend of the Spencers, the Reverend Victor Malan; the only other person there who was not family was Diana's butler, Paul Burrell . There were no cameras, no journalists, no intrusion from the outside world. Quietly the family stood round the specially consecrated plot where the grave had been dug, consumed by their own private thoughts. All the children – Diana's nieces and nephews – had been asked to write on a card a special message to Diana, something personal, something loving, words that they would remember for ever. Then, to ensure that their thoughts would always be private, the cards were sealed and placed with the coffin in the grave. It was a remarkable moment in a day of high emotion. Frances explains: 'Each child had an envelope with three cards, they wrote whatever they wanted to on one card. The cards were double-faced [i.e. the written one sandwiched between the other two] and enveloped and they were buried with her so no one ever saw a thing.'

As the Princess's body was lowered into the ground, there was a palpable feeling among the family that she had at last returned home. There was a tranquillity about the Round Oval and that brought the realization that nothing could ever harm her again. At that moment 'Diana had become a Spencer, independent and herself again,' says Frances. Beside her in the coffin were some of her most treasured possessions, including the rosary beads given to her by Mother Teresa of Calcutta, who had died only twenty-four hours before Diana's funeral. The Reverend Malan brought the service to an end with a final blessing, and a feeling of peace descended, despite the agony of loss and grief. Frances paused a moment in prayer and contemplation, thinking how lovely the island would be at first light. She realized that her daughter would always face the rising sun.

> Strange though it may seem, Diana's funeral was probably the proudest day of my life as a mother. Proud of her; my daughters, who were rock steady in their readings, and my son, who gave the ultimate tribute of brotherly love for her.

In the aftermath of the accident that killed Diana, Dodi Fayed and Henri Paul, the French set up a criminal investigation headed by Judge Hervé Stéphan and Judge Marie-Christine Dévidel. Both in their early forties and highly experienced, they painstakingly pieced together the mass of forensic evidence, police reports and witness statements. It was a complex and mammoth undertaking that required steady nerves as the demand for blame to be apportioned and heads to roll became more vociferous and more frenzied. Yet it would be two long years before the judges' report on the accident, known as 'Fatal road accident 31 August 1997 00:30', appeared with its conclusions as to how Diana, Dodi and Henri Paul came to die.

In the week following the accident, a post-mortem on the driver, Henri Paul, revealed that his blood-alcohol level was three times above the legal limit at the time of the crash. Analysis of his blood also showed the presence of prescription drugs, including the anti-depressant Prozac, which would have slowed his reactions, especially when mixed with alcohol. In addition, he was unfamiliar with the powerful Mercedes 280S, a car capable of reaching speeds of 130 mph. Yet on the night in question he drove at very high speeds during the dash from the Ritz Hotel towards the dipping and curving four-lane underpass at Place de l'Alma – long recognized as a local accident spot.

The publication of these results took the heat out of initial reports which had suggested that the crash had been directly caused by paparazzi pursuing the Princess. After the accident, however, the police had bundled six photo-journalists into the back of a van, and charged them with 'involuntary homicide and non-assistance to persons in danger' – the latter in relation to the allegation that the photographers had snapped pictures of the crashed car and its occupants rather than going to their aid. They had their press cards and driver's licences confiscated and were banned from leaving France. Although pictures of the fatally injured Princess were indeed offered for sale, newspaper editors shied away from printing them, aware that public condemnation of the publication of such images would be something from which they, or their papers, might never recover.

The only survivor of the crash was Diana's bodyguard, twenty-nine-year-old Trevor Rees-Jones, who had been sitting in the front (right-hand) passenger seat. He suffered horrific injuries to his face and chest, as well as a broken wrist. Despite being unable to buckle his seat belt in time – it was found half drawn across him – the airbag on his side of the car had taken the initial force of the crash and thereby saved his life. After many hours of operations to rebuild his face and thirty-one days in hospital recuperating, he was allowed home, still far from recovered.

Having been engaged by the Ritz Hotel, Rees-Jones's employer was Dodi's father, Mohamed Fayed, the Ritz's owner (as well as the owner of Harrods in London). Fayed initially behaved with paternal concern towards the only survivor. Once Rees-Jones was out of hospital, however, Fayed's mood darkened as the bodyguard, unable clearly to recall events leading up to the accident, started legal proceedings against the Ritz Hotel for 'failing to provide a licensed driver'. For his part, Fayed introduced a gaggle of strange and unlikely conspiracy theories in order to deflect attention away from his driver's part in the accident, claiming, 'I believe in my heart, 99.9 per cent, that it was not an accident.'

The weeks following the accident were particularly trying for Frances who, shattered by grief, was struggling to cope with constant revelations and requests for her comments on the growing speculation as the media remained fixated upon the crash and its causes. Her daughter's death was being fought over on a public stage. Particularly upsetting were the rumours that Diana had whispered a final message. Fayed contended that a nurse at the hospital had taken him to one side and told him that Diana's dying wish was that Sarah should look after William and Harry. It was a claim vehemently denied both by the hospital and by Rees-Jones's fellow bodyguard, Kes Wingfield, who was with Fayed throughout his visit to the hospital. Fayed next proceeded to institute his own investigation and would later claim, while protected by legal privilege during a court case, that Prince Philip had directed the British intelligence services to murder the Princess and Dodi in order to prevent their marriage. 'I believe there were people who did not want Dodi and Diana to be together,' he told a national newspaper. 'There was a conspiracy and I will not rest until I have established exactly what happened.'

There has been much speculation, fuelled by Fayed, as to whether his son and Diana had been planning to wed. Had they done so, then the mother of the future King – and future titular head of the Church of England – would have married a Muslim. Yet while that might have ruffled a few feathers among the British Establishment, it seems a highly dubious motive for murder, especially for one allegedly involving the Duke of Edinburgh.

Nor did the theorizing stop there. Thousands of man hours were spent searching by French police for a white Fiat car, since fragments of its tail-light had been found among the debris of the crash, although no clear connection has ever been made. Then the Libyan leader, Colonel Muammar Gaddafi, appeared on television and claimed that the crash was a plot to stop the Princess marrying an Arab, something apparently bolstering Fayed's theory. As time wore on and the official French inquiry remained silent, the public search for a reason lost all rationality. Inspector Ken Wharfe, the Princess's police protection officer for six years, has his own experienced view of what caused the accident:

> One of the most depressing aspects of the aftermath of the Princess's death is the proliferation of conspiracy theories, most saying that she was murdered by some agency or other, for one nefarious purpose or another. Yet her death is not comparable to the assassination of John F. Kennedy. There were no bullets; just a drunken driver, a bodyguard who was inexperienced in protecting such a high-profile principal, and an over-zealous boyfriend trying to impress. Like so many thousands of others each year, the Princess of Wales died in a mundane road accident.

For Frances, safely back on Seil but caught in a maelstrom of claim and counter-claim, theory and counter-theory and, above all, endless attempts to apportion blame, getting through each day became a trial. The strain began to show, and her daughters started seriously to worry about her. 'They insisted I had to have someone with me – "You mustn't be alone" – they were concerned.' Frances tried to placate Sarah and Jane, telling them, in a famous phrase of Diana's, 'You are my rocks,' while attempting to dismiss all the madness going on around her and insisting upon having her own 'space', upon being 'just Frances'. It was her way of dealing not only with her grief, but with the problems that Diana's death had brought in its wake. 'I was usually up at three in the morning playing CDs, with a large pot of tea. Well, you can't do that with someone else in the house. It's inhibiting. And there were plenty of people around here, great friends I could ring any time of the day or night. I wanted to have the space.'

It was not that simple, however. For the first eleven days after Diana's funeral, pressmen remained camped outside her home on Seil. She was desperate to go for long walks along her favourite beach, but she was adamant that she was not going to 'produce myself for a lens'. She resorted to hiding in friends' cars in order to get out at all, scuttling into them quickly as they drew up at her door. She found the physical demands of this existence quite exhausting. 'When something like this [Diana's death] happens which is totally unexpected, you are, to all intents and purposes, reasonably rested, normal, well nourished, so you have a residue of strength. But that evaporates very quickly, then you flounder, you don't eat . . . you become fairly unhealthy.'

Yet even when the press drifted away and Frances was able to get out without being pursued, she was still rarely able to be truly on her own. Going out to do everyday things became a trial, for the public mourning continued and she would never again enjoy the luxury of anonymity. It seemed that the whole world had known her daughter and wanted to talk about her death, and their own sense of loss.

> It's quite odd how many people will come up to you and say they felt very kindly and admiringly of Diana, but can you imagine if you see someone you have never met, who's a total stranger, walking around a supermarket and you happen to know their child has died . . . I've spent more time consoling, trying to help people in tears talking about Diana . . . I know that her life was so high-profile and that's very, very humbling . . . [but] it's very tough as her mum.

Always strong when together, the Spencer family tried to become more united than ever. The fiercely protective bond that Frances felt towards her surviving children intensified, now that two of the five she had borne were dead. They too were being bombarded with, and battered by, the incessant outpourings of the media and its – and the public's – apparently insatiable need for answers. Frances's unswerving loyalty was to be severely questioned in the ensuing months, however. Charles Spencer's relationship with his wife Victoria, which had been in trouble for some time, was now in terminal decline. It was also becoming embarrassingly public. Despite the fact that the couple lived a few miles apart in fashionable areas of Cape Town, matters were going from bad to worse. With divorce proceedings already in progress, Victoria had remained behind to look after the children rather than attend Diana's funeral, something that inevitably alerted the press to the idea that all was not well in Lord Spencer's personal life.

Charles's affair with Chantal Collopy had hit the headlines and it was rumoured – and reported – that he had had up to a dozen extramarital affairs during a fairly brief marriage. Although these alleged liaisons were strenuously denied by Charles's PR adviser, Shelley-Anne Claircourt, in the end the mud began to stick. Charles upped his financial offer to his estranged wife several times in an attempt to avoid being embarrassed in court, but each increase was dismissed as derisory. Victoria was requesting a lump-sum payout of £3.75 million ($5.63 million); however, her husband was offering only £300,000 ($450,000), a further sum towards expenses, and her five-bedroom bungalow in Cape Town. The gap between the two figures was immense, and a vitriolic court case loomed large. It would, inevitably, be widely reported and commented on.

Less than three months after standing in front of the world to declare his love for Diana, Charles Spencer was seated before a solitary judge playing hard ball in order to retain as much of his cash as he could. It was a dirty fight, and one that did nothing to maintain the dignity of the Spencer name.

Charles, in a sworn affidavit, claimed that there were dangers in giving larger sums of money to Victoria. In his view, his estranged wife's anorexia and drug addiction might well resurface, if she were given the means to fund the latter. He therefore proposed to limit her income as an act of caring concern. This, he said, would reduce the likelihood of Victoria falling back into the hands of unscrupulous drug dealers, and would also protect their children.

The reading of her husband's affidavit in court allowed Victoria carte blanche when it came to having her say. And she was not prepared to paint a pretty picture, either, accusing Charles of being domineering, critical and combative, as well as a philanderer. As the case progressed, the tension between the couple increased to an unbearable degree, and even more scandalous revelations were promised when her husband's former mistress, Chantal, was photographed standing side by side with Victoria on the steps of the court house. It may have been an unlikely alliance, but it threatened to tear Charles's case apart.

On 1 December 1997, Charles Spencer, perhaps rather wisely, raised his offer to his wife by £1.5 million ($2.25) and the warring parties walked out, both 'hoping their privacy would be respected'. It was a vain hope.

That same day, several British newspapers, keen to wreak revenge upon an earl who had told the world that they were largely responsible for the death of his sister, reported the court proceedings in every prurient detail. For Frances, the result was humiliating. One newspaper had obtained, and printed in full, a personal letter she had sent to her son back in February. Having flown home from a holiday spent staying with him in South Africa, her letter was note of thanks and support. She, of all people, knew what it was like to be betrayed by a parent, and she was not about to repeat history by taking sides against her son. Nevertheless, the letter was perceived as being highly critical of her daughter-in-law and unsympathetic towards her eating disorder. The most controversial part of the letter read:

. . . One of the biggest problems of anorexia is the combination of lies, mood and mind changes and irrational outpourings of self-centredness which seems to manifest itself in believing sometimes that she's pretty frail and at others that she's a lot stronger than appears . . .

Having some knowledge of the disease, Frances felt that she needed to protect her son from the effects of Victoria's anorexia. Two of her own daughters, Sarah and Diana, had suffered from eating disorders, and she knew practical advice and support were needed. Victoria was indeed a victim of the disease, and her psychological problems, if left untreated, might ricochet dangerously around the family. None the less, the letter was deemed harsh and uncaring by the media, although Frances would never have wanted to hurt Victoria, whom she had always liked. Having lost a daughter, she had not the least desire to alienate her daughter in law; equally, she was entitled to offer her support to her son.

It appeared that being 'just Frances' was not an option – at least, not where the media were concerned. In the most painful, and public, way possible, she had been given a lesson that her dead daughter had learned, to her cost, many years before: that the press may be poor friends, but they are implacable and often vindictive enemies.

CHAPTER FOURTEEN

————

Forgiveness

D IANA DIED A WEALTHY WOMAN. Her estate, worth over £21 million ($31.5 million), had to be handled with great care and sensitivity. Quite apart from the welfare of her two sons, she had had thousands of personal effects, many of them valuable, to consider when her will had been drawn up. These were not decisions that she could take lightly. To ensure that all her wishes would be carried out to the letter, she named as her executors the two women to whom she felt closest, little thinking that she would predecease them. These were her sister Sarah, whom she had idolized as a child and had later appointed as her lady-in-waiting; and her mother Frances, for whom she had always felt the profoundest love and respect.

Many commentators were to make much of the temporary estrangement between Frances and Diana in the four months before her death. Yet her will was proof that any rift was neither permanent, nor deep. It was the sort of row that commonly occurs between volatile, busy and headstrong women who also happen to be related, something that often makes any disagreement much more telling. Ken Wharfe, who for several years saw at first hand not only the closeness, but the similarities, between mother and daughter, ridicules the idea that their relationship had broken down beyond repair: 'Of course they had disagreements, as everyone does . . . but they were very much a united family. You don't entrust your estate to your family if you don't trust them.'

When pushed to comment, Frances refused to rise to the bait, saying of Diana that 'she and I knew and that's all that matters.' She felt no need to explain or defend herself in matters concerning her own daughter. She could not escape the fact that hurtful taunts about an estrangement had now, in the 'search-for-blame' atmosphere that followed the Princess's death, become part of her life, but she would deal with them in as diplomatic and discreet a way as she could.

Diana's estate included stocks, jewellery, cash (most of it from her £17 million [$25.5 million] divorce settlement), dresses, and other treasured possessions at Kensington Palace, many of them valuable. A personal 'Letter of Wishes for my Executors' was also included with her will which now reads touchingly given her sudden early death. In it she made special requests that 'should I predecease my husband he will consult with my mother with regard to the upbringing, education, and welfare of our children.' She also stipulated that her jewellery be given to her sons for their future wives, a sign not only of her close relationship with William and Harry, but also of a mother's thoughts for their future happiness. The letter was signed 'Diana' in her bold, rounded handwriting.

The will gave Sarah and Frances the power to divide up Diana's effects, after any personal bequests, 'at your discretion'. The vast majority was to be given to William and Harry, and the remainder distributed between her seventeen godchildren, something that was later to cause a good deal of controversy.

As an executor, Frances took her responsibilities very seriously. 'I do my utmost and always will to carry out her wishes,' she said. It was a desperately sad task, as well as a hard one, considering the vast number of personal notes to friends, the memorabilia of her life as well as her most private correspondence.

Throughout it all, Diana's butler, Paul Burrell, gave considerable help, and in recognition of his efforts the Spencer family decided to bequeath a generous sum from Diana's estate to him. He was also asked to sit on the board of a memorial fund, headed by Sarah, which was established shortly after Diana's death to raise and distribute money to the charities and other good causes that the Princess had either supported, or might have supported. In the six months after her death, more than £13 million ($19.5 million) was disbursed in grants by the Diana, Princess of Wales Memorial Fund. Money from the public flooded into the fund, and soon its trustees were grappling with how best to administer the vast amount raised for worthy causes. They ran into trouble, however, after accepting a sponsorship deal, worth £250,000 ($375,000) to the fund, from Flora Margarine. When this became public knowledge, there was uproar, and the deal was labelled 'tasteless' and 'vulgar' when people saw the Princess's stylized signature emblazoned on the margarine tubs, which appeared in March 1998. This tricky period was made worse when the trustees went on to strike a deal with the giant pools company Littlewoods, giving permission for Diana's image to appear on gambling scratchcards, in return for more money paid to the fund.

All too quickly a mass market emerged, desperate to cash in on Diana's image, for an association with her, however spurious or inappropriate, seemed to guarantee sales and profits. As the memorial fund struggled with how best to raise and distribute money, while at the same time protecting

Diana's memory and legacy, many unscrupulous manufacturers jumped on the bandwagon. It became hard to establish what was authentic – in other words, licensed by, and with a proportion of the proceeds going to, the fund. In May 1998 both the Princess's estate and the memorial fund filed a lawsuit at the US District Court in Los Angeles against the Franklin Mint for failing 'to obtain consent to use Princess Diana's identity and trademark' and embarking 'on a campaign to profit from Princess Diana's death'. It was claimed that the company, which sells 'collectables' largely through mail order, was exploiting her name 'like a vulture feeding on the dead'. The Franklin Mint happily sold thousands of dolls, jewellery and plates using Diana's name and image, and claimed that some proceeds from the sale were going to the Great Ormond Street Children's Hospital.* Both the executors of her will and the trustees of the memorial fund, fed up with what they saw as the constant abuse of Diana's memory by manufacturers seeking to profit not only from her fame, but from her death, had decided to make an example of one of them. It was to prove a costly decision.

Meanwhile, the carping over what the fund should or should not authorize had become too much for Charles Spencer, who himself was in the throes of establishing at Althorp a museum dedicated to his sister's memory. He complained in the press that the memorial fund had lost its way and was taking her legacy downmarket into a series of degrading enterprises. Charles's criticism appeared to be directed firmly towards his oldest sister, who was still presiding over the fund, although he deliberately made his comments while Sarah was out of the country, hoping thereby to distance her from any blame.

Frances saw at once the danger in such public declarations. In order to prevent what was being widely reported as a family rift, she stepped in quickly to smooth the waters. Interviewed by the *Daily Mail*, she strenuously denied any difference of opinion between her children, saying, 'Since Diana's death my children and I have constantly discussed how we can best care for William and Harry and protect their mother's memory. It has been a hurtful hazard that in trying to give our collective best, we have been quoted as being at odds.'

It was almost unavoidable that, given the trauma of Diana's sudden death, emotions should have run high in her family. From bitter experience, Frances knew that keeping busy was the key to recovery, and knew, too, that her surviving children were fortunate to have young children to distract them and help them focus on other aspects of life. 'I was thrilled they had children,'

---

* In November 2002, the Franklin Mint confirmed that it had donated £1 million ($1.5 million) to the hospital, matching the fund's donation.

she said, 'because children are hungry, need clothes, need the school run, need the extras.' None of them doubted that the best way to pull together as a family was, as Frances believed, by being 'totally united, willingly and definite on preserving Diana's memory and looking after William and Harry in any way that we can.'

Frequently the focus of the Spencers' attention centred not on Diana and the remembrance of her, but on Frances herself. Her children became increasingly concerned at her isolation, and expressed considerable concern at her desire for solitude. Frances steadfastly assured them that she had been living perfectly happily on Seil for many years, and that this was how she wished to carry on. There was slightly more to it than that, as she said later: 'I had to explain to them quite softly that living on my own was what was normal for me . . . I didn't for a long time feel strong enough to spend time with my children.' In the end, Sarah, Jane and Charles accepted her arguments and their fretting about her diminished.

It is hardly surprising that, for a time, she lacked the reserves of energy and fortitude to see overmuch of her children. All of them were a comfort to her, but all were a reminder of Diana and of her loss, each child displaying something of their sister through some family trait or characteristic. There was another important factor, however. They knew of the row between mother and daughter that had not been resolved before Diana died, and the anguish which, as a result, their mother must now be feeling. Worse still, public knowledge of this estrangement left Frances exposed as she had never been before. She had lived for thirty years with the stigma of having been labelled 'the Bolter'; now she faced rumour and innuendo from critics wishing to inflate her differences with Diana in the months before the fatal car crash in Paris. Many branded her guilty of ill treating her daughter, and a bad mother. For Frances this brought a desperate sense of déjà vu.

Faced with constant images of and articles about Diana in the press and on television and radio, coping with her death became even harder for the family. The obsession reached new peaks when a series of television documentaries and one-off programmes about the so-called conspiracy theories surrounding her death, or about 'the legacy of the Princess of Wales', were aired on prime-time television. Even in death, Diana continued to generate colossal worldwide interest. Sometimes it was almost too much for Frances to bear, and never more so than when faced with the astonishing crassness and thoughtlessness of some commercial interests:

> I got three long videos from a TV company – their letter said 'Examples of our work'. They're apparently doing 'The Best! The Only! The Authoritative!' documentary on Diana – and they need my help. But they aren't getting it –

I'm going to give one of my neighbours the videos so they can use them as blanks. Then they [the company] will get a postcard if they are lucky – and if I feel like it – saying 'No Thank You!'

Her determination to remain alone continued to worry her children, so that she eventually offered a compromise: she would see them all on a regular basis, but visits would be kept short. 'I felt very strongly that we were best off seeing each other very often but not spending too much time together.'

Frances, unhappy, tired, disoriented and with almost no interest in food, still tried to come to terms with her sorrow. Yet grief is an emotion that takes each individual differently, and has no timetable. Her resilience remained at rock bottom, and she compared her condition to being 'wounded'. 'One morning will be slightly better, you can make up your mind and do something for half an hour and the next day you can't do anything. It's snakes and ladders for a very long time.'

One moment of profound peace, and one she recollected later during an address she gave at a memorial mass for Diana at Oban Cathedral, was of the day after her daughter had been buried at Althorp, when she had rowed herself across to the Round Oval (as a measure against intruders, the temporary bridge had already been removed). Although nervous about talking in public when her emotions were so raw, Frances wanted to share what she had gained from the experience in the hope that to do so might ease her grief and comfort others.

Dressed in an elegant black and pink suit with a pearl choker around her neck and a large cross hanging beneath it, she spoke eloquently for ten minutes about her loss. Selfless as ever, she included the two other families who were also suffering the terrible pain of bereavement after that fateful night in Paris. Some 500 mourners heard her words of comfort:

> I come here solemnly to pray not just for my beloved daughter, but for the others tragically killed and their families . . . I know that grief has no agenda, no timetable. In life there will be dark tunnels with just the occasional rainbow. I also know that the ache will never go away, but that there will be gentler, kinder days.
>
> Charles asked if I wanted him to row me across to the island where Diana rests, and at that moment I declined. But later that morning [the day after the funeral], walking in the gardens, I was drawn to the lake. The boat looked overwhelmingly tempting so I rowed myself across to the island. As I rowed back I noticed a thin covering of weed on the water cut in two by the boat. I looked back and saw it join like a curtain as a lone swan glided past. At that point I could feel my beloved Diana was at peace. Her earthly life was short but

complete. I knew then that all she had to do was completed; and that all was well. Very well.

Her powers of forgiveness, her complete absence of bitterness and the faith which has sustained her are rare and remarkable qualities. Moreover, Frances gratefully acknowledges her own fortune: 'It is a wonderful and warming surprise to me that I have not felt, and do not feel, anger or blame toward anybody or anything over Diana's death.'

What did disturb her, however, were the continued analysis, and often reinterpretation, of the reports about Diana's medical condition after the crash and her final moments. She found Mohamed Fayed's claims about her daughter's last words and wishes especially hard to stomach. It became apparent that he believed he was being persecuted by the British government, and he continued to ram home at every opportunity the theory that his son had been assassinated by British secret-service agents to prevent him marrying Diana. He even suggested that the couple were already engaged when they died. Through the press, Frances sought to reassure a bemused and confused public on at least one point: 'She did not suffer at all. There have been many stories in the press which have led people to believe differently which has been distressing to many people. But believe me, my knowledge comes first hand from the people who cared for Diana in Paris – she did not suffer at all.'

Mohamed Fayed's dislike and distrust of the French investigation team and the British authorities and Establishment were gathering momentum, and he was now turning his wrath on the Spencers. Having lost his son in the crash, he was heavily implicated in the chaotic security arrangements surrounding Dodi and the Princess on the night of 31 August 1997. Fayed was also the employer, ultimately, of the drunk driver, Henri Paul. In these circumstances, it was Frances who should have been furious with him.

These two bereaved parents came face to face in June 1998 at the Palais de Justice in Paris, where they were to hear initial findings of the report into their children's deaths. This was the first time since Diana's funeral that they had been in the same building. It was a tense moment as both sat on the same bench, with different agendas. Fayed tried repeatedly to engage Frances in conversation by staring directly at her. She refused to be drawn, wishing to listen carefully to the judge. This infuriated Fayed who, as a lifelong friend of Johnnie Spencer and Raine (who had been appointed to the Harrods board), had never had a favourable view of Frances. To his mind, her refusal to speak to him – in part compounded by the falsehoods he had propagated about Diana's last words and wishes – proved his point exactly, and on leaving the court he launched a scathing personal attack on Frances: 'I'm a working-class guy, but she thinks she is the Queen of Sheba. If she . . . doesn't want to talk to ordinary people like me, it's up to her. She's a snob.'

That, however, was just the overture, for he now unleashed a torrent of abuse upon her. A few days later he continued the attack with a statement almost as remarkable for its inaccuracy as for its spite:

> She did not give a damn about her daughter, and her daughter did not give a damn about her. If you leave your child when she's six how can you call yourself a mother? Diana's mother thinks she is part of the royal family yet before she married Johnnie she was nothing . . . Diana's mother left her when she was six to run off with another man. As far as Diana was concerned she did not exist. Where was she when her daughter needed her?

He went on to declare that he had been so upset by the hearing's evidence he had been forced to leave the inquiry four times, while Frances remained in her place throughout – the implication being that Frances did not care, as he did, about either his son, or her own daughter. This was a slur too many for Frances. She had learned from bitter experience that there is a time to fight back. Now it had come. Forever protective of her children, she abandoned the dignified silence she had maintained for months and nailed Fayed's lie, saying what was in her heart. 'He never left the inquiry. I don't have to answer to him. Why do you think Diana made me an executor of her will? It's because I am trustworthy. And I am horrified by people who keep blethering on about being her friend. For me trust does not end with the death of a person . . .'

The investigation rumbled on, and Fayed's claims became even more dramatic and – except to those who love conspiracy theories – even more extreme. He vowed to obtain and submit to the French court a CIA file on Diana as proof positive that her death was no accident. While he, for whatever reasons of his own, pursued a lost cause, however, several families recently bereaved by an appalling fishing tragedy in Scotland, became incensed by the false depiction of Frances. Just weeks after Diana's death, the trawler *Sapphire* had sunk during a North Sea storm, leaving three families in Peterhead bereft and grieving. Despite her own suffering, Frances befriended them. The wives and mothers of the dead fishermen immediately responded to the slur on her character contained in Fayed's outburst. Isobel Stephen, who lost her twenty-nine-year-old son, Adam, told a journalist:

> My son was born on 6 July and Diana was born on 1 July, so we've [she and Frances] talked a lot about birthdays and our children. Frances is dreading anniversaries like Diana's birthday and the accident . . . Both of us found Mother's Day quite an ordeal, but she still sent me a lovely little card with a

note saying, 'Thinking of you,' and then she rang . . . We think the world of Frances. She's so kind and it's not for show – it's straight from the heart.

Mrs Stephen concluded, 'We've never told anybody about our relationship with Frances. But when Al Fayed said those things about her it made us all very angry. I felt like hitting the TV.'

By her sensible, quiet compassion, Frances demonstrated that tragedy is a universal human condition, and that it strikes randomly and regularly – and has no respect for fame or fortune. While Fayed fought an elaborate personal crusade, and other commentators aired theories about almost every conceivable aspect of the Princess's death, Frances made clear her acceptance of a tragic yet simple fact – her daughter had died in the most ordinary of ways, in a road traffic accident.

That was indeed the conclusion of the exhaustive two-year French investigation. On 3 September 1999, Judge Hervé Stéphan decided that all criminal charges be dropped against the photographers who had been present on the night of the crash. The 32-page report, compressed down from over 10,000 pages, concluded that the accident was 'due to the fact that the driver of the car was inebriated and under the effects of drugs incompatible with alcohol, which did not allow him to maintain control of his vehicle.' Henri Paul was therefore primarily responsible, but so was Dodi Fayed, albeit to a lesser extent, for allowing him (in fact, telling him) to drive. The photographers, although they escaped charges, were also implicated by their actions, which 'raised moral and ethical questions'. Furthermore, by their 'continuous and insistent presence' around the Princess, they had caused Dodi 'to make decisions that, however imprudent, were a response to being hounded'.

While Fayed, disgusted by this verdict, which contained not a scintilla of evidence of a plot to kill Diana, carried his fight to the Court of Appeal, Frances still refused to cast blame, feeling only deep sympathy for the family of the driver, marked by public opprobrium. 'My heart aches for the family of Henri Paul. I feel of all the three bereaved families his family have the sorest ache of all. I pray for all the families involved.'

Charles Spencer, on behalf of the Spencer family, thanked the French authorities for 'the time and effort they have put into the investigation and I respect the legal conclusions that have been reached.' Buckingham Palace said nothing.

If, for one grandmother of the future King, 1992 was an *'annus horribilis'*, then for the other grandmother the three years from 1996 to 1998 must have been *'anni terribiles'*.

All the setbacks Frances had suffered through the late 1980s and early 1990s seemed to reassert themselves as Diana's marriage came to an end. Being used as a constant support and repeatedly asked for advice by her daughter could at times be wearing. Nor did mother and daughter always see eye to eye on everything. From the time of her own divorce from Peter, Frances started to drink, possibly on occasion more than was either sensible or good for her, and Diana disapproved both of this and her smoking. Speaking of his visits to Seil with the Princess, Ken Wharfe recalls only friendship and hospitality, rather than over-indulgence:

> We used to go down to this oyster bed with a bottle of Pinot Grigio and enjoy ourselves. Wine was enjoyed within a social framework and there was never a problem. But I suppose if you're stuck there on your own mulling over all the problems Frances was faced with, then it's no wonder one bottle became a second bottle – but she was not a drunk.

In April 1996, as lawyers acting for Diana and Prince Charles entered negotiations over the details of the divorce, a registered letter, addressed to Frances, arrived at Callanish. It was a time of immense pressure as the royal family fought hard to distance themselves from Diana's damaging outbursts, and Frances found the role of supporting her distressed and often paranoid daughter extremely hard. Nothing had prepared her, however, for this latest in a long line of sideswipes that seemed to keep appearing out of the blue.

Frances opened the letter, and was appalled. A book, the letter read, called *Diana on the Edge: Inside the Mind of the Princess of Wales*, was about to be published. Its text suggested, as the letter went on to say, crudely, that Diana's bulimia was the result of sexual abuse as a child. The book's authors, who had sent the letter, demanded to know if Frances could confirm whether the Princess of Wales had been subjected to such violation while growing up.

Barely able to believe what she was reading, and shocked to the core, Frances took a drink to steady her nerves. She had been all but forced out of her daughter's life almost thirty years earlier, and now authors felt that they had the right to ask her, if, after she had left, Diana had been sexually molested. It was one thing for journalists and writers to publish material about her daughter, even though much of that material was biased, irrelevant, or just plain wrong; it was quite another to think that there was some sort of open season on every aspect, real or imaginary, of Diana's life. The offence and sense of violation she felt at such outrageous suggestions were overwhelming, while the implications against her former husband, Johnnie Spencer, were profoundly disturbing. These controversial, and subsequently widely discredited, views caused Frances enormous distress and led to events later that day.

Frances was stopped by a police officer in Oban after she stumbled while getting out of her car. Suspecting that she had been drinking, PC Iain Duncan and a colleague asked her to come to the police station, where a blood sample was taken. It was noted that her eyes looked bloodshot – hardly surprising, considering that the letter she had just received had reduced her to tears. The breathalyser reading, however, showed that her blood/alcohol level was over the legal limit, and she was duly charged with driving under the influence of alcohol.

During the court case six months later, Frances said of the letter, 'It was very upsetting, I cried for a long time.' She also explained why her eyes looked so bloodshot – 'I've got big eyes and they go red when I cry.' Despite the mitigating circumstances, however, the judge had to stick to the law, and imposed a fine of £400 while banning her from driving for a year. She accepted the punishment gracefully and left the court without any further comment.

Incidents that brought her to the notice of the media were becoming commonplace in Frances's life, although the pain that much of the reporting caused her never diminished. At this time, more than ever, her life and Diana's were converging. In the light of the drink-drive charge, Frances became an easy target over the ensuing months for constant smearing in the press, with many writers condemning her once more as 'the Bolter'. A whispering campaign began branding her as a drunkard. Then, as though brandishing proof that relations between the Princess and her mother were going astray, the press latched on to the estrangement between the two after Frances's *Hello!* interview in May 1997, as though it were some irreparable breakdown.

Less than four months later, Diana was killed, and throughout the following year, 1998, Frances laboured, under the often almost overwhelming burden of her grief, to rebuild her life. *Anni terribiles* indeed.

After Diana's death, it was suggested by the Palace that the title Her Royal Highness be reinstated posthumously. Returning her courtesy title was a way of reclaiming for the monarchy the Queen of Hearts and her supporters in the republican fervour that followed her death. Suggestions that Frances's comments had caused a rift of epic and unmendable proportions between mother and daughter were again scotched when the Spencers refused the Palace's offer; if the courtesy title had meant so much to Diana, they would undoubtedly have agreed. The reports of Diana's fury at losing the title had been exaggerated, her reactions not as deep as the tabloid papers would have had people believe. Ironically, by the time of her death, she had come round to her mother's view, and no longer cared about losing the royal prefix.

Buckingham Palace, back-pedalling rapidly, issued a statement, confirming that it had 'consulted the Spencer family on the afternoon of her funeral on this matter. Their very firm view was that the Princess herself would not have wished for any change to the style and title by which she was known at the time of her death. The Spencer family itself also did not wish for it to be changed.'

On 1 July 1998, on what would have been Diana's thirty-seventh birthday, Althorp was reopened to the public, having been closed for months while work was carried out on the museum to Diana's memory. Fearing problems with souvenir hunters, even rather ghoulish ones, Charles Spencer installed a high-level security system around Diana's resting place, and several slabs of metal were buried on the island to confuse anyone using a metal detector to search for her coffin. A memorial bearing a black marble silhouette of Diana had been established in the summerhouse temple, beneath which were inscribed the last words of Charles's eulogy, ending, 'Diana, whose beauty, internal and external, will never be extinguished from our minds.'

Apart from this deeply personal tribute, Charles Spencer has also converted Althorp's eighteenth-century stable block, once home to more than a hundred horses and forty grooms, into an exhibition of Diana's life and work. Although he attracted some criticism for the 'commercialization' of his sister's memory, as well as for the large increase in the entrance fee to Althorp, Charles was soon earning praise both for his efforts to mark her life and work and for the sensitive nature of the design and content of the exhibition, which occupies five rooms.

Even today, six years after Diana's death, people often leave the exhibition in tears, perhaps moved by the carpet of dried aromatic petals strewn across the floor (widely but wrongly assumed to be from flowers left in tribute at Kensington Palace and Althorp after the Princess died), or by the sight of her extraordinary wedding dress, or messages from people of all ages and stations of life in several books of condolence from all over the world laid out for people to read. Most simply absorb the atmosphere in silence, reflecting on what had once been, and what might have been.

Having once loathed the place, Frances is now a frequent visitor to Althorp, glad to spend holidays and weekends there in the company of her son and daughters and her grandchildren.

She walks round the grounds and, when the house is open, wherever she goes people nod, stare and point cameras in her direction. As she strolls from the main house towards her grandchildren playing in a fenced-off private area, several visitors run towards her. Close enough to touch her, some want to talk while others still feel the need to hug. Frances refuses no one.

To the sounds of the children playing in the background, she attempts to extricate herself from the small crowd. Ever polite and understanding, nevertheless the strain shows a little in her face. A film crew in the grounds hurries to capture the moment. A walk that should have taken Frances a matter of minutes has turned into an epic engagement.

Diana's burial at Althorp changed the character of a place that held many unhappy memories for Frances. By a bitter irony, the death of her daughter meant that she was now able to draw a line under that part of her life, a time when she had been a viscountess trapped in a fading marriage. She could at last forgive the main players in the drama, for Johnnie, eighth Earl Spencer, and Ruth, Lady Fermoy were both long gone. Althorp had become, for her, a very different place in the twenty-first century; it was finally 'cosy, comfy' and full of children's laughter. It was also safe in the hands of her son, Charles.

Frances was about to embark upon a new stage of her life, although it was one that she had never expected to have to face. She felt no bitterness over her daughter's death, and apportioned no blame for it; instead, a year after the accident, she was ready to begin again, aware that the focus of her life had shifted.

'Now we live without Diana,' she said.

CHAPTER FIFTEEN

Like Mother, Like Daughter

SINCE THE DEATH OF THE PRINCESS OF WALES, many have seen in Frances the woman Diana would have become. Physically they were strikingly similar – tall and long-legged, with large azure eyes and a luxuriant shock of blonde hair. At 5 feet 10 inches they were the same height and build, both elegantly tall. Diana's habit of walking with her head tilted down was often thought to be the result of an adolescent embarrassment at being taller than her suitors, while others claimed that it was because she did not want people to see her facial expressions. Her habit of keeping her eyes downcast led quickly to her being dubbed 'Shy Di.' Frances, however, says that once Diana came into the public eye she became worried that journalists would attempt to misquote her, and so made sure that she was never overheard whispering, while by keeping her head down 'no one could ever read her lips'.

As Diana moved towards her forties, comparisons between her and her mother were made with increasing frequency. This was hardly to be wondered at, for Frances had been a huge influence in her life. Theirs was above all a lively and open relationship, in which both women would speak their minds, or 'spit it out' as Frances puts it. She adds: 'Well, of course one has arguments. Who on earth wants a wishy-washy mother? There are occasions when you have to admit that you may have been right or may have been wrong, [although] I do think repetitive apologies are a form of self-pity.'

Frances's emotional attachment and commitment to Diana were unquestionable. They found it easy to be in each other's company because they shared so many characteristics. Both were independent and high-spirited, although Frances had the edge when it came to repartee, as Ken Wharfe notes: 'I don't think the Princess had the wit her mother had but they enjoyed each other's company.' And they loved to laugh – the sound of Diana's giggles mixed with Frances's throaty laughter, once heard, could never be forgotten.

Both Frances and Diana had been born in the master bedroom at Park House, to the left of the grand sweeping staircase, overlooking the cricket pitch. Rumours that the room is cursed may have some basis in truth, as Frances explains: 'Until this day only three people have been born there: my son, my daughter and myself, all in the same room and I'm the sole survivor. It's really curious and one can only have a question mark about it.'

At some point after the Spencers left, the Sandringham Estate leased Park House to the Leonard Cheshire Trust, and it is now an hotel for the infirm. Frances returned briefly to take a last look round before the house was converted. 'I couldn't get through the front door and I remembered a broken window lock so I climbed in. One of the workmen recognized me from a long time ago and exclaimed: "I think I've seen a ghost."' Frances laughed, replying, 'No . . . it's just me!'

Frances and Diana both grew up at Park House, and both went to the same school, West Heath, in Kent. As young women, they moved in the same aristocratic and royal circles, and even their social life was similar, for they loved ballet, opera, and evenings with their girlfriends. They even shared a friendship over two generations. Frances and Susie Barrantes became friends as teenagers; a generation later, Diana was instrumental in introducing Susie's daughter, Sarah Ferguson, to Prince Andrew, and thereby gained a much-needed friend and ally within the royal family. Sarah herself explained that 'Our mothers had been in school together, where Mum and Frances had some legendary burping competitions. Diana and I hit it off and soon we were lunching together once a week.'

Although both demonstrated a caring side to their natures from an early age, despite the privilege to which they had been born, that wild capacity for naughtiness in Frances was very much a part of Diana's character. Once, staying at Balmoral, and extremely bored after dinner, she and Sarah Ferguson, still in their evening gowns and grand shoes, skidded and bumped quad bikes over the immaculate greens of the golf course. Then, discovering the Queen Mother's Daimler unoccupied and with the keys in it, Diana clambered in, donned a chauffeur's hat and started the engine. Sarah, who climbed in with her, remembers the occasion fondly: '"Faster, Smithers!" I commanded. Diana sank her foot down, and we did gravel spins all the way around the castle. We eased the Daimler back into the garage – no one had seen us; we never got caught for that one.'

Of her schooldays, Diana said, 'I was very naughty in the sense of always wanting to laugh and muck about rather than sit tight looking at the four walls of the schoolroom.' (After one incident at West Heath, which ended with the arrival of the police, Frances said to Diana, 'I didn't think you had it in you.') The Spencer children's nanny at Park House, Mary Clarke, was made aware of her mischievous nature from the start, and found she needed a firm hand to control her. Diana was known for throwing any new nanny's clothes on to the rooftops, as well as for being behind a habit of locking them in the lavatory.

At home, Frances remains mischievous, and still has a girlhood penchant for fancy dress. Her photograph album contains page upon page of comical pictures of her with a group of women friends, all dressed in leotards, stockings and tiaras. Shots of one raucous weekend away show Frances playing Neptune, her long legs clad in fishnet tights, and a fishing rod in her hand. She is glad of a chance to let her hair down, and especially to laugh. Sometimes, however, the funniest moments happen in the most unexpected places. On one occasion she had to attend a funeral on one of the Hebridean islands, which meant rising at 4.30 a.m. for the journey, since ferry crossings would be involved. Not at her most sociable at that time of the morning, she headed for the ferry's lavatory to put the final touches to her hair and make-up in preparation for such a solemn occasion. As the boat rolled and pitched, however, the door jammed and Frances was locked in tight. She banged on the door and yelled for help, but the ferry's engines drowned out her cries, and no one came. Resourceful as ever and determined not to be defeated, Frances, dressed in solemn mourning, managed to climb out of a window 'the size of a microwave', emerging on deck with a huge smile on her face. Naturally she made the service with not a hair out of place and no ladders in her tights.

Perhaps Frances's greatest gift is her natural ease with people, something that Diana undoubtedly inherited from her. From the moment Frances looks at someone and begins to talk, she communicates on their level, without pomposity or airs and graces. She will say unexpectedly ordinary things to break the ice, such as how her grandchildren insist on this or that cereal for breakfast when they come to stay, or how inept she is when she struggles to use a computer. This has the effect of immediately breaking down a person's reserve, allowing him or her to see beyond the courtesy title and the royal and aristocratic connections to the person beneath. Frances is 'grand' only when using her title may lend credibility and bring much needed publicity to a cause, as when she demonstrated with a placard to save a local school. There can be no doubt that Diana acquired the ability to talk to 'ordinary' people and enjoy their company from her mother. Ken Wharfe recognized this gift in both women: 'The great thing about the Princess was she came into the royal family as a commoner and she maintained her roots. She capitalized on her strengths, which were getting to the heart of ordinary people. This was a quality that she inherited from her mother.'

Yet sadly, both also came up against the other side of public admiration – indeed, adoration in the Princess's case – when they recognized people's often impossibly high expectations of them. Frances sums it up thus: 'I can't give them more than myself, and sometimes I think, "Gosh, they think I am going to wave a magic wand or something."'

It is true that, in both mother and daughter, their care for others masked in each a will of steel. Both were very much their own women, perhaps even to their own detriment. Diana showed her mettle when she absolutely refused quietly to accept her husband's infidelity, feeling herself being used as a 'hired womb'. She struggled, too, to bring the royal family headlong into the modern age, and it is a bitter irony that that process of modernization only really got under way after her death – and to some extent because of it.

Frances's search for love saw her facing an Establishment determined to demolish her character, while her mother turned against her simply to retain favour with the royal family, and that same Establishment. The experience almost destroyed Frances, yet she came back stronger, to form loving relationships with each one of her children.

Whereas Diana had her mother to turn to for advice and emotional support throughout her life, Frances was all but abandoned after her divorce from Johnnie. Her father long dead and her mother wholly unsympathetic, she had only Peter for support, and as a result was forced to look inward for her strength, in time becoming more self-reliant and more trusting of her own judgement. As painful as this process was, it gave her enormous reserves of sympathy and good sense, as well as a wealth of experience to tap into when Diana needed her. At thirty-six, however, Diana did not have the years of experience, and much less the wisdom, that Frances had acquired by the same age. By then Frances had given birth to five children, of which one died shortly after birth; lost another child to a miscarriage about which she kept silent; married twice; been forced to fight through the courts for custody of her children, and lost; suffered the rejection of her own mother; become a stepmother and moved away to live on a distant island. Yet during those dramatic and often disturbing times, Frances had found love. Although that love later soured, what remained was a complicated, intriguing and amusing woman with a growing sense of self-worth and of peace within and around her. In contrast, Diana's experience of life was cut short, although she showed signs of maturing, however late, into a strong, resilient woman like her mother. She might even have remarried, as Frances did, for at the time of her death she was still searching for love, and for the happiness she hoped it would bring.

There are other parallels. Both women fought to save their marriages, although both were forced in the end to recognize that being less famous than their partner is something that many men find hard to live with. Of her second marriage and its subsequent end, Frances said:

I think the pressure of it all was overwhelming and finally impossible for Peter. They [the press and public] didn't want him, they wanted me. I became Di's mum and not his wife . . . It's not self-pity or excuses, it is fact. I've seen exactly the same thing happen in other family marriages like Di's and Charles's. I do firmly believe that sort of pressure can't be sustained.

If Seil became a haven for Frances and also for her youngest daughter, holidays there also highlighted their love of children and their capacity for bringing out the best in them. These were happy times, made all the more idyllic because they allowed Diana to escape, if only for a time, the sadness of her marriage and the pressures of the Palace.

To a considerable extent, their absolute ease around children came from the childlike qualities that stayed with Diana throughout her life, and which Frances will always have. This 'Peter Pan gene' imbued mother and daughter with a sense of spontaneous fun. Diana delighted in taking her children on theme-park rides at home and abroad, or in watching them hare round on go-karts. Frances on her frequent trips to Lourdes with the Handicapped Children's Pilgrimage Trust would amuse the children by dressing up, sometimes, improbably, as Barbie, complete with 'satin shimmering peachy-pink jump suit and a long blonde wig'. Once, on the morning after one of these displays, a child asked Frances where her hair was. Thinking quickly, Frances replied, 'I cut it before breakfast.' The child retorted, 'You looked like a lady last night – but now you don't.' By this time Frances had pulled 'a scarlet baseball cap emblazoned with "Forever Friends"' over her eyes – 'not exactly designer chic for OAP grannies,' she laughed. 'It's covered in badges while I keep the rather more risqué ones firmly in the drawer.'

Certainly motherhood brought out the best in both women. They were liberal and loving with their children, while insisting on impeccable manners and respect for their elders and for traditional values. Yet both also recognized that making mistakes is part of growing up, necessary steps towards becoming a rounded person, but also a humane one. They set out to be friends with their children, rather than someone to be feared, a distant figure brought to the nursery just before bedtime, as had been the norm for upper-class children in Frances's era, and was the way that Prince Charles had been raised. They hugged and kissed their children, and were generous with their time and their praise. Spending time with them was a joy not a duty, so that as parents they were involved, interested and committed. Frances, having lost custody to Johnnie, was determined that her ties with her children would not be severed, and succeeded triumphantly, against considerable odds.

She has formed close relationships with all her grandchildren, seeing them all regularly and having considerable influence with them. There are happy

Christmas celebrations every year at Althorp, where members of each generation of the family meet. Of the family home that Charles has made of the great house, she says:

> I call it his Croft House and there are plenty of adult grandchildren and family to hang on to. The biggest grandson is 6 feet 7 inches. When I'm with him he calls me 'Shorty' and people look at him, not me. I look like a little dwarf beside him. You can't miss him. When he goes to Territorial Army camp he sleeps in a sleeping bag wearing his socks plus a bin liner.'

Relationships with men were not so straightforward, however. Both women married older men when they were almost the same age – Diana only just twenty and Frances not yet nineteen. Both had difficult relationships with their fathers-in-law; Jack, the seventh Earl Spencer, was a cold, unemotional man, while Prince Philip had little time for the fripperies of the most photographed woman in the world. These men walked in a society of duty and subjugation, a place that Frances and Diana found they had to escape in order to survive. Their husbands by comparison aged before their time, were often bullying, and refused to change their ways. Both women left their marriages by different routes, but the result was the same – freedom for their spirits to 'sing openly'.

It is an irony that Frances and Diana, both sharp of mind and fiercely independent, were born into a world in which women were subservient. They struck out against the established ethos of that world and each forged a route for herself, albeit at considerable personal cost. Having lost the first custody case, Frances attempted to divorce her husband on the grounds of cruelty only months before the 1969 Divorce Reform Act came into effect, at a time when proving cruelty within marriage required more substantial evidence than is the case now. As has been said, Erin Pizzey's fascination with the treatment of women in that era culminated in her writing a novel, *In the Shadow of the Castle*, based to some extent upon what she had read and heard about Johnnie Spencer's marriage and the treatment meted out to Frances. Through her novel, Pizzey, a leading campaigner on behalf of battered women, resolved to unveil the secret power held by the aristocracy and demonstrated in their ability to manipulate the legal system. As she says, of Frances's efforts to divorce Johnnie for cruelty: 'In those days you couldn't get a divorce, particularly on grounds of cruelty, unless you had masses of physical evidence. You just think to yourself this is why it [physical abuse of women] goes on, because at the top it's completely hushed up.'

Frances ultimately paid a high price for her temerity, losing her children. At that time, however, for a woman to accuse her titled husband in a court of law of such behaviour was unheard of. She was probably the most unexpected and unwitting pioneer for women's rights at that time. Pizzey believes that Frances suffered greatly because of the attitude taken by the courts in response to Johnnie's well-mustered counter-charges. As she says: 'Frances is a good mother, I imagine, or tried to be . . . My heart goes out to her, partly because in the world in which I live and work that was one of the most gross miscarriages of justice, which today still continues.' (Diana was herself to work for the cause of battered women, at one stage visiting a family refuge in Chiswick, west London, which, coincidentally, had been established by Erin Pizzey in the 1970s.)

Diana too struck out against the paternalism of the royal courts and palaces that had existed for centuries. She took on unpopular charities, insisting that her children accompany her on visits to shelters for the homeless and similar projects, rather than just on sanitized official visits; refused to accept her husband's mistress, unlike previous royal consorts in history; and spoke openly of her own fears and phobias. The image the public had of her was of someone real – warm, certainly, but also fallible, vulnerable and human. This is how her mother is, and how she raised her children to be.

Never afraid to become involved in difficult or unpopular issues that others, including the royal family, shied away from, Diana brought a new sense of purpose to her life when she lent her name and her patronage to unfashionable causes. By comparison, Ken Wharfe said of Frances: 'If you look at the charitable works that Frances has done without all the razzmatazz of her daughter, she has worked tirelessly and has done so all her life.'

Frances instilled in her children, and her youngest daughter in particular, a powerful sense of wanting to contribute to the world they lived in – not just by meeting dignitaries and shaking a few hands, but by offering practical support, especially to charities with low profiles, and those often held in low regard. Both women were drawn to the experience of working with and becoming close to some of the most disaffected or dispossessed groups in society. From the homeless to the handicapped, the diseased to the dying, Diana and Frances would always try to lend their time, their presence, their labour and their experience.

Like her daughter, Frances is prepared to go to extraordinary lengths to help, from getting up at 6 a.m. to tie hundreds of individual tartan bows for a charity, to speaking her mind about the erosion of fishing rights and its effect on local industry in Scotland. Just days before Diana's death a close friend drowned in the River Spey, and when asked by his widow if she would help by writing a tribute to be read at the funeral, Frances selflessly offered to read the address herself, making a 200-mile trip to do so. She publicly withdrew her support from the Conservative Party in view of their policies on commercial fishing rights, and undertook a local crusade against changes to fisheries law which seemed likely to make it far more difficult for fishermen to earn a living. As patron of the Mallaig and North West Fishermen's Association she has long been a champion of the underdog, as EU regulations and the effects of over-fishing continue to undermine what is still an important industry in Scotland. One secretary of the association commented: 'She often demonstrates her commitment to the fishing industry. She gives a lot of time and effort, not only on the political side but on the pastoral side of our association as well. She has managed to win the respect of the fishing industry here, despite some initial reservations.'

For Frances, as for Diana, sitting on the sidelines making small talk and looking pretty was never an option. Both felt a strong need to become involved and to work to effect change – to 'make a difference', as Diana put it.

Yet accompanying this tremendous energy and zest for life, themselves harnessed to a powerful sense of duty, there was also a darker side. Constant giving can mask insecurities, while to understand emotional pain in the way that Frances does, and Diana undoubtedly did, one must have felt it personally. In short, true empathy is born of experience. 'Pain is very personal,' says Frances, 'but when you have experienced it you know what it feels like.'

Both women's marked ability to empathize with often desperately unhappy or sick people was born of experience. On many occasions after doing their separate good works, Diana or Frances would return home alone, to a solitary dinner in front of the television. Each had given of herself throughout the day, but there was no one waiting for them at home to hear how things had gone or what they were feeling. In the course of the day each might have seen and heard much suffering, but there was no one to share their experiences with at night, to allay their anxieties or bolster their courage. Paradoxically, while the people they had tried to help thought Diana and Frances marvellous women who led glamorous and exciting lives, away from the spotlight there were, for both of them, times of deep unhappiness and loneliness. Characteristically, however, Frances refuses to pity herself, remarking, 'We all get bruised but I've never, ever envied anybody who experienced life as a warm bath. The bruises are necessary for happiness and knowing what happiness is, and not taking life for granted.'

At times of near unbearable strain, both women turned inward on themselves; in addition, Diana had for a time punished herself through binge eating followed by purging. Such actions might have been seen, to use a cliché, as cries for help, save that they were often undertaken secretly and alone. The public persona could not, at times, have been more different from the private. Diana admitted that 'I hated myself so much I didn't think I was good enough, I thought I wasn't good enough for Charles, I wasn't a good enough mother – I mean doubts as long as one's leg.'

Frances echoed these insecurities when she said, 'When you've had a long, hard time, the natural feeling is that you don't believe you can cope – which means you don't believe in yourself.'

Some similarities between Frances and Diana, though perhaps less arresting, were nevertheless quite marked. Both enjoyed close relationships with their younger brothers, to whom they displayed an almost motherly concern for their welfare. As a child, Frances found a natural ally in Edmund, three years her junior, and they undoubtedly shared a strong and trusting kinship. She described him as her 'little treasure', and was devastated by his suicide at the age of forty-five. They had enormous fun as children: 'we just knew every prank and made our own high spirits.' Sensitive by nature, Edmund would often ask Frances's advice long after they had grown up, and he trusted her judgement. He remained a favourite uncle of Diana's and his loss was deeply mourned. He is buried next to baby John, in a quiet corner of Sandringham churchyard, and his gravestone bears the same simple inscription, 'In Loving Memory'.

Charles Spencer's personality is very different from his uncle's. Confident and self-assured now, as a child he had clung to Diana's skirts and lived in her shadow, for she was outgoing and athletic where he was shy and studious.

Diana and Charles remained close right up until she was killed, although, as has been seen, they had the occasional row. She visited him after he moved to South Africa, and became close to his children, whom she loved. Despite their typically Spencer-like quarrels, Diana confirmed that she 'was never jealous of him. So I understand him.' For Charles, however, the unreality of his sister's death is hard to deal with. Even three years after she had been buried at Althorp, he was to say, 'I often think I must ring and tell her this and then I realize instantly that's not possible. I would want to tell her funny things – she had a good sense of humour – and positive things.'

In a curious twist that would have amused her, the tables have been turned, for now it is up to him to protect his elder sister.

Diana's passing has not diminished the bond between her and her mother. After her death, as Frances sorted through her daughter's belongings at Kensington Palace, she felt the other's presence. In the eerie susceptibility of recent death, Frances thought she could hear Diana impatiently drumming her fingers and wryly muttering, 'Oh . . . get on with it, Mum.'

CHAPTER SIXTEEN

Power of the Matriarch

FRANCES HAD BEEN FEELING TIRED and rather off-colour for many months. The effort of getting around began to cause her concern, although she initially put it down to the trials of growing older. It was more an irritant than a serious worry, she hoped, until she began to feel a slight, but noticeable wobble in her legs when she stood up. She tried to dismiss this as nothing more than an attack of light-headedness, or perhaps the effect of a nasty virus, but it continued and gradually worsened, becoming both persistent and troublesome. Shortly afterwards, while alone in the bungalow, she tripped over the edge of the sea-grass matting and fell heavily, wrenching her body and banging her head on the way down. Shocked and in pain, she could feel the swelling come up around her eyes. She called the doctor, who came and found that, despite the bruising, there was nothing broken, and told her to rest. 'I couldn't go out for over nine days,' she says. 'I ached all over.' As her black eyes began to fade she noticed that her face was still sore and discoloured. So she called out the doctor again who was highly amused 'when he realized I had been putting haemorrhoid cream on my face rather than the lotion prescribed! It went bright luminous and my skin is very tender pink. Hardly Max Factor!'

Her balance continued to deteriorate, and matters were made worse because she began to find eating increasingly difficult. She was having to chew her food many times before swallowing, otherwise she would feel that she was about to choke. Frances also knew that her speech was being affected. Sometimes she found it hard to articulate her words – the sounds would blend into each other so that people could not understand what she was saying. ' I was afraid,' she says honestly. 'Not of dying – but I am afraid of pain.' There seemed to be no pattern to the symptoms; they were random, almost chaotic, and crept up on Frances when she least expected them. They impinged upon her life, and were a sharp reminder of her own mortality. As she approached the age of sixty-five she described that imminent birthday as 'one to forget.' Always an active woman, she found the thought of infirmity quite shocking.

Too proud to admit that she had a problem, Frances kept her symptoms secret for a long time so as not to alarm anyone, especially her children. She hoped that the condition was transient, the result perhaps of stress or exhaustion, and tried to believe that it would fade over the following months. Yet no matter what she tried, nothing seemed to help.

She fell over again and again. Her legs just refused to do what she asked of them. Towards the end of the year 2000, she finally had to admit to herself that she needed help. Looking down across the sea from her sitting-room window she could make out the neat whitewashed building that housed the doctor's surgery.

Although nervous before seeing the doctor, Frances knew that it was impossible to go on as she was. In the event, her visit to the surgery was something of an anti-climax. After describing her symptoms and a brief chat, it was decided that she needed to be referred to a specialist. She realized that now the children had to be told. If they saw a photograph in a newspaper of her going into hospital, they would be dreadfully worried. She decided that, in telling them, she would make light of it – understate her symptoms, protect them from unnecessary fretting.

Frances underwent three weeks of extensive medical tests, and then saw a neurosurgeon. She travelled to London for more tests and consultations. In hospital for a brain scan, she was told to remove all her jewellery and made to lie absolutely still. As the nurse moved away, it dawned on Frances how absolutely alone and vulnerable she was. 'It's scary stuff. They put your head in a vice. It's hell. It's very noisy,' she complained afterwards. Confined inside the claustrophobic MRI (magnetic-resonance imaging) scanner, she suddenly felt very exposed as the machine took electronic images of her brain for thirty minutes.

Back home on Seil, waiting for the results of the scan proved just as nerve-racking. The experts had told her that such tests are used as much to eliminate the presence of a dangerous condition, as to identify others, but even so her mind ran through every frightening possibility. She prayed for strength. She talked with Janey. She tried to push the illness to the back of her mind and keep busy with other things, going to church, working on her charity projects. She pottered about in the kitchen, always a place that helped her to relax, making pot after pot of strawberry jam and orange marmalade, spooning them into recycled jars. Yet even that was becoming more difficult, and now she was frightened of falling and burning herself while carrying one of the heavy pans of scalding liquid.

By the time of her next appointment with the consultant in London, her nerve had begun to fail her and she felt she needed moral support, enlisting the help of her daughters Sarah and Jane. The three of them entered the clinic together, hoping that by acting in concert any potential bad news would be diluted, and then digested and discussed in detail. Her daughters' presence certainly made Frances feel more secure, for by now she had, understandably, become frightened – 'I took my daughters. I thought they could understand better than me.'

The results were conclusive. They showed that Frances has a progressive disease which affects her muscles. When they learned the news, in spite of the seriousness of the moment, and perhaps because of their collective anxiety, their first reaction was humorous. Sarah joked, 'What about HRT [hormone-replacement therapy]?' The consultant replied, 'No, that doesn't make any difference.' Then, with a perplexed look on his face, he added, 'Either way, I don't know whether to put her on it or take her off it.'

Frances was asked whether she wanted to see a speech therapist to try to improve her diction. Proud as ever, she replied emphatically, 'NO I do not.' Thinking that the hospital was trying to push her into treatment plans that she did not need, she exclaimed, 'You really are greedy, you lot.'

She had been hurt by suggestions that her slurring was in fact drunkenness, yet she refused to go public with her illness. She did not wish to 'come out', as she put it, just yet. She did, however, agree to aromatherapy and physiotherapy, both of which she found relaxing as well as therapeutic. She was also given an unexpected, if slightly embarrassing, boost when, in the middle of treatment, the physiotherapist, while examining her legs, blurted out, 'My . . . what a pair of pins you have!'

Frances's condition is not life-threatening, but it is limiting, and has also meant changes to her lifestyle and to the bungalow to accommodate her declining mobility. It is very important that she keep her bones and muscles exercised, although movement will become harder as the disease progresses.

For a woman who loves walking along the beach and hiking through the countryside, or flyfishing for salmon on the River Dee, the restrictions took some getting used to. Frances coped, however, aware that the illness was not life-threatening and reconciled to curtailing some of her usual physical activity. She took pleasure in simple things, in the company of family or visits to art galleries in Glasgow followed by a leisurely lunch, a favourite jaunt, especially when accompanied by a couple of her friends. She started to entertain more at home, as well, often lighting some of her huge array of scented and what she calls 'Catholic-kitsch' candles for atmosphere. It just takes her a little more time to do the cooking than before, because she can no longer flit around the kitchen as quickly as once she did.

Knowing that working her muscles and bones was important, she took up an exercise regime, since that was at least a positive step. Over a period of months she had her bungalow extended, and installed a step machine and an exercise bike in one of the new rooms, which became a kind of mini-gym. It enables Frances to work out every morning to a training programme carefully devised by her specialists, and designed to strengthen those famous legs.

The modifications to Callanish went a great deal further than a simple extension, however. The property has been transformed both inside and out. The sea-grass matting has been replaced by smooth wooden flooring which is easy to move across and has no edges to trip over. There is now a self-contained flat for grandchildren, guests or extra help if Frances ever needs it; two extra bedrooms with two single beds in each; a white fitted kitchen and cheerful combined sitting and dining area, in which there is a comfortable sofa, and a second bathroom. Light floods the bungalow from windows set into the roof, reflecting off the cream-painted walls. Large paintings, both modern and traditional, dominate some of the walls. The garden has been altered to remove the cumbersome steps that led to the front door, replaced with a new, gently sloping pathway. Frances marvelled at the amount of hardcore it took to get the area around the house level – 'tons of the stuff' – but is delighted with the results.

Meanwhile, Charles Spencer had become concerned that his mother's illness would progress more quickly unless some of the pressure was taken out of her life. He suggested appointing a public-relations consultant to handle the calls to her home from the media and others. Frances declined, however, still determined to keep as much control of her own life as she could. Despite her disability, she wants to continue, as far as possible, as before, while her philosophy remains to live every day as fully as she can.

In her typically straightforward fashion, she decided to inform those whom she considered important to her of her illness, and set about doing it herself. In a modest and upbeat fashion, she wrote: '. . . the intellectual part of my brain (bet that is small!) is absolutely fine and healthy, and the extensive blood tests have eliminated the possibility of having various, heavy illnesses.'

She went on to reveal the full nature of the illness, saying that she now suffered impaired balance and slurred speech, while injecting as much humour into her letter as the situation allowed. 'I hope to be both safe and independent,' she went on, adding, 'The condition is permanent and untreatable.' In conclusion, she wrote, 'I think it is fantastic that I don't have a life-threatening illness.'

Undoubtedly, the death of Diana and the stress of dealing with her own grief, quite apart from coping with the voracious and importunate media, had taken their toll. As Frances adjusted to the physical limitations of her illness, the mental anguish of losing Diana continued. Her mantra had become simply, 'You have to endure what you have to endure.'

It was fortunate that she has been blessed with such inner resilience, for her views are now more than ever sought since Diana's death, and especially over Mrs Camilla Parker Bowles. Speculation in the tabloids remains very high as to whether the latter will become the next wife of the Prince of Wales and consequently stepmother to Frances's grandchildren, Princes William and Harry. As a result, Frances is constantly asked her opinion on many aspects of her former son-in-law's relationship with his mistress of many years. Whether Camilla is a potential stepmother or not, Frances has no intention of giving up on her grandsons.

It can be said that disdain for Camilla Parker Bowles is one thing that Frances shares with the Queen. For this woman was not simply a problem within the Windsor and Spencer families – at times, if the newspapers were to be believed, her presence in Prince Charles's life seemed to threaten a constitutional crisis. The mere fact of her existence scandalized both the Court and public opinion, and continues to be a source of embarrassment to the monarch. It seems clear, too, that recent concessions from the Queen allowing Camilla to enter royal circles are far more a sign of resigned acceptance and of responding to the advice of courtiers, especially those in Prince Charles's camp, than of any growing liking or approval.

Yet neither the Queen nor Frances, despite their own feelings, can force her to go away. Marriage looks unlikely without the Sovereign's permission (which seems equally unlikely), leaving Charles with the prospect of having to wait to be crowned King before marrying his mistress. There is another option open to him, namely a morganatic marriage, whereby Camilla would become his wife in name only, but she would have no claim on his property or his title, much less the succession. She would thus never become Queen Camilla, although she would be the wife of King Charles III.

Frances has little interest in, nor does she particularly care about, the personal happiness of the man who drove her daughter to despair. Camilla, however, irks her. Having been a thorn in Diana's side, she is now a persistent source of irritation in Frances's life. For Frances and the Queen, both in their own way powerful and influential women and both sitting at the head of polarized families now linked for ever by ties of blood, Mrs Parker Bowles remains *persona non grata*.

Frances vents her spleen by saving particularly savage newspaper cartoons of Charles and Camilla to giggle over with friends. She knows her behaviour is childish, but finds a certain satisfaction in mocking the couple who damaged and humiliated her daughter so publicly. Polls taken immediately after Diana's death showed Camilla's popularity to be at rock bottom; only 8 per cent of British people thought that she should even be considered as Queen. In the immediate aftermath, it was also reported that she suffered the humiliation of having bread rolls thrown at her by customers at her local supermarket. Even now, long after Diana's death, the road to public acceptability for the Prince and his mistress will be a long and stony one.

Being told that Camilla is being kept out of the limelight is dismissed by Frances as being 'fine'. She wants nothing to do with Mrs Parker Bowles. Despite having an extraordinary capacity for forgiveness, she offers no sympathy or understanding to this woman. Frances may live hundreds of miles from Highgrove, but the Prince is not unaware that she is still a forceful and formidable woman. Since Diana's death, and since he received the rough end of Frances's tongue at Prince Harry's christening, he is careful of upsetting his former mother-in-law, not least because his sons feel the utmost love and respect for her.

The Prince of Wales's charm offensive after Diana's death had begun with the judicious placing of stories designed to show what a good father he was. To be fair, he had always been a caring parent, and he redoubled his efforts, quick to be seen on photo shoots with the boys. He even started to include Frances in his plans, inviting her to Highgrove to spend time with William and Harry. She accepted, maintaining a pragmatic civility with the Prince while being more than happy to take any opportunity to see her grandchildren.

Her focus remains firmly on the boys. When, because of her illness, writing became too tiring, she improved her computer skills, sending them emails as a way of keeping in contact.

Fortuitously, in the mid-1990s Frances had bought a substantial property in Falkland, in Fife, some way north of Edinburgh. This ancient and beautiful village is tucked away at the foot of the Lomond Hills, and Frances had spent a winter in a rented cottage in the heart of the village opposite the magnificent Falkland Palace, a hunting lodge for Mary, Queen of Scots that boasts the oldest real-tennis court in Britain.

Not surprisingly, for it is charming as well as historic, Frances had fallen in love with the village and, after some help from local estate agents, had found Ladywell House, which had been fairly recently renovated as a luxury bed-and-breakfast establishment. While Frances had no intention of using the place to accommodate paying guests, it was exactly what she was looking for, with plenty of bedrooms (ten in all, as well as five en-suite bathrooms) for family and friends. She also made it available for the bereaved fishermen's families she had befriended in the year of Diana's death. She has used it regularly as a place in which to entertain and relax, but buying it was also partly symbolic of her moving on after her devastating divorce from Peter. It was a bold decision at the time, and one she has never regretted.

For Frances, Ladywell House is the perfect retreat, as well as a peaceful haven away from the spotlight. She keeps many of her family photograph albums here, and will spend happy hours looking back fondly at the pictures of her late father, Maurice Fermoy, with Francis, his identical-twin brother, and of her sister Mary and late brother Edmund as children at Park House.

It also provides a change from the quiet of Seil, for Falkland is a busy village in a relatively well-populated area of Scotland. There is, too, a second advantage, although Frances did not know it when she bought the house: Falkland is just twenty miles from St Andrew's, where William is studying History of Art at the university. Indeed, Frances's presence near by was of considerable comfort to William when, during his first term at St Andrew's, he found himself going through a particularly troublesome time, and considered changing to Edinburgh University. The house has also proved to be a perfect base for one of her granddaughters, Laura Fellowes, who also studies in Scotland and who is particularly close to her cousin William, and for many of her other grandchildren. Its size means that Frances can accommodate up to twenty people without too much trouble.

Frances encourages all her grandchildren to mix with each other and to keep in touch, despite the differences in their ages which range over twenty years. Furthermore, almost the only benefit of Diana's death is that it has brought the family closer together. Although a titled family, the Spencers show far less regard for rank and position than do the Windsors, and rarely stand on ceremony, with the result that younger children do not feel too intimidated to talk freely with their elders. Frances visits South Africa when Charles and the children are there, and maintains close ties with her son's former wife, Victoria. Since her illness, too, she goes more often to Althorp to be with Charles's children during the school holidays, looking after all four of them, enjoying the banter across the breakfast table as she works out who likes what to eat. Always good with children, she maintains that the world would be a better place if we learned from their outlook, from 'what they feel and see, which is usually loving, protective, fun and realistic. I wish adults had more of a child's mind and vision, it's healthier.'

Frances is also a regular source of advice within the family, though, unlike many grandparents, she is a mentor rather than a meddler, as she has shown more than once. On one occasion a close friend of Sarah's teenaged son, George, died, and in his grief and anger the boy refused to go to church. Sarah insisted that he should go with the family to worship, but to no avail. At the end of her tether, she telephoned Frances, urging her mother, not altogether politely, to 'do her Catholic bit'. Frances called George and spoke to him at length, but realizing that he was very angry, thought it best to leave him alone to work things out for himself. This did not resolve the problem for Sarah, however, while being told to back off by her own mother was not a solution she received well. The two women had one of their many frank and brisk discussions – or, as Frances put it, 'Sarah got bolshie.' The argument culminated with Frances warning Sarah that if she kept pushing George she would have to cope with the consequences. 'If you win this one you can take the credit for it, but if you fail, you'll have that responsibility too.' Perhaps it was the recognition that at least half the problem stemmed from Sarah that made Frances's advice so valuable, but in any event it seemed to work and peace was restored.

On what would have been Diana's fortieth birthday in July 2001, her marriage came under scrutiny once again. By then she had been dead for almost four years, yet the media's feverish interest in her seemed scarcely to have diminished at all. With whom had she been in love before she died? Had she been pregnant? Had she been about to leave Britain to live in America?

That month also coincided with what would have been the twentieth anniversary of Diana's wedding to Prince Charles. Frances was inundated with calls from journalists and her unease turned to anger at what she considered exploitative news angles that had no basis in truth. Was it not time, she asked, to leave her daughter in peace?

The myths and fanciful theories surrounding Diana's life particularly upset Frances. When that life ended at the age of thirty-six, she had been a divorcée heading in a new direction. Frances found the obsession with Diana turning forty extremely distasteful. She had been pestered with requests from newspapers and television companies for months beforehand. 'They seem hell-bent on illuminating the fact that she would have been forty next weekend,' she told a friend. 'Well, if you die you are without age, aren't you?' To her, speculation seemed so pointless: 'This summer it would have been her twentieth wedding anniversary. Since she wasn't married when she died, would she have been celebrating this summer?'

The question was not supposed to receive an answer.

CHAPTER SEVENTEEN

Indecent Exposure

IN THE AUTUMN OF 2002, just a few weeks before the trial of Paul Burrell, Diana's former butler, was due to start, Frances shuffled stiffly into her kitchen. She had just driven home down the windy roads from the supermarket in Oban, and was carrying a mountain of heavy plastic bags. Shopping was not an easy task for her, but it was one she still enjoyed, and her many friends were touched by her determination to remain a part of the local community, despite her illness. Gingerly placing the bags on the ceramic tiles of the kitchen floor, she walked awkwardly into the sitting room and turned up the volume on the CD player. Back in the kitchen she reached over to the large fridge, pulled open the heavy door, and picked up a carton of milk. She intended to make a pot of tea and some lunch once she had unpacked all the bags.

Whereas once she would have turned from the fridge and walked over to pick up another bag without a second thought, now she had to concentrate hard, thinking all the time about her co-ordination. She swivelled round like a child taking its first tentative steps, holding on to the fridge to steady herself. She held on tight, frustrated by the time and effort it took to do such simple things.

Without warning, she felt her right foot disappearing from under her. She had accidentally stepped on one of the plastic bags, which on the hard tiles acted like a skateboard beneath her foot, making her slip face-first towards the floor's unyielding surface.

Frances, unable to break her fall, landed with terrible force. She lay momentarily dazed but perfectly still, trying to assess the damage to her body. Surprisingly nothing hurt – for a moment. Then a dreadful throbbing started in her head, and she saw blood spattered all over the cold white floor, mingling with the yoghurts and bread and making the red printing on the bags seem even more vivid.

She managed to roll onto her back and moved her hand tentatively towards her face, afraid but also curious to learn the damage, and felt warm blood leaking from the bridge of her nose and trickling between her eyes. Blinking, she was fairly certain that the dreadful pain meant that she had broken her nose. Gazing upwards through one blood-blurred eye, she could make out the notes stuck to her fridge door. Still dazed, she could just see a card reading 'Ferguson Hair and Beauty', a copy of the guidelines issued by the Press Complaints Commission, and a booklet on how to work her security system. None of these were of any use to her now, and, unable to move, she cursed the fact that the telephone was in the sitting room. She had no means of contacting anyone from where she was lying, but fearing that she might be concussed, she did not dare to attempt standing up until her head cleared. Instead she gathered all her strength and yelled, 'Help – can anyone help?' but the languid sounds of Celine Dion coming from the sitting room drowned her cries.

Outside, a builder working on alterations to the bungalow thought he heard an unusual noise. He lit a cigarette, but, hearing nothing more, assumed he was imagining things and got on with his work. Moments later, he heard the noise again. Curious, he put down his tools and walked towards the bungalow. He rang the doorbell and waited, but no one called or came to the door. He looked towards the garage, and could clearly see an Audi saloon. Frances was obviously at home, but dare he peep in through the window of a house occupied by the late Princess of Wales's mother? Then he heard a cry, this time louder and more insistent – it was definitely a woman calling.

He was wholly unprepared for what he saw when at last he peered in through the kitchen window. Frances was lying motionless on the floor, and there was a widening pool of blood next to her head. 'Oh my God . . . She's been attacked!'

'Only by a plastic bag,' Frances joked later. Even so, the scar on her nose was still quite pronounced and tender to the touch as she travelled down to London in October. Her fall had shaken her badly, although luckily there was no serious damage other than to her nose. By then, however, it was the last thing on her mind. For weeks, she had been anxiously waiting to learn whether she was needed at the Central Criminal Court, better known as the Old Bailey, for the Burrell trial, which had already been delayed so as not to coincide with the Queen's Jubilee celebrations in the summer. The Spencer family had lived with the trial hanging over their heads for more than two years. In the event, Frances, Sarah, Jane and Charles would all be called to give evidence, although it had been agreed that no one from the royal family would be asked into the witness box.

'Operation Plymouth' – as the police investigation was codenamed – could be traced back to the night after Diana's death. With her immediate family spread all over Britain or in South Africa, the Prince of Wales, having just returned with Diana's body from Paris, contacted Michael Gibbins, Diana's financial adviser, and asked him to lock up her apartment in Kensington Palace; no one was to enter until further notice. Gibbins refused, however, believing that this would 'have been a totally unreasonable thing to do'. Such was the emotional trauma of the time he became concerned that Diana's butler, Paul Burrell, who had also returned from Paris, where he had dressed the dead Princess, might take his own life if he was refused admittance to the Palace, where he too lived. At around 3.30 a.m. the following morning, Burrell backed his blue Ford Escort estate car up to the door of the Princess's apartment at Kensington Palace, jumped out and scampered up an alleyway. A short while later he reappeared carrying a deep-brown wooden box, possibly made from mahogany and measuring about one foot by two, which he put in the car before disappearing again to return with two evening gowns wrapped in plastic. He opened the rear door of his car and carefully placed them alongside the box.

This curious little charade did not go unnoticed, however. A police protection officer on duty at the palace, finding this sort of behaviour in the dead of night highly suspicious, confronted Burrell, demanding to know what on earth he was doing. The butler, obviously aware that it was a strange time at which to be carrying out house removals, said that he had been asked by Lady Sarah McCorquodale to take certain sensitive items of private property out of the building and destroy them. The only reason he was doing it in the early hours of the morning, he said, was to avoid attention – 'so it was done discreetly.'

Unconvinced, and still suspicious, the officer allowed Burrell to leave but passed the information on to Scotland Yard, which in turn later contacted Sarah at her Lincolnshire home to check that the butler's explanation was legitimate. To the contrary, however, she immediately denied giving him any such permission. She checked with Frances, but neither she nor anyone else in the family had authorized Burrell to remove Diana's property from her apartment. With their suspicions raised, the police made further delicate inquiries over the following months.

In the meantime, Burrell had been asked to work alongside Sarah on the memorial fund that was being set up in Diana's name. At first, he was regarded as a vital member of the committee, but after a time he became more outspoken and apparently determined to take centre stage, and concerns were voiced as to his motives. 'Paul lost sight of what the Memorial Fund was about,' said one source close to members of the fund's committee. 'It certainly wasn't about Paul Burrell becoming a celebrity and using the Memorial Fund to promote his own self-importance. They [the other members of the committee] were not happy about that, which he believed was an attempt to do him down.'

In December 1998, less that two months after running the New York marathon as the fund's event and fundraising co-ordinator, Paul Burrell left amid recriminations. The fund's chief executive, Andrew Purkis, claimed that the former butler 'would dearly love to be even more of a media personality' and that this was causing 'tensions'. Burrell, however, refused to accept a different role, and informed committee members that he had decided to go to America to consider his future.

Some time later, Burrell's name cropped up with Scotland Yard again after a tip-off to the Specialist Crime Unit, which was conducting an investigation into the alleged theft from Kensington Palace of a solid-gold, diamond-encrusted model of a dhow, said to be worth £500,000 ($750,0000), one of the more ostentatious gifts to the Prince and Princess of Wales. The police, however, were completely unprepared for what they were about to uncover.

Just before daylight on the morning of 18 January 2001, Burrell's Georgian house at Farden in Cheshire, which he shared with his wife and two boys, was raided by police. In a strategically planned operation designed for maximum shock effect, both uniformed and plain-clothed policemen, armed with a search warrant, pounded on his door and demanded entry. Clad only in his dressing gown, a bleary-eyed Burrell, still half asleep, carefully unlocked his door and peered out to find a row of grim-looking figures staring back at him. As he appeared at the door, one of the officers reportedly shouted, 'We've come for the Crown Jewels!' Burrell, visibly distressed, was too traumatized to do anything other than stand back and let them in.

Increasingly nervous, he watched as the police officers' perplexed expressions turned to astonishment. On almost every surface, in almost every corner, there were pictures, memorabilia and valuable items belonging to the late Princess, many of them signed with her name. It seemed that they had found an Aladdin's cave of stolen goods.

Detective Chief Inspector Maxine de Brunner of the Metropolitan Police's Specialist Crime Unit clearly thought that they had hit the jackpot, and ordered her officers to undertake a full search. Unfortunately, they had not come properly equipped for an intensive search. On reaching the first floor they discovered a trapdoor leading to a loft, but astonishingly, had no torch, and the detective chief inspector, who suffers from a fear of heights, was unable to climb the ladder. None the less, those bold enough to poke their heads through the trapdoor found a spectacular haul. Fourteen hours later they re-emerged from Burrell's home with more than 300 items of clothing, ornaments, photographs, jewellery and papers crammed into dozens of black rubbish bags.

By now Burrell's obvious distress was affecting his wife Maria and his two sons, Alexander and Nicholas. A doctor was called to see if the former butler required medical aid, but it was decided that 'no psychiatric treatment was needed'. He was then taken to the local police station in Runcorn for questioning, and released on bail sixteen hours later while investigations continued.

Detective Sergeant Roger Milburn, second in command of the operation, expressed the amazement they had all felt at what had been found. 'If I had known,' he said, 'I would have brought with me a photographer, a video-camera operator, a full search team and a removal van.' In the end, it required thirty-six pages of A4 paper to list everything of Diana's that had been found in the house. Included in the haul were a blue Versace dress; signed CDs; negatives of photographs of Diana; framed photographs of Prince William with the model Naomi Campbell; a Cartier clock; a writing desk; a portrait of William and Harry; a metal wine cooler; a coral bead necklace; Diana's monogrammed pyjamas; a jewellery box; a floppy disk containing files of Diana's personal accounts; a key to Kensington Palace; and thousands more photographic negatives, many of William and Harry. Even so, the police still managed to overlook a kingfisher ornament, which had been a wedding present to the Prince and Princess of Wales from the US President at that time, Ronald Reagan. Unfortunately, however, neither photographic nor video evidence was taken.

Seven months later, it was the turn of the Prince of Wales to receive a visit from the investigating officers. In an effort to shore up their evidence against Burrell by securing royal backing, they told the Prince that they had photographs of male servants in royal employ wearing dresses that had belonged to the Princess, and also informed him that Burrell's bank balance had unaccountably soared. In fact, the first allegation was based on unsubstantiated hearsay, with no factual evidence to back it up, and the second was because police had failed to realize that Burrell was enjoying the proceeds from a bestselling book about royal entertaining that he had written, and also from his new career as an after-dinner speaker. Ironically, later on the day his house was raided Burrell had been due to address guests at a black-tie dinner organized by Cheshire Police, which had to be cancelled at short notice. The upshot of the police's interview with the Prince, however, was that having previously refused to be drawn into the investigation, fearing that William and Harry would become involved, he now appeared persuaded.

Similarly, the police persuaded both Frances and Sarah that, as executors of Diana's will, they were pivotal to the case if the prosecution was to proceed. Charles Spencer, as guardian to the young princes after Diana's death (although by 2001 William was no longer a minor), was also interviewed in connection with the investigation.

Two weeks later, on 16 August, Burrell, on the advice of his solicitors, voluntarily walked into London's West End Central police station, bringing with him a statement running to thirty-nine pages, which he later said officers paid scant regard to. Within an hour he had been formally charged with stealing 342 items, over an 18-month period either side of 31 August 1997 (the day of Diana's death), belonging to the Princess's estate, to Prince Charles and to Prince William. The estimated value of the haul was in the region of £6 million ($9 million). On the following day, Diana's former butler and self-styled 'rock' was remanded at Bow Street Magistrates Court on conditional bail.

Burrell, an inoffensive looking man with an easy smile and cropped brown hair lying atop a moon face, found the pressure almost too much to bear. The skin on the soles of his feet blistered, he started to drink too much, and found it necessary to take medication for depression and sleeplessness. Things became so bad that he contemplated committing suicide by taking an overdose of paracetamol.

Born into relatively humble circumstances in the mining village of Grassmore in Derbyshire, the son of a lorry driver and canteen worker, Paul Burrell became enraptured with the glamour and prestige of royalty after going on a family trip to see the Changing of the Guard ceremony at Buckingham Palace. Even then, as a small boy, he told his parents, 'I want to work here one day.' Ironically, he might never have done so but for the intervention of his mother, who later secretly destroyed a job offer from the cruise-ship operator Cunard, which had arrived at the same time as the one from the Palace. Ken Wharfe, who knew Burrell, wryly comments, 'Burrell has chronic red-carpet fever and he will die from it.'

Burrell joined the royal household in 1976 as a trainee footman, and within a year was appointed personal footman to the Queen. Although he was at one stage caught up in a police investigation into homosexuality among the crew of the Royal Yacht *Britannia*, he was cleared of any involvement, and retained his job. Later he became the under-butler at Highgrove, living in a grace-and-favour cottage on the estate and working for both the Prince and Princess of Wales. After the couple separated at the end of 1992, he moved on to work exclusively for Diana. It appears that the Princess was initially reluctant to have another butler at Kensington Palace, but was persuaded by her then head butler, Harold Brown. Brown moved on to work for Princess Margaret, at which point Burrell was promoted head butler to Diana.

By the time the case came up at the Old Bailey on 14 October 2002, Burrell, dressed in a well-tailored suit and an Hermès tie, looked close to a nervous breakdown; it was, after all, more than a year since he had been charged, and nearly two years since police had raided his home. Almost immediately the trial was halted and a new jury sworn in, something that only served to heighten the tension among the press and public, as well as all those involved in the case.

Not unnaturally, Frances was also worried. After two years of waiting she was now going to be called as one of the main witnesses for the prosecution. It was not something she was looking forward to, but she knew she had a duty, as Diana's mother and as an executor of her will, to try to reclaim her daughter's possessions on behalf of the boys.

It was said at the time that Frances had been press-ganged into the witness box, but nothing could have been further from the truth. In fact, she had been offered the chance of submitting a doctor's note, citing her ill health, which would have exempted her from giving evidence and all the anxiety that went with it. She categorically refused, saying she wanted to use the trial not only to tell the facts, particularly after all that had been said in the press, much of it untrue, but also publicly to 'out my illness'. Many of Burrell's allegations, reported at length in the media during the long run-up to the trial, were deeply upsetting, and Frances was adamant that she was going to attend court, not least because she felt that it was important 'to counter his [Burrell's] claim that he was Diana's "rock", adding, with absolute certainty, 'because he was not'.

Ken Wharfe backs Frances in this, laughing at the suggestion that Burrell was Diana's sole 'rock', as the former butler liked to imply. It was a term the Princess commonly used in approval of anyone who had helped her. To Wharfe, it would be ridiculous to suggest that Burrell was the only person to have the term bestowed upon them; 'She even called me her rock,' he says.

The case was opened by counsel for the prosecution, William Boyce, QC, who suggested that Burrell's days at Kensington Palace may well have been numbered, and that he had taken to admitting privately that he wanted to find better-paid employment aboard. According to counsel, after Diana died Burrell had exaggerated his closeness to her, thereby securing his own position, as well as a considerable measure of public sympathy, and perhaps enhancing his future employment prospects. Yet Burrell was nowhere near as close to the Princess as he purported, the court was told, and motives other than those contained in his much-reported defence – that he was keeping the Princess's property safe for her sons – were coming into play when he took items belonging to Diana. William Boyce added, 'I simply pause a moment to ask you to consider the value of one CD autographed by Diana, Princess of Wales.'

The implications were clear – Burrell was rewriting history in order to elevate the importance of his own position, and in the process had hoped to make money out of memorabilia connected closely to the dead Princess. Matters looked ominous for the forty-four-year old who, despite having no claim upon Diana's estate, nor even a mention in her will, had already been given a generous £50,000 ($75,000) payment by Frances and Sarah, as Diana's executors, in recognition of his work. There had been genuine concern for him; Frances, noting how affected Burrell was by events leading up to Diana's funeral, had lent him a cross and chain to wear on the day to 'keep him safe'.

Giving evidence, Lady Sarah McCorquodale said that she had decided to offer Burrell a memento from among Diana's belongings. 'I had offered anything he would like to take,' she said. 'He said he would not because his memories were in his heart, and that was all he needed.' Unbeknown to her, however, he had already secretly removed many items belonging to Diana's estate, and would acquire a great many more.

Burrell had been horrified by the allegations made against him, but had when questioned given the police conflicting reasons for his acquisitions, although always claiming that his only purpose had been to help and protect Diana. At one stage he stated:

> I realize issues may be raised about some items – correspondence, computer disks and personal artefacts. I have made no use of these items whatsoever, they have been stored carefully in my attic, I never intended to use them. At some point I intended to do what was appropriate with them but the horrific events of her death made me sure that to hold on to the items was the only safe way of protecting her memory.

He said that he had been the conduit for several of Diana's secret liaisons, and that she had trusted him with important aspects of her private life. 'I very quickly became her closest male confidant, and knew all her secrets as far as I am aware.' By describing himself as Diana's 'rock', he had provided a reason why she had rewarded him by passing on clothes, CDs and trinkets for which she either had no need, or which she felt she would like him to have.

When she died, Burrell had, he said, maintained a constant vigil at Kensington Palace, adding that he had provided 'succour to members of the royal family, the Spencer family and the Princess's friends to ensure they were able to deal with the situation.' Furthermore, although deeply traumatized, he had had to bring the Princess's bloodstained clothes from the accident back from Paris to Kensington Palace in a hospital refuse bag. He had then stored them in a fridge there before burning them.

These and other revelations, while interesting (and occasionally somewhat gruesome), showed the enormous power that Diana still wielded, even in death. They also provided a considerable insight into life at Kensington Palace and the power struggles therein. Burrell, however, was holding back his most damning allegations to attack what he had viewed as the disintegrating relationships between Diana and her mother and oldest sister.

Promoting himself to the position of the Princess's moral guardian, he had apparently felt it his duty to protect her possessions and her reputation, above, and perhaps even from, her own family. He claimed that in the aftermath of Diana's death Frances and Sarah had shredded papers, medical records and sensitive material that belonged to her sons. While he conceded that 'her executors were entitled to remove items,' he took the view that they were in fact using their time at Kensington Palace to get rid of 'personal and important documentation'. These papers, he believed, should in due course have been passed to Prince William and Prince Harry, and he added, sententiously, 'Such action was the only way to preserve her memory.'

He then went on to twist the knife, saying that on one occasion he had listened in to a telephone conversation between Diana and her mother and had been shocked to hear Frances unable to contain her anger at her daughter's choice of men (a reference to the fact that both Dodi Fayed and Hasnat Khan were Muslims). It was 'a hate-filled, personal attack,' said Burrell, which had left Diana 'crumpled on the floor and vowing never to speak to her mother again'. He also alluded to differences of opinion between himself and Sarah, whom he dubbed 'Sarah McCrocodile'.

The sensational allegations Burrell had made against her in court placed Frances right back in the forefront of the news again. Then, on the following day, she was called to the stand. Despite the awkwardness of her movements, for she was leaning heavily on a stick, she insisted on walking into court with dignity. She was driven to the Old Bailey and entered the court holding the arm of a smiling CID officer. 'I had to laugh,' she said, 'because I was on the arm of an unknown man, who was rather gorgeous. I said to him, "I'm slow at getting out of cars – so I'm going to teach you a trick." He looked at me rather oddly. I said, "Look as if you are gliding me past the press into the court, and I'll hang on like hell, trying to go straight." I added, "By the way, I think we look wonderful together" – that's why he was laughing.'

It proved to be a rare moment of light relief for Frances in what was to become a harrowing and deeply unpleasant experience. Sitting in Court Number 1, which had once seen the trials of the Yorkshire Ripper and other vicious criminals, she was forced, in the most public arena, to relive once more her daughter's death, and to suffer the ignominy of having to defend her relationship with her child. For an hour and fifty-five minutes Frances, clutching a crucifix in her left hand, stoically delivered her evidence from the witness box – never once looking at Burrell, who was only seven paces away, while the most personal aspects of her life were probed.

In order to discredit Frances's relationship with Diana, Burrell's counsel,

Lord Carlile, QC, opened up the matter of when they had last spoken, suggesting that it might have been as long as six months before the Princess's death. It was an easy blow, and one intended to inflict maximum embarrassment. Frances admitted that it had been four months. 'There were sometimes ups and downs,' she said, but 'it was normal family behaviour.' To suggest that her relationship with Diana had been anything other than loving and trusting, she said, would be ridiculous. And, under oath, she vigorously refuted allegations that she had disapproved of her daughter's boyfriends.

The early days after Diana's death, she said, had been 'very emotional, very gloomy', especially the time she had spent at Kensington Palace sorting through her daughter's effects. She told the court that her main consideration had been to look after both her grandsons' best interests, and that it remained so. The idea that she had in some way sought callously to destroy material important to her daughter's memory, while allegedly drinking wine, was anathema to her. 'I shredded a very small number of a very large amount of correspondence,' she said. 'None of it was from members of the royal family.' She estimated that she and Sarah had destroyed, in total, not more than a hundred documents, mostly thank-you notes from people like ladies-in-waiting.

She went on to say that many valuable items such as family photographs should have been held at Althorp, rather than at Burrell's home. And while she conceded that Diana would happily hand out small gifts not identifiable as being hers, she would never have allowed items belonging to royalty to leave her possession.

Aware of the seriousness of the trial, Frances nevertheless joked gently with the jury when she was told that Andrew Morton had been wrong when he had written, in a new edition of *Diana: Her True Story* published after the Princess's death, that Diana had been buried in a Catherine Walker dress. 'I don't read Andrew Morton's books,' Frances replied, smiling as the court erupted in laughter. Neither had she read *Princess in Love*, the book James Hewitt had written with a journalist, detailing his affair with the Princess. No doubt she regarded the Hewitt book as 'outrageous', suggested Lord Carlile. 'Is that the title?' she replied, to more laughter.

Her evidence over, Frances walked out of court with her head held high, hoping that she had convinced the jury. She had told the truth, had behaved with dignity, had got through the day. She had, however, been deeply shocked by Burrell's accusation that she had disapproved of Diana's association with Muslim men. 'That really upset me,' she told a friend, 'I would never ever say that.' Yet there was nothing more she could do, except wait for the verdict. Like the rest of the nation, she had no inkling that events were about to take a dramatic turn.

On 20 October, while the trial was still in progress, the Union flag atop Buckingham Palace was flown at half-mast between 8 a.m. and sunset. The Queen had granted this once unheard-of gesture in memory of the victims of the terrorist bombing of a nightclub in Bali, in which hundreds of young people had died. It was a concession she had first made to her subjects after Diana had been killed. Now it is followed to show respect at profound moments, as after the terrorist attacks on New York and Washington on 11 September 2001, and the death of her own mother the following year. Neither the gesture, nor its connection with Diana, still dominating the headlines five years after her death, was wasted on the press and public.

On the following Friday, 26 October – the ninth day of Burrell's trial – the Queen and the Prince of Wales were sitting in the back of a Rolls-Royce on their way to St Paul's Cathedral and a memorial service for those who had died in the Bali bombing. It was early evening. They were anxiously discussing the case at the Old Bailey. As they talked, the Queen mentioned to an incredulous Prince of Wales that she had granted an audience to Paul Burrell a few weeks after Diana had been killed, and that he had told her that he was looking after some of the Princess's papers for 'safe keeping'. The Prince, to his credit, immediately recognized the importance of this information, and instructed his Private Secretary, Sir Michael Peat, to inform the police straight away.

The trial of the Princess of Wales's former butler collapsed, the prosecution's carefully constructed case blown apart by the Queen's sudden and total recall. Burrell said that his private audience with the monarch had lasted for three hours, during which both had remained standing. Others remain deeply sceptical of this claim, believing it unlikely that the Queen would countenance such a lengthy audience with a servant, let alone stand for the entire time. Burrell also said that Her Majesty had nodded sagely as he told her of what he was doing to protect Diana's memory, and, somewhat bizarrely, had warned him to beware of 'dark forces' at work.

Yet by revealing that she had known of Burrell's activities, the Queen demonstrated that she had been party to his actions. Since the Queen had been aware, and had not taken any disapproving action, then the £1.5 million ($2.25 million) case became irrelevant. The collapse of the trial was a bitter pill for Frances and the Spencer family to swallow, and a public humiliation for the police and the Director of Public Prosecutions. On the Monday morning, following hours of legal argument, the prosecution admitted defeat and Burrell walked from the court a free man. William Boyce stood in court to announce that 'The prosecution has concluded that the current trial is no longer viable.' Diplomatically, he added: 'Her Majesty had no means of knowing until after the trial had started of the relevance to the prosecution of the fact that Mr Burrell had mentioned to Her Majesty that he had taken items for safe keeping.' At the time and subsequently, cynical observers suggested that there was more than an element of 'convenient amnesia' in the Queen's delayed recollection, and that she became fearful that Burrell was about to expose details in court about the royal family, and the Prince of Wales in particular, which would inevitably be reported in the media. The Queen, it could therefore be construed, stepped in to protect the House of Windsor.

After weeping with relief on the shoulder of his barrister, Burrell emerged on the steps of the Old Bailey to announce triumphantly, 'The Queen broke for me. I'm thrilled.' He dashed off with his lawyers for a champagne celebration at Luigi's in Covent Garden, a restaurant which, ironically, had been a favourite of the Princess's.

Charles Spencer was in the middle of a visit by Nelson Mandela to Althorp when the news came through. Asked by a journalist if he had any comment to make on the day's sensational development, he replied laconically, 'Not really.' His comment was not just a masterpiece of understatement, but of self-control. The only public announcement from the Spencers was deliberately muted. 'The only concern of the family has been that Diana's private possessions be returned to her family so they can be held for Prince William and Prince Harry. We are very hopeful that this will happen as soon as is practicable.'

Behind the scenes, however, things were very different. Frances was seething at how she had been portrayed, nor had other members of the family escaped, all having been vilified or belittled in the course of Burrell's evidence. Worse was to follow. The collapse of the case meant that Burrell was free to sell his story to newspapers; he received £300,000 ($450,000) for it from the *Daily Mirror*, and a further £100,000 ($150,000) for an 'at home' with *Hello!* magazine. Over the following weeks he systematically exposed Diana, her love affairs, her children and all the senior members of her family. This information from the self-styled 'keeper of the secrets' was lapped up by the British public and syndicated worldwide. Frances took it particularly hard. She had endured a two-year investigation, poring over police photographs and descriptions of Diana's property and reliving grief-filled hours at Kensington Palace in the days after her daughter's death. She had been made to justify her right to sort through her dead daughter's effects, as any mother, let alone an executor, would automatically do. She had suffered all this, with the world watching, in open court, where the statements made are protected by legal privilege and can be printed by any newspaper that sees fit to do so. Justice seemed hard to find.

Yet for the sake of family unity, she knew that she had to keep a lid on her feelings in public; 'dignified silence,' she called it. She recognized that voicing her concerns and her disgust and anger would inflame an already volatile situation. Privately, however, she was incensed. She believed that the Queen had been content to sit back and watch the Spencers being 'humiliated' in court and in the press. Throughout the trial, the only word from the House of Windsor had been uttered behind closed doors. Reported to the court, it had brought about the collapse of the prosecution's case, thereby denying the Spencers their hope of finding vindication through the conviction of Paul Burrell for theft.

In effect, Frances was biting her tongue on strong words that echoed even stronger feelings, feelings that reached back decades and which, if articulated publicly, would rip open old wounds and create even further sensation. The tentative and fragile bonds that held the two families together were being stretched to breaking point.

The whole Burrell saga had taken years to come to court, yet it had ended so quickly and unexpectedly that it almost seemed an anti-climax. This fight for what was right, hampered at every turn by legal argument, misunder-standings and ineptitude, had resolved nothing for Frances. The entire case had been an ordeal. 'I had to look at every exhibit during the trial, so that was like reliving Diana's death again,' she says angrily.

For her, the injustice was made doubly stark and unbearable now that doubts about her role as a mother had been aired and were gathering pace. Depicted in court and in the press as an uncaring, detached, self-righteous bigot, Frances, even with her faith, found it hard not to become profoundly resentful and distressed.

The days immediately after Diana's death had been some of the hardest she had ever endured. Just having to walk into the apartment in Kensington Palace had been almost unbearable. Smelling her daughter's scent, seeing her pictures, touching her clothes and being surrounded by her most precious possessions made the loss all the more real, and thus all the more difficult to bear. Everywhere was Diana. Yet there was no more Diana.

As Frances opened doors, diffidently pulled out drawers and looked in cupboards, she glimpsed the private life of her daughter. These were Diana's things – notes, cards, gifts, frivolities that her mother was never meant to see – the collections of trinkets and trivia that say so much about a person. There were her favourite toiletries, her books, CDs, jewellery and, of course, the collection of stuffed animals she had kept since childhood. Frances had looked at her daughter Sarah, and they had sat quietly together for a moment on a sofa before beginning their task.

There was no question that their sole priority was the welfare of William and Harry, and Frances insisted that they must be asked if there was anything special they wanted to keep in memory of their mother. The two women, the mother and sister who had known and loved Diana all their lives, were unarguably the right, and possibly the only, people capable of doing this. They, more than anyone, could capture the spirit of Diana for her children. Before anything was touched, therefore, the young princes were given a last chance to claim for themselves what they wanted from among their mother's effects.

Paul Burrell was in the apartment when Frances and Sarah arrived to begin their grim work, and appeared to have everything in hand. Frances, not knowing quite where to start, turned to him for support, and asked how she could help. Burrell disappeared for a moment and, returning, 'gave me four sacks of mail to sort through.' She 'organized it into groups – there was a pile for and from the children; lots of girlie letters and bread-and-butter letters.' This painful task took hours, but once the material had been sorted she handed it all back to Burrell, apart from 'letters I thought the boys might like to read later in life,' and a large bundle of thank-you notes ('bread-and-butter letters'), mundane invitations and run-of-the-mill messages. She took the bundle of irrelevant notes and shredded them, aware that even such transient correspondence had a value, especially since Diana's death, and that they would certainly be put on the market if they fell into the wrong hands. 'I was NOT shredding history,' she asserts furiously, a reference to what had been said about the shredding in court. Burrell took the remaining correspondence and disappeared with it.

Later, when 'Paul suggested I put bin bags of Diana's clothes into my car,' Frances complied, seeing nothing abnormal in a family taking a loved one's clothes to keep or do with as they saw fit. After all, who else could be expected to sort through and take care of Diana's personal effects? As Frances says, 'That wasn't unusual. I am her mother.'

Grateful for his help, both Frances and Sarah wanted to show their gratitude to Burrell, and therefore, as executors, arranged for the terms of Diana's will to be altered, with the result that he was bequeathed £50,000 ($75,000) from her estate for all that he had done throughout this trying time. They had no reason to suspect his motives might have been anything other than genuine. Having been Diana's butler for several years, an important position of trust, he would be expected to have had a good working relationship with her.

It therefore came as a huge shock to the Spencers when, many months later, they were informed by the police that hundreds of Diana's possessions were being stored in Burrell's home. His explanation in court that Frances could not be trusted with her own daughter's belongings came as a double blow. 'His position went to Paul's head,' she says. 'Diana only wanted to use him in an administrative capacity, like a PA. He would contact so-and-so on her behalf . . . but then he would make sure they all came back through to him and so he made himself indispensable.'

Ken Wharfe, who had no axe to grind and, being an officer of the Metropolitan Police, was not on the Princess's payroll, watched the goings-on from a dispassionate point of view. He says, 'I've known Paul for a long time and professionally he was very good – he was a very good butler.' Wharfe became concerned, however, with how far Burrell was prepared to go to keep control of Diana's diary and thus her life, finding him somewhat 'manipulative' and a man with his 'own agenda'.

Frances found Burrell's controlling ways equally exasperating. She suspected that the butler was screening her calls to her daughter, and became frustrated when he seemed to be deflecting them. 'In his room, Paul could see when her light was on to take a phone call. I begged her to get a scrambler.' When she did get through to Diana, the calls would be spent in conversation; there was no screaming and shouting, as Burrell later claimed. 'If Diana phoned late at night for advice, we'd talk and laugh, but I'd only give an opinion if asked.'

When Frances, over the telephone, heard Burrell say, 'Princess Diana needs you. She needs contact with her mother,' it took a good deal to contain her anger, for she believed that he was holding all the strings and appeared to be controlling all contact between mother and daughter. Her fury almost erupted at the way he would try deliberately to patronize her. 'Sometimes Paul would call me and say "The Princess wants you to know how much you helped." I didn't need him to affirm our relationship. This was insulting!'

After the court case, Frances, through gritted teeth, realized that she would have to content herself with knowing that 'He's just obsessed with Diana.' Burrell himself later admitted the truth of this judgement.

CHAPTER EIGHTEEN

Beyond Betrayal

A s Frances left the Old Bailey after giving evidence, she felt a cold hand touch her shoulder. Looking round, she found herself face-to-face with a serious-looking policeman. 'What now?' she thought. 'Surely they don't want me to go back into court again?' Frances could not contemplate another grilling by Burrell's counsel. She was already exhausted by the day's events and needed to rest. There would be no chance of that now, however.

'I'm afraid we have some bad news,' she was told. Fed up with the continual pressure she had faced for so long, she replied wearily, 'What a surprise . . .'

The policeman took her to a quiet part of the court, and she felt herself go cold as he told her, 'You've been broken into. Your house in Seil, it's been ransacked.' This seemed like a joke in the worst possible taste, and her hackles rose. 'I'm going home,' she said. 'Now!'

'I'm afraid that's not possible, Mrs Shand Kydd. The forensic team are still there looking for clues to the burglars. It's a crime scene at the moment. It would be far better for you to remain in London as planned, so they can finish their job.'

Frances, who had by now had enough of being told what to do, flared up. 'Well, tell them I'm coming!' she fumed. She had been away from Seil for only twenty-four hours – 'the most expensive one-night stand I've ever had' – but her presence in London had been broadcast around the world. Since it was well know that she lived alone, some enterprising thief or thieves had taken advantage of her absence. Now she had to face feeling vulnerable in a world that normally keeps her safe – her own home.

Seil has always been a place where the local people, trusting by nature, leave their back doors and cars unlocked. Most of the five-hundred-strong population know each other by sight, if not by name, and any outsiders are soon noticed. Even so, with the increasing number of casual tourists and day-trippers making their way over the famous Atlantic Bridge connecting Seil to the mainland, outsiders have become harder to monitor. The islanders are protective of their famous resident, and the burglary at Callanish was a blow that struck at the heart of their community. Nevertheless, and despite considerable sympathy for Frances, no one would be pushed into changing a way of life so attractive that it has seen this tiny community grow from just a hundred people when Frances arrived more than thirty years ago. The island's souvenir shop, just yards past the bridge and opposite the pub, has an honesty bowl for anyone wishing to buy the postcards on display. There are no policemen on the island – the nearest being fifteen miles away in Oban.

Yet despite this feeling of trust and safety, Frances had often experienced unwanted attention as part and parcel of her life on Seil. Aware of her high profile, she had installed a £5,000 ($7,500) state-of-the-art security system comprising alarms and closed-circuit TV which also recorded to video. This had the added bonus of providing her with a few moments that appealed to her sense of humour and of the absurd. She explains why:

> I know why the media has the opinion I like being a recluse and don't like going out. It's all because I can ignore them when they doorstep me here – I see them on my close-circuit television. They see my car is here and hear music – which I play all day long – but I don't come to the door because I can't be quoted if I haven't spoken. The mirth for me comes from seeing them arrive.
>
> All reporters visibly put their shoulders back and straighten up. The girls fiddle or do something or other with their hair to make themselves look better. But it's really the male reporters who are my chief enjoyment. It seems to be mandatory to check their flies! When I look back on the video of that I certainly get plenty of laughs.

That day at the bungalow, however, she was not finding anything very amusing. The burglary had a distinct air of professionalism about it. The telephone line had been cut and the alarm disabled before the intruders had gained entry.

Her housekeeper, Jenny, had discovered the break-in on the Thursday morning, only hours after Frances had left for London. The burglars, by watching reports about the Burrell trial on television, knew that Frances was hundreds of miles away, so their only obstacle was getting past her surveillance system; once that was disabled they could deal with the locks. After they had driven along the steep and winding road and sneaked up to the secluded bungalow, they were able to take their time. Having cut all the wires, they gained entry by quickly crawling inside through a ground-floor window. Inside the house, they closed the heavy curtains in the sitting room, shutting out Seil and any prying eyes, before busying themselves emptying drawers and cupboards.

They showed no respect for Frances's belongings or memories, but ruthlessly tore the house apart, looking for valuables. Luckily photographs of Diana, William and Harry, as well as a large one of the Round Oval at Althorp in a curved brass frame, were left untouched, but other precious family shots lay damaged or broken on the floor. The burglars, frustrated by the number of locks and bolts, took an axe to one of the tables in an attempt to find out what was inside its drawers. A deep gash was left in the surface, but the solid lock refused to give. Hidden safely inside was Diana's postmortem report, which was one of the first things to come to Frances's mind when she heard of the burglary. If that had been taken and had got into the wrong hands, it would have caused a furore.

Her valuable collection of Herend pottery, lovingly arranged on a dresser behind the large chesterfield sofa in the sitting room, was also untouched, but the intruders had soon discovered what they were looking for – her collection of jewellery, much of it unique and extremely valuable, as well as irreplaceable.

The contents of the house had been scattered everywhere and the whole place left looking like 'a tip', its usual orderliness replaced by violent chaos. Yet even at the dreadful moment of seeing the violation of her home, Frances managed to feel relieved that nothing of Diana's had been stolen. Her daughter's memory remained intact. However, over £90,000 ($135,000) worth of her own precious jewellery, including a pearl and diamond choker, a gold anchor brooch and a small antique floral brooch, had been stolen, among many other pieces. It was an appalling discovery. The missing pieces, Frances says, included, 'items of value and, more importantly, sentimental value – which remain in my heart – pieces which belonged to my grandparents and a ring given to me by my father.'

The only jewellery she was left with was what she had worn to London for the trial – a cross on a chain around her neck, a beautiful eternity ring of rubies and sapphires to commemorate her two dead children, John and Diana, and a brooch given to her by the people of Dunblane.* 'I feel completely violated,' Frances said, as she surveyed the mess.

As if that discovery were not enough, her misery was compounded when she realized that the missing jewellery had not been insured, so that she would never be able to replace the pieces, or have copies made, even if she

---

* In March 1996, a disgraced former Scoutmaster, Thomas Hamilton, had taken four guns into the primary school at Dunblane, near Stirling, and opened fire on a class of five- and six-year-olds, killing sixteen children and a teacher, and wounding twelve, before killing himself. In the aftermath of this appalling tragedy, Frances had given her help and her support to the shocked people of the small community.

had wanted to. She was later asked why she had listed two engagement rings among the missing items. 'Johnnie's ring was Spencer jewellery, so that went back to the family, and Peter had two rings made for me, one that I didn't like but kept,' she explained. 'And he then had another one made. And I kept both.' Stoically, she tried to compensate for her loss by remembering the 'forty years' enjoyment of wearing it'.

The local police, determined to find the culprits, alerted other forces around the country, but leads were hard to come by. In early November 2002, around thirty officers, armed with a search warrant, stormed into a jewellery trader's home in east Glasgow. They had received a tip-off that Frances's valuables might be hidden inside the brickwork. After four hours of pulling panelling off walls with crowbars and using endoscopic cameras to look inside the wall cavities, nothing was found. They left, empty-handed and embarrassed, while the poor trader, thoroughly traumatized by the raid, had to be resuscitated by an ambulance crew.

The trail went cold but, desperate to revitalize the case and prompt memories, Oban Police contacted BBC TV and requested a slot on its crime-solving programme, *Crimewatch*. This features details and reconstructions of crimes and appeals to viewers for help and information by asking them to call on secure lines, guaranteeing to protect their identity; it has had some remarkable successes over the years. At first Frances was unsure about taking part, 'as doing this sort of thing makes me nervous,' but she eventually agreed, aware that 'it brings people to the phones'.

The BBC was glad to oblige, and offered to fly Frances down to appear on the show. She, however, still feeling shaken after the burglary, and no longer confident of her speech on live programmes, declined with a joke, saying that she would only get on an aeroplane if she was 'given a parachute', preferring to make an appeal by telephone. On the day before recording the message, she had said, 'It's no cigarettes and coffee for me,' her vulnerability suddenly apparent as she added, 'I hope my voice, which is a bit peculiar, holds up.'

In the event, Frances did better than even she had hoped, recording the message at the first attempt – 'a oner', as she called it. She told a national audience that 'A bracelet and earrings were tangible links to my deceased children, as was the ring my father gave me, and also the pearl choker which I wore to the weddings of all my children. I don't think they can bring happiness to anyone but me because they are too steeped in emotion.'

She read her appeal for help from pre-prepared notes, hoping that it would not sound stilted, and was happy to hear after the programme had been transmitted that the police had received around twenty new leads. Sensitive to the overall purpose behind *Crimewatch*, she could not help feeling that her slot had at least offered some 'light relief' in a 'grim programme concerning so many murderers and muggers'. She was, too, recovering her sense of humour, laughing when she said, 'I wound the Oban policeman up when he got back [from appearing on the programme] – he was the only officer with any hair on television that night!' Sadly, to date none of her property has been recovered.

Frances's concentration was, not surprisingly, sometimes amiss during the traumatic period immediately after the collapse of the Burrell trial and the burglary. One day as she was driving to Oban in her Audi, she skidded on a patch of oil on the road and clipped a bridge parapet near Kilninver. Her car spun out of control and flipped over.

'The roof of my car caved in by six inches. I'd overturned and was hanging upside down like a bat,' she remembers. Aware that the engine was still running, but unable to reach the ignition key, she flicked the transmission to 'Park' mode. Then she became terrified by the danger from leaking petrol and the realization that the car might catch fire or explode unless she could turn off the ignition. Held by her seat belt, which she could not undo, she carefully stretched for the keys, managing to manoeuvre herself into a position to silence the engine. She was held in place by her belt for nearly twenty minutes, with the blood rushing to her head, until another motorist drove up and, startled by what he saw, hit his own brakes hard. He leapt out, smashed the window of her car and wrenched the buckled door open.

'I was shouting "Get me out of here,"' says Frances, but worried that he might injure her further by carelessly pulling her out of the wrecked Audi, he calmly replied, 'I'm afraid to move you.' Frances desperately waved her arms around to indicate that nothing was broken and shouted back, 'Look, I'm okay.' At this the motorist undid her belt and she wriggled out like an eel, just as the police arrived.

'Do you want anything?' she was asked.

'Yep . . . I could really do with . . . a cigarette,' came the reply.

There was considerable relief all round, for she was obviously not badly hurt. As is standard procedure after car accidents, however, the police asked Frances to take a breathalyser test. It proved negative and Frances, unwilling to cause any more fuss, declined any immediate medical attention, saying that once she got back home she would call her local doctor. She was later diagnosed with severe bruising down one side, and shock; 'I was aching and shaking,' she says laconically.

The Audi was towed away to the local garage and hidden inside. Even so, before the end of the day a photographer was seen hanging around, trying to get pictures of the smashed vehicle. The garage owner told him in no uncertain terms that he was definitely not welcome.

By the evening, Frances had become irate, angry at how Burrell had twisted her relationship with Diana, and furious at the public's perception of her after his damning testimony. She had been stripped of her dignity in court, violated by burglars in her own home and her declining health had taken a further battering both from stress and that day's events. In the heat of the moment, as she sat in Callanish recovering from the accident, all her feelings about Burrell flooded to the surface. Bruised, humiliated, affronted, and finally at the end of her tether, she exploded to a friend over the telephone, 'I could kill that man!'

Once she had calmed down, however, she realized that there was little she could do. She refused to compromise her dignity by entering into a humiliating public row – and Burrell seemed hell-bent upon keeping himself at centre stage. By contrast, she herself was desperate for a quiet life. Trapped in an impossible situation, she resigned herself to hoping that matters would return to some semblance of normality.

She had been proved right in one thing, however. Despite being married, Burrell later admitted during a television interview that he had 'in a way' been in love with Diana. For Frances, Burrell's obsession with her daughter could only intensify her sense of injustice.

In the weeks that followed, Frances did what she could to secure her home, bringing in more electronic security to help fend off potential robberies – as well as unwanted visitors – while trying to strike a balance between peaceful living and turning her home 'into Fort Knox'. At Christmas, she engaged the burglar alarm, locked her doors and set off for Althorp, glad to see the back of 2002.

The New Year refused to bring any better news, however. Rosa Monckton, one of Diana's closest friends, published a highly critical article in the *Daily Telegraph*. She had not seen eye to eye with Frances and Sarah for some time and complained in her piece about what she saw as Frances's interventions in the wake of Diana's death, writing bitterly that, 'her executors, principally her mother and elder sister [did not] properly understand the true nature of the relationship between Burrell and the princess. His role in her life was as confidant and protector.'

She believed that Burrell and Diana had been interdependent upon one another, and while feeling that the butler had acted wrongly in storing Diana's belongings in his attic, she could understand his motives. He was, she said, 'reacting to a set of circumstances impossible to explain to an outsider'.

She then took a direct swipe at both Frances and Sarah, claiming that they had not acted 'honourably' and had 'suppressed' and 'ignored' Diana's letter of wishes, attached to her will, which set out how she had expected her money and property to be divided. It also appeared that the Bishop of London, the Right Reverend Richard Chartres, the third executor of the will, had known nothing of the letter. Rosa Monckton continued, 'Hijacking Diana's memory is one thing, her chattels, quite another, and both the executors and Burrell, in his more naive way, are guilty of this.'

Her grievance appeared to hinge upon the interpretation of how Diana's godchildren – of whom Rosa Monckton's daughter, Domenica, was one – should benefit. The Princess's separate letter of wishes had been written on the day after she signed her will. In it she asked her executors to 'divide, at your discretion, my personal chattels, between my sons and my godchildren. The division is to be three quarters in value to my sons and one quarter between my godchildren.'

As a result of her divorce settlement, by the time of her death, Diana's estate had risen to £21 million ($31.5 million), rather than its estimated £1 million ($1.5 million) when she had first signed the will. Considerably more money was therefore now at stake. Frances and Sarah, however, had learned that the letter of wishes was not legally binding, and had it legally set aside a couple of months after Diana's death. Sarah had then driven round the country and herself delivered a gift to each of the Princess's seventeen godchildren. Rosa was furious when her daughter only received what she described as a 'tatty brown box containing some pieces of Herend china wrapped in an old newspaper accompanied by a cute demand [from Sarah] for a receipt.' If that was 'all [Domenica] is given to remember her godmother by', it was, she thundered, an insult.

Then, in February, the society magazine *Tatler* waded in to the fight, splashing the word 'Betrayed' across its cover with, in only slightly smaller type, 'Diana's godchildren and their missing inheritance'. Heavy with sarcasm, the article criticized both Frances and Sarah for their handling of the will. The magazine estimated that each of the seventeen godchildren should have received in excess of £300,000 ($450,000),* rather than the 'meagre trinkets' that had been delivered to their doors. 'The executors chose their heirlooms with care. One, a cheap watercolour, had written on the back that it was a 'gift to the Princess of Wales from Argos plc [a cut-price retailer]'. Another proudly proclaimed that it was a present to the Princess of Wales from the Women's Institute in Caernarfon.' The article continued, 'A watercolour courtesy of Argos is hardly a memento to remember anyone by, except perhaps the chairman of Argos.'

---

* A figure reached by dividing one quarter of the total estimated value of Diana's estate by seventeen; however, by the time the taxes had been paid the estate, although handsome, had been considerably reduced.

Quoting an 'old friend' of the Princess's, the piece went on, 'The one thing about Diana that all her friends know, is that she always knew what she wanted. And she usually got it. She would be livid if her final wishes were overturned.' The gifts ranged from a carriage clock to paintings, a decanter and china.

Legally, it can be argued that 'personal chattels' refers to furniture, ornaments, clothing and other more-or-less portable possessions. Frances and Sarah had acted at their discretion, as allowed under the will and specifically requested by Diana. They had preferred to follow the instructions in that will, in which Diana had listed individual items as bequests to be distributed among her seventeen godchildren. Whatever Rosa Monckton or the *Tatler* might say, they had acted perfectly legitimately.

To be fair, a part of the problem had been caused by Sarah herself, albeit unwittingly. She had spoken during the Burrell case, after arriving looking chicly sombre in a green chiffon scarf and sage jacket, and with her dense, short, distinctive auburn hair fashionably but neatly styled. She had taken the stand immediately after her mother, answering questions about Burrell in a succinct and businesslike fashion, speaking clearly and confidently. The questioning had then turned to the matter of the godchildren. In reply, she said that as all these children were young, she believed that they would prefer a gift to remember Diana by rather than money. When, however, it was suggested that the godchildren, despite outward appearances – some of them were titled, or had titled parents – were not all wealthy, Sarah feistily and truthfully, if perhaps ill-advisedly, countered with, 'There are not many paupers in there.'

When her remark was reported in the next day's press, many of the parents of Diana's godchildren saw red, outraged by such a comment. Murmurings of dissatisfaction turned to outright hostility among some of them, who saw the decision taken by Frances and Sarah as a deliberate attempt to cut their children out of the will and deny them a large sum of money.

Solicitors acting on behalf of Frances and Sarah agreed that the Princess's will had been altered by a court order, but that this had been done legally and correctly. They added that her will had been made four years before she died and did not take into account either the money she received after her divorce, or the extraordinary consequences of her death. In 1996, when Diana's will was updated, Patrick Jephson, who was no longer her Private Secretary, having left earlier that year in acrimonious circumstances, very properly resigned as an executor of the will and was replaced by Sarah. She was a natural choice to replace the courtier, since she was a well-trusted member of Diana's own family. Sarah had on occasion served as lady-in-waiting to her younger sister, and the two women had always been extremely close.

Diana's trust in her mother had also remained firm, for Frances was named as an executor both in 1993 and again after the changes were made to the will in 1996. She saw no reason to dismiss the woman whom she most trusted, and who, she knew, would always have her best interests, and her children's, at heart.

Some of the parents of the Princess's godchildren remained unperturbed throughout the row, and were grateful for the bequests. Sophie Straker, a former flatmate of Diana's and the mother of her godchild Camilla, offered words of comfort. 'I'm happy with the situation as it currently stands. Camilla got a very nice, thoughtful memento, and the rest [of Diana's estate] has gone to the boys.'

And that, to some, was indeed the point. As her sons, William and Harry had rightfully received the lion's share. Sarah and Frances had both acted legally in trying to protect the princes' inheritance and Diana's memory.

As is often the way with such things, the row over the godchildren eventually fizzled out. Unfortunately, however, another was brewing. By the summer of 2003 the Diana, Princess of Wales Memorial Fund had lost both its legal case and a subsequent appeal in California's US District Court against the Franklin Mint, which immediately responded by counter-suing the fund for £16 million ($24 million) on the grounds of 'malicious prosecution'. Frances, along with the her daughter Sarah and the Right Reverend Richard Chartres, was now potentially in the unenviable position of becoming personally liable for huge sums of money. What had started as an aggressive attempt to protect her daughter's image and the princes' inheritance over a dispute surrounding a Diana doll, plates and jewellery, has so far ended in disaster. An immediate freeze has been made on all payments to the 127 charities that benefit from the fund, which now not only faces a £4 million ($6 million) legal bill, but also the fact that its philanthropic future – indeed, its continued existence – remains in doubt.

The whole episode of the godchildren left Frances shaken, and yet she was criticized in the media for keeping her own counsel, refusing to speak on the matter. Despite the negative press and the months of stress, she continued to live quietly, seeking solace and support in the closeness of trusted friends, her family and the church. This is a path she tends to pursue when things become too much, rather than seeking professional help. For although she is a deep thinker, she has no strong interest in psychoanalysis, nor much real faith in it. It is not a course that she believes has helped either her or her children – especially Diana. To this day, she remains dismissive of counsellors, who she says 'dig up the past.'

None the less, Frances accepts that counselling may be helpful to many people, but it is not something to which she feels drawn. She even rejected offers of anti-depressants or other medication to help her to get through the initial period of grief after Diana died. That, she believed, would only delay the inevitable. For her, it became important to face her grief head on, and immediately. 'I knew that as time went on I wasn't sleeping, but to take sleeping pills was kind of self-indulgent, and what was it going to do for me?' It was, she felt, pointless, and possibly even more destructive, to delay with drugs what she felt at the time of Diana's death, only to suffer all those feelings later on.

On 20 January 2003, her sixty-seventh birthday, Frances invited seven friends to Callanish and cooked dinner for them. She bemoaned not being able to get around as easily as once she had, at last admitting that her 'mobility is not so good these days'. Yet finding, as always, an opportunity to laugh at her own predicament, she smiled, 'But I do ricochet off the walls quite nicely!'

CHAPTER NINETEEN

Role Royal

'WASN'T WILLIAM GREAT?' Frances asks. 'Succinct, bold, brave and dignified. I was thrilled to bits because there has been such a build-up. I just lived on answerphone.' Only the night before she had watched her royal grandson on television in a film about his gap year, the year he had taken off between leaving school and starting at university. For over ten weeks, aged just eighteen, he had been in Chile as a volunteer with Raleigh International, a charity that sends young people to work in underprivileged communities in the Third World. The film showed him caring for young children, completely at ease, unmindful of his title or position and content to knuckle down and help wherever required. He was shown pulling on a pair of rubber gloves to clean the lavatory in his hut-like accommodation, carrying logs on his shoulders and hammering posts into the hard earth. It had been a formative experience for the young prince, and the programme marked the first time the public had seen him in such a light. Frances was proud of him. William was living up to all expectations; he was, as Frances put it, 'becoming his own man.'

Even before his year away from formal education came to an end, William made it clear that he wanted to study at the University of St Andrew's, on the east coast of Scotland. Indeed, he had been so taken with the university town that in a back-to-front way he had first chosen the place, and then found a course that he wanted to take – in his case, Art History. Frances could not have been more pleased, for her house in Falkland is only a half-hour's drive away from St Andrew's.

When Diana's boys had been small children, Frances had spent many happy hours with them on Seil. Now that they were older, it was reassuring to her to know that their mother's death had not diminished Frances's presence in their lives. William was now much closer to Frances and, away from Eton and Highgrove, the way was open for him and his grandmother to see each other more often and to talk about Diana, and what she might have thought and advised. Frances delights in her maturing grandson, although she finds it hard sometimes to ignore in him the striking physical similarities with Diana.

From the day William was born, Frances refused to accord him special privileges. He was to be treated like all her other grandchildren, in as unaffected a way as possible. While she acknowledged his destiny, she instinctively knew that it was important not to let his rank and position override the need for ordinary good manners in his person. Having grown up on a royal estate and later seen, and to some extent been part of, Diana's meteoric rise, Frances knew that her grandson carried a heavy weight of other people's expectations. That knowledge, however, only made her believe more passionately that William should lead as normal a life as possible. He needed the chance to develop naturally, and to know his own mind, before being subjected to the inevitable politicking of the royal courts, the machinations of a fickle media and the vagaries of public opinion.

By the same token, Frances won William's respect from the beginning, not least because she was not afraid to chastise him when, like all children, he got out of line. If he was cheeky 'she would give him a clip round the ear,' says Ken Wharfe. Certainly she has never been afraid either to speak her mind, or to speak the truth. Her way of dealing with children is to ensure that any discipline is balanced with 'enormous affection.' She is liberal, but she is not a pushover.

An independent streak, coupled with a certain fearlessness, has always led Frances to question tradition and convention. She follows her own instincts when dealing with children, rather than what has always been said or done. Somewhat unconventionally for someone close to seventy years old who is an aristocrat, she says, 'I feel that the perception that adults are always right is incorrect. I believe the reverse to be true. Adults through experience should be able to conceal, overcome or keep in check their own faults. We all have our own faults from birth right through to the grave and I feel children should be treated as equals rather than making out adults are better.' It is an interesting philosophy, in someone who long ago accepted the need for the monarchy to move more rapidly with the times and to embrace modern culture. When William accedes to the throne doubtless these beliefs, which were also shared by Diana, will be apparent in the substance and style of his reign.

Frances's influence was obvious from the early days of Diana's marriage when, casting aside the formality and stuffiness of the royal family, she would insist on taking William and Harry to everyday events like theme parks and public concerts. They were encouraged to play with their Spencer cousins on family holidays, and generally to let off steam in the manner typical of boys their age. When they stayed with Frances on Seil, she would always try to fit in a trip to one of their favourite places, the SeaLife Sanctuary. Turning up unannounced meant that they often toured the sanctuary completely unnoticed – a rare luxury for the princes and their mother, but also a sign of the respect for her privacy that Frances commands in her home town.

In keeping with this more relaxed style of parenting, the boys were encouraged to go to tea with friends after class, just like other schoolchildren, the protection officers keeping a respectful distance. They also saw something of what life was like at the opposite end of the spectrum, away from the privilege and palaces. They were taken by Diana on a tour of the streets of London among the homeless and drug-addicted, and visited hostels and shelters. That too was a part of Frances's legacy to her daughter, never to ignore the less fortunate, and to count one's own blessings.

Throughout their teens, Frances maintained contact with William and Harry. During term time, when they could not speak on the telephone, she relied on letters to show them her love. Rather more publicly, she wrote a message for William at the time of his confirmation at St George's Chapel, Windsor, and lit candles for him in Oban Cathedral. She wanted him to know that she was thinking of him and offering prayers for his future. Just fourteen days after Diana's death, when Harry became a teenager, she again lit candles in Oban Cathedral and wrote a poignant but uplifting message praising his courage. Three years later, watching William on television as he turned eighteen, Frances saw what a balanced young man he had become, a man fit to be king in a new era.

Dedicated as she is to maintaining the two princes' privacy, Frances rarely makes a comment about either of them. She knows only too well the pitfalls of life on the global stage in the glare of the media, and when it comes to talking about the boys, other than in the simplest generalities, she has drawn a line. She has often experienced the backlash that can follow the uttering of a few well-intentioned words, and has been misrepresented in the press more often than she cares to think about. 'I sometimes think I am at risk even when I'm asleep,' she says, only half-jokingly.

The family's elevation to royalty, through Diana, has given Frances a certain power behind the throne. In their long history Spencers have been lords, advisers, equerries to royalty, but none has been as close to the ermine-trimmed coat tails of power as she is today. Ironically, the wife whom Johnnie Spencer discredited all those years ago has returned to prominence and with her own indelible place in history. Yet the price has been high. Her mother's desire to stay close to royalty led to Frances losing custody of her children; her own marriage to Peter Shand Kydd was suffocated by the cult of Diana; the two families – the Windsors and the Spencers – once neighbours, are now all but sworn enemies; and her daughter, a princess, was at first almost destroyed by unhappiness, and then died tragically young.

If it is her sense of justice, coupled with a refusal to be silenced, which sometimes gets Frances into trouble, then the same fervour has been passed on to her children and grandchildren. William refuses to use his courtesy title of His Royal Highness while he is a student at St Andrew's University. Although he had been expected to employ it officially after he reached the age of eighteen, he is aware that it will be years before he accedes to the throne, and so asked the Queen for permission to delay its introduction. For the time being he wants to be known as plain William Wales. Frances, a woman whose ancestry spans American pioneers and Irish opportunists, sees this as a step in the right direction. Although respectful of tradition, where it deserves respect, she rejects both snobbery and stuffiness. She once remarked to a friend after a stay at a very upmarket, and rather self-consciously 'grand', Scottish country hotel, 'If you like rules, you'll love it there!'

Frances's life in Scotland is a distant world away from that of William's other grandmother, Queen Elizabeth, whose aloof style is rooted in duty, protocol and palaces. She only touches her subjects when wearing gloves, and when the Australian Prime Minister unthinkingly put a gentlemanly arm around his monarch, his action made front-page headlines in Britain, to the general accompaniment of cries of shock and horror at this over-familiar act. For Her Majesty, her mysterious and glacial metaphorical armour provides a natural blanket of security, and a defence against those who would come too close. Such attitudes, however, are now being challenged as many from the old school of royalty, among them the Queen Mother, Princess Margaret and Frances's own mother, Ruth, Lady Fermoy, are no longer alive. The Queen has become increasingly isolated, and to many of her subjects her *modus operandi* appears outdated, outmoded and unnatural. Many also consider that her personal inflexibility has been responsible for creating a progressive shift in popularity away from the monarchy. Since Diana's death there have been increasingly vociferous calls for royalty to adapt or face extinction.

William's future is already mapped, and has been since his birth; he is a son and heir born to the country's highest destiny. The sudden death of his mother when he was an impressionable fifteen-year-old made life much more difficult for him, not just because of his loss, or because he was catapulted into the public eye as a result, but also because Diana's radical attitude to the monarchy had included specific plans for him, which fell by the wayside when she died. Yet her ideas continue, many of them through the influence of her mother.

So far, William has responded to his position in a dignified way and with quiet resignation. He has never felt any particular love for the formality and pageantry that surround his future role, but he is slowly adapting to his responsibilities. Aware of his mother's ambivalent attitude towards the media – a mixture of antagonism and fascination – he is treading a considered public path. Frances, who has dealt at first hand with the media for more than twenty years, has long recognized the pressures that come with position. Aware of her family's vulnerability to the press after Diana's marriage, when her own son, Charles went to Oxford in the 1980s she asked the broadcaster Gordon Honeycombe, a friend of hers and Peter's, to provide her son with advice on how to handle the press attention.

Like William, Frances lost a parent as a teenager, albeit in altogether different circumstances. Yet that experience has informed her decisions as to how she can help to fill the emotional chasm left by her daughter. Although she never tries to replace Diana she can and does provide a vital link to the Princess. As matriarch of the Spencer clan, the love and respect of her children is, she believes, not just necessary to her life, but a fundamental part of it. In return, Charles Spencer acknowledges his mother's considerable influence, referring to 'the intricacies of such a close relationship'.

William at just twenty-one displays similar characteristics to his maternal grandmother. He has chosen to lead as near to a normal existence as he can, hoping to live a relatively subdued student life at university. He says, 'I just want it to be somewhere I can relax – my own space. I've got to have a stereo – got to have music. I love my music.' Sounding ever more like his mother and grandmother, he adds, 'I don't deliberately select my friends because of their background. If I enjoy someone's company, then that's all that counts. I have many different friends who aren't from the same background as me and we get on really well.' Ken Wharfe saw this at first hand:

> When William was at Wetherby School [his prep. school in London] he was completely unfazed by who he was. He'd turn up and his mother was in a track suit, while the other mothers would be in their haute-couture outfits at eight-thirty in the morning. One kid came up and said to William, 'Is it true you know the Queen?' William, off the cuff, said, 'Don't you mean Granny?'

Frances's dispiriting experience with her own mother taught her a harsh lesson. In rebelling against her mother's austere Victorian values, as well as her snobbery and passion for doing the 'done thing', she adopted a more liberal and sympathetic attitude. In fairness to her mother, she does admit, 'I suppose with hindsight I was a totally nightmarish child.' But this naughty side of her nature has been put to good use as she can 'recognize certain aspects of my grandchildren's misbehaviour'. In short, and unlike so many people, in growing old she has not forgotten what once it was to be young.

She believes, too, that praise works better than criticism, a view that Diana felt was severely absent within royal circles. The Princess regularly complained that her good work was often ignored, but that any small mistake was pounced upon.

Frances works hard to maintain good relationships, especially for her grandchildren's sake. It is not an accident that she and Peter Shand Kydd remain good friends, and he is obviously equally good at retaining friendship even after love has gone. His third wife, Marie-Pierre Becret, who never met Frances, and from whom he was divorced in 1995, subsequently changed her surname to Champagne in an attempt to avoid the attention of being married to Diana's stepfather. In the summer of 2003, however, Marie-Pierre, who now hires out her property in Provence as a holiday home, appeared also to have resolved her past differences with Peter.

When contacted, she admitted intriguingly, 'Peter is here with me now, okay? He is not in the same room. He is in bed now. In my studio.' She went on to say, 'As you know we're divorced and I do not want to talk because it has been so bad in the press when we divorced. The press has been so bad about me and I'm a very simple – well maybe not – but honest woman and I just don't want anything. There are so many things I am terribly hurt by over the last twelve years. The rubbish that has been written about me and about him. I do remember Peter being approached about Diana and the person was really ruthless and Peter slammed the phone down. But the past is the past and Peter doesn't belong to me.' As for Peter Shand Kydd himself, his reply remains as consistent as ever: 'I have never talked in forty years and I am not about to start now.'

His silence can be assumed with absolute certainty, and by the same token Frances will do everything she can to protect him. He is a man who has commanded the loyalty of all three of his wives, and remains on good terms with these very different women despite the trauma of divorce. Now approaching eighty, he can reflect that he has achieved his goal – to maintain almost complete anonymity despite having been so closely associated with Diana and the Spencer family for so long.

Frances does seem, more than most people, to understand that friendship needs to be kept in good repair. When her former daughter-in-law, Victoria Spencer, announced she was pregnant again, aged thirty-seven, her daughter Kitty told Frances, 'Mummy's having a boy – yuk!' and wrinkled up her nose. Frances ticked Kitty off, although she understood this childish rush to judgement. She does, however, maintain a close connection with Victoria, despite her divorce from Charles, and always sees the children when they return to England in the school holidays. Victoria told *Hello!* magazine that she had met her new partner, Jonathan Aitken, through friends after her stints in a South African drugs rehabilitation clinic. It is typical of Frances that she worries that the strain of battling addictions might have a detrimental effect on the relationship, although she hopes not. Touchingly, she refers to Victoria's new baby as one of her grandchildren.

For more than thirty years, Frances has been at odds with the Establishment, even though the pinnacle of that establishment, the royal family, is now part of her blood line. Diana has been at the heart of many of these conflicts. The first encounter came when the courts ruled against Frances and, catechizing her as an unfit mother, took her children away. The next came when Diana, as a nineteen-year-old, elected to marry Prince Charles, the heir to the throne of the United Kingdom. For Diana, perhaps even for most people, this was a dream come true, but Frances could see the pressures ahead, and it was not long before her daughter was truly miserable, and had been abandoned by the Palace.

When Diana married, Frances gained a measure of fame but lost her identity, becoming to most people the 'mother of the Princess of Wales', rather than a person in her own right. Her own life was changed for ever by her daughter's much publicized existence, and by her sudden death. Diana became the idol of a nation, bringing beauty, glamour and, above all, warmth to an anachronistic institution. In death, however, Diana was lost to everyone. For Frances, the guilt she felt because she and her daughter had not spoken for several months only made the parting harder to bear. Frances clung to the belief that she would one day be reunited with her daughter. Furthermore, as much as the thoughts of a grieving nation were a huge comfort to her, they were also a constant reminder that she had shared her daughter with millions of people. Although she knew that she must accept their condolence, and their sorrow, with grace, inside she also knew that her pain was unique. As she explains, 'For many people, Diana's death simply became a matter of state, but wasn't she also my daughter?'

In the end, this is the reason why the apparent indifference of the Queen rankles with Frances. Her Majesty's personal style dictates that she maintain a physical and emotional distance from her own sons and daughter.

There is, too, an undeniable generation gap between the Queen and Prince William. She represents the sovereignty of the nation in all its pomp, whereas he is the living legacy of the 'People's Princess'. One royal aide sums up the Queen as someone who 'doesn't really understand things because she has never been out there, never been a normal human being, didn't go to school, never mixed with real people, never suffered indignities which real people have to deal with all the time.' By contrast Frances, although she lives off the beaten track, has the spirit and energy of someone in tune with modern life.

She loves popular culture, enjoys pop as much as classical music, uses email and is even learning to text message on her mobile phone.

Frances would not trade places. She has expressed, and understood, emotion from an early age, without either embarrassment or mawkishness. She has been touched by life and has responded accordingly – by fighting back, by learning from experience, and by trying to profit, at however great a cost, from that experience. She has buckled, but she has never broken. She lives among, and can often inspire, 'ordinary' men and women. She ran a successful business in Oban for many years, got her hands dirty farming for a generation, and has involved herself in the life of the community around her. While she may have been born to privilege, she has never taken it for granted, and she certainly does not live a life of luxury. She has no full-time servants, courtiers, PR spin doctors, or secretaries to arrange her life. Her small home on Seil is pleasant and comfortable, but it could never be described as grand or ostentatious. She is, as she has always been, 'just Frances'.

And what of the future for Frances? Back when she was a carefree young girl kicking off her shoes to dance on the roof of Park House, the prospect of such an extraordinary life would never have crossed her mind. As a teenage debutante 'doing the Season', she hoped, like most young girls, for a happy marriage and healthy children. The first eluded her, and of her six pregnancies there are only three children who survive. Her life has been a road of extremes, of both soaring highs and plummeting lows. She has endured some of the greatest tragedies that life can hold, yet has also lived the very best of times. Her youngest daughter married into the most prestigious family in the world, and she herself mixes in circles most people can only dream of. She has tried to make the most of every stage of her life, good and bad. Ask Frances Shand Kydd what she thinks, and she will say that she has been blessed, and that her life is 'wonderful'. Even her infirmity she tries to view as just another challenge.

Always she has been herself, whether riding in an open landau with his Royal Highness the Duke of Edinburgh, or protesting outside a local primary school unjustly earmarked for closure. As Ken Wharfe shrewdly observes, 'Frances came into the royal family as a commoner and she maintained her roots. She didn't become embroiled in the royal issue but realized her weaknesses and capitalized on her strengths, which she got from ordinary people. This was a quality that she passed on to her daughter.'

Frances's mind and spirit remain as sharp as ever. The mother of the late Princess of Wales and grandmother of an heir apparent to the throne cannot retire from those roles. She keeps up to date, and that keeps her young, as her family can attest. Not long ago, she was staying in London, visiting both her daughters, Sarah and Jane. Aware that she had to keep her wits about her because her family are much given to teasing each other, she waited for the comments to begin flying around. Jane's daughter, Laura, was also there, as Frances recalls:

> Laura was wearing a small denim top and a Chinese jacket which she got from an Oxfam shop for a quid. And Jane says 'Laura are you wearing a bikini top under that?' And Laura replied 'Yes.' And Jane, with a horrified look on her face, says, 'Look at your feet!' I looked down and Laura was wearing her brother's black bedsocks – he's so tall he has to put socks on because his feet come out of the end of the bed. Jane looked disgusted and said, 'You do not have dinner with your Grandmother wearing bedsocks and a bikini!'

At which Frances, as quick as a flash and only just suppressing a smile, said to her granddaughter, 'I think your choice is inspired!'

Yet there remain many less attractive legacies of her position. Besides the CCTV cameras and other security measures, the internal doors in the bungalow on Seil have deadlocks, a security precaution introduced in the days when Diana regularly stayed there with the boys. Worse, her privacy is compromised, for the media – as well as the merely curious – know where to find her. Yet her high profile does at least allow her to help those in need, and she remains an ardent believer in doing what she can for others, supporting many smaller, less popular charities.

The Queen can pass on to William the trappings of monarchy, but it is Frances who will give his role life. Her sense of purpose, her natural affinity with people, her understanding – despite her disdain for it – of the Establishment, and her refusal to lead anything other than her own life, show strength and a strong sense of personal responsibility. While Prince Charles may have his toothpaste squeezed out on to the brush for him by a servant, Frances can at least, she says, somewhat wryly, 'wash my own hair'.

Once Diana's glamour was no longer there to paper over the cracks in the royal display, the Windsors found themselves back where they had been before she had married the Prince of Wales. The people saw the monarchy in terms of 'them and us'. It irked them that senior royalty could avoid paying tax, and were able to obtain many privileges for peripheral members of the royal family. There seemed to be an excessive amount of freeloading at the taxpayer's expense. In 1996 the cost to the nation of the monarchy was £53 million ($79.5 million). A year after Diana's death it had been reduced by £15 million to £38 million ($22.5 million to $57 million). Before then, however, for the first time in forty years the Sovereign agreed to pay income tax. She also consented to bear the cost of restoring Windsor Castle after it had been badly damaged by fire in 1992, giving permission for a part of Buckingham Palace to be opened to tourists for a few weeks in the summer to raise the money.

After fifty years on the throne the Queen is an aloof figure, arguably as cut off from the people as on the day when she was crowned. Her role has been dictated by an antiquated system of belief entrenched in the legacy of the days when Britain ruled a vast empire. She has done little to change that, resolutely refusing to move with the times, and finding it hard to respond to a society that has changed beyond her recognition, for the general respect for royalty (or sycophancy towards it, depending upon your point of view) of the early 1950s has long since evaporated.

When, in 1998, the Royal Yacht *Britannia* was taken out of service the Queen wept, even though she had not shed a single public tear over Diana's death – something that did not escape the notice of either the press or the public. Picking up a child or walking through a field sown with landmines are not actions that would occur to Her Majesty, or that she has any desire to perform. Yet even so, Diana's influence has made the Queen and the royal family more responsive to change, while the tide of public emotion since her death has come to mark a watershed in the Windsors' history. In the end, it came down to whether to take responsibility for updating themselves, or risk sweeping changes imposed by the government at the behest of the people, the Queen's subjects.

As one royal insider noted:

> The Princess threw the white gloves away and would pick out some screaming old lady at the back and talk about the rent bill. These were all Spencer qualities, whether you like it or not. She wasn't given a book about how to perform royal duties by the Queen; not one single person said, 'This is what you do.' She took the bit between her teeth and dealt with [her duty] in the only way she could, based on her own experience of life.

Yet despite the fact that Diana is the face of the modern monarchy, her memory is slowly being phased out of the royal family. This is very hard for the Spencer family to bear, especially Frances, because she knows just how much Diana contributed to elevating royalty in the public consciousness. The Queen rarely mentions Diana, and when, in April 2003, a guide responsible for tours at Sandringham was asked if a recent portrait of the royal family included Diana, his response was, 'Who?'

There is a proverb that Frances likes and laughs over: 'Fear not the path of truth because of the lack of people walking on it.' Witty yet intense, with a strong sense of right and wrong, she is a woman who has grown and matured as a result of tragic loss. She has, too, the very thing for which the Windsors have to work so hard – a sympathetic charisma. It is that quality, more than any other, which has endeared her to the people she loves.

And they to her.

～

I have done the state some service, and they know 't;
No more of that. I pray you, in your letters,
When you shall these unlucky deeds relate,
Speak of me as I am; nothing extenuate,
Nor set down aught in malice: then, must you speak
Of one that loved not wisely but too well . . .

William Shakespeare, *Othello*, Act V, Scene 2

Bibliography and Sources

BOOKS

RICHARD BARBER, *Earl Spencer, Saint or Sinner? A Biography*, London, André Deutsch, 1998

NIGEL BLUNDELL, *Windsor v Windsor: Charles and Diana: The Inside Story of Their Divorce*, London, Blake Publishing, 1995

SARAH BRADFORD, *Elizabeth*, London, Heinemann, 1996

PIERS BRENDON and PHILLIP WHITEHEAD, *The Windsors: A Dynasty Revealed*, London, Hodder & Stoughton, 1994, Pimlico, 2000

TIM CLAYTON and PHIL CRAIG, *Diana: Story of a Princess*, Hodder & Stoughton, 2001

MARY CLARKE, *Diana: Once Upon a Time: Her Nanny's Story*, London, Sidgwick & Jackson, 1994

LADY COLIN CAMPBELL, *Diana in Private: The Princess Nobody Knows*, New York, St Martin's Press, 1992

NIGEL DEMPSTER and PETER EVANS, *Behind Palace Doors*, London, Orion, 1993

JONATHAN DIMBLEBY, *Prince of Wales: A Biography*, London, HarperCollins, 1994

ANNE EDWARDS, *Diana and the Rise of the House of Spencer*, London, Hodder & Stoughton, 1999

ALISON GAUNTLETT, *Prince William*, London, Parragon, 2003

GORDON HONEYCOMBE, *Year of the Princess*, London, Michael Joseph, 1982

P. D. JEPHSON, *Shadows of a Princess: Diana Princess of Wales 1987–1996*, London, HarperCollins, 2000

PENNY JUNOR, *Charles: Victim or Villain?*, London, HarperCollins, 1998

ROBERT LACEY, *Majesty: Elizabeth II and the House of Windsor*, London, Hutchinson, 1977

ANGELA LEVIN, *Raine and Johnnie: The Spencers and the Althorp Scandal*, London, Weidenfeld & Nicholson 1993

ANDREW MORTON, *Diana: Her True Story – In Her Own Words: 1961–1997*, London, Michael O'Mara, 1997

ANDREW MORTON, *Diana: Her New Life*, Michael O'Mara, 1995

JOHN PEARSON, *Blood Royal: The Story of the Spencers and the Royals*, London, HarperCollins, 1999

ERIN PIZZEY, *In the Shadow of the Castle*, London, Hamish Hamilton, 1984

TREVOR REES-JONES, *The Bodyguard's Story*, London, Little, Brown, 2000

MARY ROBERTSON, *The Diana I Knew: Loving Memories of the Friendship Between an American Mother and Her Son's Nanny Who Became the Princess of Wales*, London, HarperCollins, 1998

SARAH, THE DUCHESS OF YORK with JEFF COPLON, *My Story*, London, Simon & Schuster, 1996

THOMAS SANCTION and SCOTT MACLEOD, *Death of a Princess: An Investigation*, London, Weidenfeld & Nicolson, 1998

INGRID SEWARD, *The Queen and Di*, London, HarperCollins, 2000

SALLY BEDELL SMITH, *Diana in Search of Herself: Portrait of a Troubled Princess*, London, Random House, 1999

KATE SNELL, *Diana: Her Last Love*, London, André Deutsch, 2000

CHARLES SPENCER, *The Spencer Family*, London, Viking, 1999

MICHAEL THORNTON, *Royal Feud: The Queen Mother and the Duchess of Windsor*, London, Michael Joseph, 1985

GRAHAM TURNER, *Elizabeth: The Woman and the Queen*, London, Macmillan, 2002

A. N. WILSON, *The Rise and Fall of the House of Windsor*, London, Sinclair Stevenson, 1993

KEN WHARFE with ROBERT JOBSON, *Diana: Closely Guarded Secret*, London, Michael O'Mara, 2002

CHRISTOPHER WILSON, *The Windsor Knot: Charles, Camilla and the Legacy of Diana*, New York, Pinnacle Books, 2002

PHILIP ZIEGLER, *King Edward VIII: The Official Biography*, London, Collins, 1990

OTHER SOURCES

Those who spoke to us are listed in the Acknowledgements on page 9. The following newspapers and magazines were also consulted:

Daily Express	*Mail on Sunday*
Daily Mail	*News of the World*
Daily Mirror	*Scotland on Sunday*
Daily Telegraph	*Sunday Express*
Evening Standard	*Sunday Telegraph*
Hello!	*Woman's Own*

Index